Journal of a Mad Man

Journal of a Mad Man

The Wisdom of Ecclesiastes

Derrick McCarson

Foreword by
Dennis Thurman

RESOURCE *Publications* · Eugene, Oregon

JOURNAL OF A MAD MAN
The Wisdom of Ecclesiastes

Copyright © 2014 Derrick McCarson. All rights reserved. Except for brief quotations in critical publications or reviews, no part of this book may be reproduced in any manner without prior written permission from the publisher. Write: Permissions. Wipf and Stock Publishers, 199 W. 8th Ave., Suite 3, Eugene, OR 97401.

Resource Publications
An Imprint of Wipf and Stock Publishers
199 W. 8th Ave., Suite 3
Eugene, OR 97401

www.wipfandstock.com

ISBN 13: 978-1-62564-475-6

Manufactured in the U.S.A.

This book is dedicated to my first born son, Daniel. It is my prayer that you will love wisdom and "remember now thy Creator in the days of thy youth."

Contents

Foreword by Dennis Thurman | ix
Acknowledgments | xiii

1 The Journey of a Desperate Man (1:1–3) | 1
2 The Circles of Life (1:4–11) | 13
3 The Search for Meaning (1:12—2:11) | 24
4 A Brief Glimpse above the Sun (2:12–26) | 36
5 The Mystery of Time and Eternity (3:1–15) | 47
6 Crooked Justice (3:16—4:3) | 57
7 Overcoming Loneliness (4:4–16) | 68
8 Wise Words for Worshippers (5:1–7) | 78
9 Beware of the Money Trap (5:8–20) | 87
10 Satisfaction Sold Separately (6:1–12) | 97
11 Taking the Bitter with the Better (7:1–14) | 105
12 The Balancing Act of Wisdom (7:15–29) | 118
13 Wisdom for a Warped World (8:1–17) | 128
14 Straight Talk about Life and Death (9:1–10) | 140
15 Reckoning with Murphy's Law (9:11–18) | 149
16 How to Spot a Fool (10:1–20) | 160
17 Living on the Edge (11:1–10) | 174
18 Passing the Final Exam (12:1–14) | 183

Bibliography | 197

Foreword

Someone has well said, "We live life forward, but we understand it backward." Solomon would have nodded his head in agreement. He discovered near the end of his journey that traveling at warp speed, searching for fulfillment in the world, took him at last to what he once knew but had forgotten: "Now all has been heard; here is the conclusion of the matter: Fear God and keep his commandments, for this is the duty of all mankind" (Ecc. 12:13).

It is a message that resonates with our culture—where people are so full, they are empty. We are gorged with stuff, satiated with sensual delights, and yet with a gnawing hunger that cannot be filled with anything in the material universe—all that is, "under the sun," as Solomon equates it repeatedly. The old king was the man who had everything, and yet enjoyed nothing—at least not for long. The shiny toys, the expensive baubles, all quickly lost their luster. The haunting cry of David's son echoes in the chambers of our own soul, "'Meaningless! Meaningless!' says the Teacher. 'Utterly meaningless! Everything is meaningless'" (1:2).

Solomon sped down one dead-end after another, running head-on into a crash with futility, while ignoring that narrow, steep path where there was almost no traffic, until the Prodigal Prince rises up from his moral pigpen and heads to the Father's house. He learned from his mistakes. That was smart—befitting this monarch of prodigious, proverbial wisdom. It is smart to learn from your mistakes, but it is smarter to learn from the mistakes of others!

That is what Derrick McCarson helps us to do! He masterfully takes us on a tour of Ecclesiastes, giving us a close-up of the spiritual wreckage of a materialistic life. With keen insight, breadth of research and captivating illustrations, we have a roadmap to guide us to true satisfaction—the opposite direction of Solomon's folly. We are pointed to an intimate relationship with the Creator—the One who can make us a new creation in Christ!

The time to remember that Creator is when the heart is young and tender. There is no need to pursue a reckless excursion into evil, with its momentary thrills, that are extremely overpriced! Indeed, Jesus posed the rhetorical gem, "What good is it for someone to gain the whole world, yet forfeit their soul?" (Mark 8:36)

The author of this commentary has proven wiser than Solomon, in heeding that counsel while a lad. It was my privilege to watch young Derrick McCarson as a boy in our children's ministry, and to see the quiet, unassuming fellow, mature into the bright, capable young man he is today. It was my joy to see him answer the call to preach and participate in his ordination service. For a period of time he served as an intern in our youth ministry. Now, he is pursuing the purpose for which God has placed His hand on him. Derrick shepherds the flock of God called Liberty Baptist Church that gathers each Lord's Day, just two miles down the road from our facilities at Pole Creek Baptist Church in Candler, North Carolina. There he faithfully proclaims the Word of God.

I have known his father and mother, Joe and Linda, and have seen first-hand what the nurture of Christian parents can mean in shaping a life. But, God has no grandchildren! Like all believers, there must be a personal experience of regeneration that makes us a child of God. Derrick has had such an encounter with the Eternal One—the evidence is clear—and now wants to take hold of all that for which God has taken hold of him—to paraphrase the Apostle Paul in Philippians 3:12. Solomon chased after the wind; Derrick is chasing after the Spirit!

Derrick McCarson maps out for us the path to abundant life. He graphically shows us the Devil's detours, and the consequences of those who traverse them. The caution signs are large enough for any who wish to read them. They are emblazoned in the book of Ecclesiastes. One of the verses in Ecclesiastes bemoans what many a student has felt in school, "Of making many books there is no end, and much study wearies the body" (12:12b). Yet, this commentary is a book that demands to be studied and promises refreshment for all who will apply its message.

To drink from the well of truth is to never thirst again (John 4:14). Too bad that Solomon spent so much time drinking from a golden goblet, the intoxicating beverages that leave you worse the next day and craving for more. Thankfully, he finally awakened to the futility of that and quenched the thirst of his soul with God.

We should all be grateful to Derrick McCarson for offering us that life-giving elixir from God's Word. The other alternative is the poison Solomon drank. That is indeed madness and folly (1:17).

God's heart breaks for those who reject His way. "My people have committed two sins: They have forsaken me, the spring of living water, and have dug their own cisterns, broken cisterns that cannot hold water." (Jeremiah 2:13)

We should be grateful for a teacher named Derrick who shows us the error of another "Teacher, son of David, king in Jerusalem," (1:1). This young commentator presents a clarion call to truth in the Son of David, Jesus Christ! Drink deeply!

Soli Deo Gloria,
Dennis Thurman
Senior Pastor, Pole Creek Baptist Church

Acknowledgments

WRITING A BOOK IS like running a relay race. It's a team effort which requires the diligence of others to help cross the finish line. I would like to express deep gratitude to the insight of my mother-in-law, Trudy Rogers, for helping me proof read and edit this book. I would also like to thank my dear wife, Caitlin McCarson, for all her prayers and support. As Solomon wrote, "of making many books there is no end; and much study is a weariness of the flesh" (Ecc. 12:12). Your help through this process has made the journey to completion that much more enjoyable.

1

The Journey of a Desperate Man (1:1–3)

SEVERAL YEARS AGO AS a teenager my family took our annual summer vacation to Garden City, SC. If memory serves correctly, I was probably in the ninth grade and my real interest on that trip was learning how to master the skimboard—a thinly polished panel of wood which glides across the surface of the waves as they wash up on the beach. However, it wouldn't be the skimboarding that would ultimately capture my attention that trip but a tourist trap that turned into an unforgettable spiritual lesson.

Along the main highway, not far from where we were staying, there were several attractions whose primary mode of survival was preying upon the impulses of tourists with cash to spare. Mini golf courses, souvenir shops filled with novelty beach towels and NASCAR t-shirts, ice-cream parlors, video arcades, and water parks lined the strip. Among this smorgasbord of entertainment there was an interesting place called "Maze Mania."

Imagine a labyrinth constructed of twelve-foot-high walls spanning an area about half the size of football field. On the roadside was a towering neon sign emblazoned with a cartoon logo of a mouse in athletic gear running off with a piece of cheese. From the backseat of my parent's Buick Regal this place was reminiscent of an obstacle course off the Nickelodeon game show Double Dare and I was ready for a physical challenge.

I finally convinced Mom and Dad to let us go check it out. There was a buzz of excitement as we wheeled into the parking lot. Upon further investigation, I learned that the premise of Maze Mania was simple. For ten dollars you gained admission and once inside the goal was to find the cheese in the middle of the maze (which was nothing more than a sophisticated hole-puncher disguised as a block of cheddar), get your card stamped, and then find your way out. If you could navigate yourself out of the maze in less than ten minutes you could win a t-shirt declaring that you were a "Maze Maniac."

Feeling confident that I was up to the challenge I laid my hard earned grass-mowing money down and entered the gauntlet. About forty-five minutes later I emerged exhausted, sweaty and vowing that I would never return. Turns out, Maze Mania was one of the worst torture devices ever created. It had to be the brain child of an evil scientist with crazy Einstein hair who took pleasure in experimenting on his test subjects.

Once inside the maze you were totally on your own. There was no sense in asking for direction because everyone was equally lost. There was no map, no friendly guide to tell you where to go. There were kids in there crying because they had been in there for who knows how long looking for a way out. I remember seeing one kid trying to climb out of the maze over the walls as if he were escaping a POW camp. Images of Steve McQueen and *The Great Escape* raced through my mind. On top of that, it was insufferably hot and there was no relief from the boiling South Carolina sun. Kids were dropping dead from exhaustion like we were on the Bataan Death March (Okay, perhaps a slight exaggeration).

After what seemed like hours, I began to panic because in my mind I was thinking, "Will I ever see my family again? Am I going to die in this God-forsaken maze?" Just when I thought I'd found my way out I would inevitably come to a dead-end or a place that I had already been. Frustration eventually gave way to despair. I got the distinct feeling that all I was doing was going around in circles.

Those feelings of madness, frustration, and hopelessness that I experienced wandering through that maze encapsulate the emotional morass of Ecclesiastes. Except in Ecclesiastes the journey is through the maze called "life." Each one of us has felt the frustration, monotony and even the despair of being trapped in a world that seems to be rigged to our disadvantage. Life can be like a maze that is full of dead-ends, cul-de-sacs, and endless corridors.

Philosophers tell us that every human being is hard-wired to search for the answers to life's big issues—origin, purpose, morality, meaning and destiny. Questions like, "Does God exist?" "Is there life after death?" And of course, "What is the meaning of life?" have been troubling the minds of the wise and unwise for ages. It has been called, "the existential vacuum"—the universal void inside each one of us that aches for fulfillment and answers to help us make sense of our existence.

In the introduction of Rick Warren's mega best-seller, *The Purpose Driven Life*, he describes a survey done by Dr. Hugh Moorehead, a philosophy professor at Northeastern Illinois University. Moorehead wrote to 250 of the world's leading thinkers, scientists, writers, doctors and intellectuals asking a simple question: "What is the meaning of life?" Some offered their best guesses. Others gave cliché responses: love, family, happiness, work, achievement, etc. Still others candidly admitted they were clueless. In fact, several of the intellectuals even asked Moorehead to write back and tell them if and when he discovered the purpose of life![1]

The book of Ecclesiastes is a deep, philosophical look at the question, "What is the meaning of life?" Dr. David Jeremiah has written, "The book of Ecclesiastes is an inner road map of Solomon's search for satisfaction—a testament to one man's journey for meaning on earth. It stands unique within the Bible as a classic of real-world, everyday philosophy, seen through the eyes of the most powerful, influential, and educated man in the world at the time."[2]

This book is raw, brutally honest and unapologetic in its conclusions. Many times you might step away from the text depressed, perplexed, or troubled with the same feelings of emptiness that Solomon dealt with. Bible expositor, Philip Ryken adds:

> We should study Ecclesiastes *because it is honest to the troubles of life*—so honest that the great American novelist Herman Melville once called it "the truest of all books." More than anything else in the Bible, Ecclesiastes captures the futility and frustration of a fallen world. It is honest about the drudgery of work, the injustice of government, the dissatisfaction of foolish pleasure, and the mind-numbing tedium of everyday life—"the treadmill of our existence." Think of Ecclesiastes as the only book of the Bible written on a Monday morning. Reading it helps us to be honest about the problems of life—even those of us who trust in the goodness of God. In fact one scholar describes Ecclesiastes as "a kind of backdoor" that allows believers to have the sad and skeptical thoughts that we do not usually allow to enter the front door of our faith.[3]

As we study the pages of Solomon's ancient journal you will find that at first it's like reading the thoughts of a cynical, pessimistic, fatalistic mad-man who was trapped in the maze of life. Yet, if you are able to pierce

---

1. Warren, *The Purpose Driven Life*, 19–20.
2. Jeremiah, *Searching for Heaven on Earth*, xvii.
3. Ryken, *Ecclesiastes*, 14.

through the fog of confusion and the initial doom-and-gloom of Solomon's pontifications you will find this book to be most relevant to the nitty-gritty existence we know all too well.

The Preacher of Ecclesiastes (1:1)

The author of this book identifies himself twice, once in 1:1 and again in 1:12, as "the Preacher." He was the son of David and the King of Jerusalem, none other than the wisest man who ever lived (besides Jesus Christ), Solomon. The Hebrew title which is translated "the Preacher" is *Qoheleth*. Some translators prefer the title "Teacher," "Philosopher," or even "Quester." The Hebrew root of the word *qoheleth* literally means "to gather, collect, or assemble." Some scholars take this as a reference to the way the author collected various wise sayings and proverbs into one book.

Moreover, the name of the book "Ecclesiastes" comes from the Greek word *ekklesia* which is the common New Testament word for "church." An *ekklesia* was the assembly of believers who gathered together for the public worship of God and to hear the teaching of the Scriptures. Essentially, the title "Ecclesiastes" is the Greek transliteration for the Hebrew word *qoheleth*.

Thus, it appears that Solomon has taken up this pseudonym "the Preacher" like the way Samuel Clemens took up the penname Mark Twain. Solomon is preaching to us his personal account of all that he learned over his lifetime in the pursuit of pleasure. Ryken even suggests, "Ecclesiastes is his [Solomon's] memoir—an autobiographical account of what he learned from his futile attempt to live without God. In effect, the book is his final testament, written perhaps to steer his own son Rehoboam in the right spiritual direction."[4]

We can understand Solomon's life in three stages. One of my Old Testament professors helped students understand the different seasons of Solomon's life by relating it to the progression of a day—sunrise, noonday, and sunset. In the morning of this life, Solomon produced a passionate, and often erotic, study of romance in the Song of Solomon. In the noonday of his life, he wrote Proverbs—a collection of pithy sayings and wisdom giving heavenly rules for earthly living. Finally, in the evening of his life came Ecclesiastes—a regretful retrospective looking-back over the wreckage of his life. This journal is an attempt to warn others not to detour onto the broad road of destruction that he went down.

But who was Solomon really? First off it's important to realize that Solomon was born out of David's illicit affair with Bathsheba (2 Sam. 11).

---

4. Ibid., 16–17.

After the terrible fallout of David's adultery with Bathsheba and murder of Uriah, we learn that the child which was conceived from David's one-night-stand died soon after birth (2 Sam. 12:15-18). After that tragic incident, David and Bathsheba conceived and bore another son, Solomon (2 Sam. 12:24-25). David ended up fathering twenty children with multiple wives. Toward the end of his life, "the man after God's own heart" had fallen away from the Lord and there is little evidence from the Bible to suggest that David had much positive influence on his son Solomon.

To say that Solomon came from a dysfunctional family is an understatement. The turmoil surrounding young Solomon is best revealed by examining the blunders and power hungry plots of his brothers, all of whom had desires for the throne of their father. First, there was Amnon, David's eldest son. He raped his half-sister, Tamar, and then banished her from his presence. It was David's duty to punish that crime, but he did nothing (2 Sam. 13:1-20).

A second brother, Absalom, was infuriated by Amnon's actions and the passivity of his father. He boiled with rage for two years, finally concocting his own plan for revenge. Absalom got Amnon drunk at a feast, then had him murdered for raping Tamar (2 Sam. 13:23-39). He was now heir to the throne, but he kindled David's wrath with his vengeful actions. Absalom fled to Geshur, remained in exile for three years, then returned to Jerusalem to try to take the throne from David by force. In the end, Absalom died a humiliating death hanging from a tree by his hair (2 Sam. 18).

A third brother, Adonijah, also considered himself fit for the crown. He prepared chariots, horseman, and arranged for a public demonstration of his power where he named himself the next king. However, he did all this without the approval of David, the High Priest or the Lord. Nathan the prophet, hearing of these events, went to Bathsheba and warned her to tell David what was happening. Her speech spurred the king into action and David anointed Solomon as his successor (1 Kings 1:5-27). Solomon was only eighteen when he assumed the throne.

Reality television has got nothing on Solomon's tumultuous upbringing. He lacked godly examples in his life. Yet with the daunting task of leading a nation weighing on his shoulders, amazingly Solomon sought after God's wisdom. In 2 Chronicles 1:7-13, we learn how this man received his giftedness on the eve of his ascension to the throne:

> In that night God appeared to Solomon, and said to him, "Ask what I shall give you." And Solomon said to God, "You have shown great and steadfast love to David my father, and have made me king in his place. O Lord God, let your word to David

my father be now fulfilled, for you have made me king over a people as numerous as the dust of the earth. Give me now wisdom and knowledge to go out and come in before this people, for who can govern this people of yours, which is so great?" God answered Solomon, "Because this was in your heart, and you have not asked for possessions, wealth, honor, or the life of those who hate you, and have not even asked for long life, but have asked for wisdom and knowledge for yourself that you may govern my people over whom I have made you king, wisdom and knowledge are granted to you. I will also give you riches, possessions, and honor, such as none of the kings had who were before you, and none after you shall have the like." So Solomon came from the high place at Gibeon, from before the tent of meeting, to Jerusalem. And he reigned over Israel.

Think of it, Solomon literally received a blank check from God. What would you have chosen? Riches? Long-life? Superpowers? The truth is that it took wisdom to ask for wisdom, and God blessed Solomon more than any other king. Solomon needed no brain trust because according to 1 Kings 4:29, "God gave Solomon wisdom and very great insight, and a breadth of understanding as measureless as the sand on the seashore."

The crown jewel of Solomon's kingdom, and arguably his greatest masterpiece, was the building of the temple in Jerusalem. He got to do what his father David longed to do—erect a permanent house for God. Second Chronicles 3–4 spell out the magnificence of Solomon's temple. It was one of the wonders of the ancient world. The footprint of the temple spanned about two football fields in length and it glittered with gold. This project was truly an engineering marvel. First Kings 6:7 says that all the stone used to build the temple was cut and pre-fabricated in the quarry so that "neither hammer nor axe was heard in the house while it was being prepared." In other words, the block for the temple was hewn and smoothed so precisely that masons cut it out of the mountainside, transported it into Jerusalem, and fitted the stones together. You just thought modern man came up with the idea of modular homes!

Keep in mind those were in the days before cement and mortar, so the blocks had to fit together tightly. On top of that it was all done by hand—no power tools and no computers. When you factor in all the building materials—including the cedars, the gold, and the manpower—scholars estimate that to build the temple again today with all the opulence that Solomon did, it would be over $100 billion. By contrast New York's Yankee Stadium, which opened in 2009, came in at $1.5 billion as the most expensive sports venue built in the United States.

We also know that Solomon was a man who had tremendous appetites and the resources to satisfy those hungers. Solomon had so much money it was just plain silly. Second Chronicles 1:15 tells us that Solomon "made silver and gold as common in Jerusalem as stone." When I read that verse my mind goes back to the Duck Tales cartoons where Scrooge McDuck is swimming around his vault of treasure. Solomon had deep pockets and also a sexual vigor than most men fantasize about. The Bible tells us in 1 Kings 11:3 that Solomon had 700 wives and 300 concubines. Solomon had more one-night escapades than James Bond.

Solomon personally presided over a forty year season of unparalleled peace in Jerusalem. Free from the consuming rigors of military command, he had time to think, to write, to enjoy the pleasures of peace time, and to accumulate wealth from the empires of the world. The riches of every kingdom were at his disposal. He had all the brains and all the bucks a man could want. Ironically, all these factors combined to make Solomon a very unhappy camper once the bills came due from his reckless and cavalier lifestyle.

The Problem of Ecclesiastes (1:2)

"Vanity of vanities! All is vanity." If you came to Solomon for a light-hearted and uplifting message of encouragement, then this isn't the book for you. This is the preacher's synopsis of human experience. He will also end the book with this same refrain (12:8). In fact, this phrase will surface more than thirty times throughout the pages of Solomon's journal. Taken from the Hebrew word *hevel* it carries the thought of smoke, vapor, nothingness, emptiness, futility, and meaninglessness. Chuck Swindoll comments in this way:

> Being interpreted in today's terms, life is a wisp of vapor, a puff of smoke, a hollow empty ring, soap bubbles that float around then pop, a mouthful of cotton candy that dissolves in seconds and leaves us hungry, zero, zilch. That is the way Solomon described how he felt before he took his journey, while he endured his journey, and after his journey was over. Nothing satisfied. There was nothing he saw, attempted, discovered, produced, initiated or concluded as a result of his lengthy search that resulted in lasting significance or personal satisfaction. As the saying goes, "When you get to the top, you find out there is nothing there."[5]

---

5. Swindoll, *Living on the Ragged Edge*, 3.

I remember reading about Sir Edmund Hillary, the first man to climb to the summit of Mt. Everest in 1953. Someone asked him what it was like when he reached the roof of the earth and stood there on the precipice of Everest, over 29,000 feet high. He said, "For a moment there was a fleeting moment of triumphant ecstasy, then there was a sinking feeling of desolation. Where could I go from there? What mountains were there left to climb?"[6]

In 2005 the popular news documentary, *60 Minutes*, sat down and interviewed the quarterback of the New England Patriots, Tom Brady, who at the time was twenty-seven years old and had already won three Super Bowl rings. The football commentators were already talking about inducting him into the NFL Hall of Fame. Tom Brady told the interviewer, "Why do I have three Super Bowl rings and still think there's something greater out there for me to do? I mean a lot of people would say, 'Hey man, this is it. I reached my goal, my dream in life.' Me, I think: God, it's gotta be more than this. I mean this can't be what it's all cracked up to be. I mean I've done it. I'm twenty-seven. And what else is there for me?"[7]

There is no greater disappointment in life than to strive after something that you think will bring you satisfaction only to find out when you finally get there that it doesn't fill the void. Solomon had reached the peak of economic, political and academic success and found out that it was all in vain. His bank account was worth billions, but his soul was totally bankrupt. His mind was filled with libraries of wisdom, yet he stood dumbfounded by the mysteries of life. His stomach was always full, yet he still hungered for more. Solomon was a walking contradiction. Philip Yancey adds:

> Ecclesiastes endures as a work of great literature and a book of great truth because it presents both sides of life on this planet: the promise of pleasures so alluring that we may devote our lives to their pursuit, and then the haunting realization that these pleasures ultimately do not satisfy. God's tantalizing world is too big for us. Made for another home, made for eternity, we finally realize that nothing on this side of timeless Paradise will quiet the rumors of discontent ... Ecclesiastes sets forth the inevitable consequences of a life without God at the center, and the pitfalls it warns against endanger the believer as much as the pagan. King Solomon, the shadow figure behind the book, offers the best example of all.[8]

---

6. Hilary, quoted by Abba Eban, *Abba Eban: An Autobiography*, 609.
7. Schorn, "Transcript: Tom Brady, part 3."
8. Yancey, *The Bible Jesus Read*, 160–161.

Solomon figured out what so many of today's sports superstars, famous actors, and business moguls discover when they reach the top: a little money is never enough, a woman is never pretty enough, clothes are never fashionable enough, cars are never fast enough, gadgets are never modern enough, houses are never furnished enough, food is never fancy enough, relationships are never romantic enough, one achievement is never enough. Life is never enough. It's like going to the beach and drinking a mouthful of saltwater—it only makes you thirstier.

The Perspective of Ecclesiastes (1:3)

Here is a mind-boggling statistic—astronomers tell us that the sun has a diameter of 865,374 miles (1,392,684 km). Roughly speaking that's 109 times greater than the diameter of Earth. Yet If I take a dime in my hand and hold it close to my eye, it will block out the sun and I will see nothing but that small, shiny coin. Obviously, the sun dwarfs a dime, but because the coin is so close it blocks from my sight something incomparably greater.

In much the same way the daily realities of life may be neither big, nor ultimately important in the grand scheme of things, but because they are close to us they obstruct our vision. The danger is that the closeness of this world blocks out the infinitely vaster prospect of the glorious world which is beyond.

This illustration describes the myopic and limited perspective of Ecclesiastes. In 1:3 you will notice another key phrase of the book, "under the sun." It is an expression that repeats itself over twenty-five times in the book and it explains to us the vantage point from which Solomon is writing. His view of life is totally horizontal; there is no consideration of heaven. This is what life is like apart from God and the best secular man can hope for. Heaven cannot be seen because it is being obstructed by Earth. Bible teacher Ray Steadman writes:

> The book clearly states at the outset that it is limiting itself to that which is apparent to the natural mind. One of the key phrases of the book is the continual repetition of the words, "under the sun." Ecclesiastes is a collection of what man is able to discern only in the visible world. The book does not take into consideration revelation that lies beyond man's powers of observation. It is an inspired and accurate report, for it records the things which people actually believe bereft of worldview which includes God. The book is not merely a collection of ancient philosophy, for what it talks about is universal and timeless. Here is what you

will hear in soap-operas, in political speeches, in the halls of secular academia, or on the streets of any city. In this book the philosophies by which people attempt to live are brought out for honest consideration and serious critique.[9]

Notice also in 1:3 that Solomon asks the rhetorical question, "What does a man gain by all the toil at which he toils under the sun?" This question is intended to be answered with a resounding, "Nothing!" Solomon has in mind here the idea of profit or surplus which is left over from a business deal. You can read between the lines and see that at the end of all life's problems, paychecks, purchases, and pleasures that there is little to show for all our efforts to "get ahead."

As we do a flyby of this book from 25,000 feet it's important to get an overall feel for how it is put together. The structure of Ecclesiastes can be broken into three distinct sections:

- *The problem is stated* (1:1–11): In the prologue the thesis is clearly stated that there appears to be no satisfaction in the world. As the Preacher observes things from the ground level existence, tethered to Earth, he sees the endless cycles of life. The sun rises and sets, the wind blows round and round, the waters evaporate and then fall in the rain storms, and one generation of humanity overtakes another. There is a sense of cosmic indifference to the universe. It was here before we came, and it will be here, unchanged, after we have gone. Life is vanity and a chasing after the wind.

- *The problem is studied* (1:12–12:8): This is the main body of Solomon's quest as he searches for satisfaction in the world. However, fulfillment remains elusive in everything he tries. In this section Solomon rolls up his sleeves and does some wild living. He tells us his observations, feelings and thoughts from all his endeavors. The Preacher also takes his readers down several thought provoking rabbit trails. Being a jack of all trades, Solomon is going to touch on nearly every area of life—money, politics, philosophy, work, sex, death, injustice, aging, relationships and wisdom. The Preacher-King isn't looking to give us simple answers. Instead, he does a good job to raise many issues and leave them unresolved.

- *The problem is solved* (12:9–14): In the end, Solomon concludes that ultimate satisfaction is found in fearing God and keeping His commands. He finds out that humanity has an infinite capacity for happiness, but that appetite cannot be filled by mere finite things. Only the

9. Stedman, "The Search for Meaning."

fear of the Lord leads to meaning and contentment. Fearing God is a wise way to live because it takes into account the inevitability of divine judgment and eternity.

As Solomon works through the problems of "under the sun" living you will notice that a handful of themes run through the journal and continually resurface. These thematic elements tie the book to together and bring cohesiveness to what seems like an unstructured stream of consciousness. Examine the chart below to see how these underlying themes weave in and out of the text.

Theme	Scripture
The vanity of riches	2:11, 2:18, 4:8, 5:10, 5:13, 6:1-2
The certainty of death	2:14-15, 3:19-20, 5:15-16, 6:6, 8:8, 9:2-3, 12:6-7
Enjoy life	2:24, 3:12, 3:22, 5:18-19, 8:15, 9:7-9
The sovereignty of God	3:11, 3:17, 5:10, 7:13-14, 8:17, 9:1, 11:5
Fear the Lord	3:14, 5:7, 7:18, 8:12-13, 11:9, 12:13-14
Injustice and oppression	3:16, 4:1, 5:8, 7:7, 8:11, 8:14
Wisdom and folly	1:17, 7:1-13, 7:19, 9:16-18, 10:1-20
The limits of human reason	3:11, 3:21, 6:12, 7:23, 8:16-17, 11:5

Remember Maze Mania? There was one detail I purposefully left out that I need to tell you. Built above the maze was an observation deck. It was a place where parents who were not in the maze could sit and watch their kids wander aimlessly around the labyrinth of wood and concrete. As I went from one dead-end to another, I can remember looking up at the deck and seeing my father. I thought to myself, "If only I could look down from his perspective I could see the big-picture and eventually find my way out." I waved at my dad in confusion and yelled for directions, but no matter how much pointing and coaching I received, I was still stuck. My viewpoint was crowded by screaming kids, blazing sunlight and walls in every direction. If only I could get above it all. That's what Ecclesiastes is all about. It is one man trapped on earth trying to get an eternal perspective from heaven. He cannot see the forest for the trees. He cannot rise above the sun.

The great English evangelist John Wesley once preached his way through Ecclesiastes. In his personal journal he described what it was like to begin that series of sermons. "Began expounding the Book of Ecclesiastes," he wrote. "Never before had I so clear a sight either of its meanings or beauties. Neither did I imagine, that the several parts of it were in so exquisite a manner connected together, all tending to prove the grand truth, that there is no happiness out of God."[10] All the oases of the world which promise pleasure are merely mirages. Only in God do we find the sweet waters of joy and everlasting life which bring gratification to our thirsty souls.

---

10. Wesley, quoted by R.N. Whybray, *Ecclesiastes*, The New Century Bible Commentary, xii-xiii.

2

The Circles of Life (1:4–11)

In one of his books, Dr. David Jeremiah tells the gut-wrenching true story of Thomas "Toivi" Blatt—a holocaust survivor. He writes:

> The Sobibor Nazi concentration camp was set in the scenic woods near the Bug River, which separates Poland and Russia. The natural beauty of the setting stood in stark contrast to the stench and horror of the camp, where torture and death awaited every man, woman and child who arrived there.
>
> On October 14, 1943 Jewish slave laborers in Sobibor surprised their captors by using their shovels and pickaxes as weapons in a well-planned attack. Some of the Jewish prisoners cut the electricity to the fence and used captured pistols and rifles to shoot their way past German guards. Hundreds of others stormed through the barbed wire and mine fields to the potential safety of the nearby forest.
>
> Of the seven hundred prisoners who took part in the escape, three hundred made it to the forest. Of those less than one hundred are known to have survived. The remainder were hunted down by the Germans and executed.
>
> One of the survivors was a man named Thomas Blatt—or Toivi, as he was known in his native Poland. Toivi was fifteen years old when his family was herded into Sobibor. His parents were executed in the gas chamber, but Toivi, young and healthy, was a prime candidate for slave labor. In the confusion of the escape, Toivi attempted to crawl through a hole in the barbed wire fence but was trampled by prisoners who stormed the fence. As a result, he was one of the last to make it out of the camp.

Toivi and two companions set off in a nightmare journey through the dense woods. By day they rested beneath the camouflage of brush and branch; by night they fought their way through a black expanse of tree and foliage. They were driven both by youthful vigor and fear; by determination and desperation. Most significantly, they were propelled by that elusive thing they had now reclaimed: *hope*.

What they needed and craved was a guide—someone who could read the stars, who knew north from south, east from west. These were city boys lacking in outdoor skills.

After four nights of stumbling through the cold forest, the three boys saw a building silhouetted against a dark sky in the distance. Could it mean sanctuary? Perhaps a woodsman to help them towards safety? With hope and growing gratitude, they hurried forward.

As they got closer, they noticed that the building they had seen was a tower—a familiar tower. It was part of the Sobibor concentration camp! The three boys had made one giant circle through the woods and ended up exactly where they started.

Terrified, horrified, they backed into the waiting arms of the forest once more. But only Toivi lived to recount their awful experience.[1]

I think Toivi's circular journey through the unforgiving wilderness is a microcosm of the frustration and futility that many feel as they struggle through the daily grind. If life seems like one big hamster wheel or a never-ending treadmill where you exert lots of energy but never go anywhere, it's because it is according to Solomon. Oh, and that light at the end of the tunnel is not a safe passage, it's actually an oncoming train!

Solomon has already made the point that all of life is like a sputtering balloon that is quickly deflating. Imagine that I take a balloon out of my pocket—this balloon represents your life at birth. By filling the balloon with oxygen from my lungs I'm providing a visual illustration of your lifespan. I now clasp the end of the balloon with my thumb and index finger, holding it in the air—this is the sum total of your life's potential. As I release the pressure of my fingers, the air begins to escape at a quickening rate. In a mad rush to jettison all the gaseous contents, the balloon sputters and smacks as it erratically whirls through the air. In a matter of seconds the balloon's potential is exhausted and it lies shriveled up on the ground.

Got the picture? That's the message of the opening lines to this book, "Vanity of vanities. All is vanity!" From his "under the sun" vantage point,

---

1. Jeremiah, *Searching for Heaven on Earth*, 1–2.

Solomon argues that life, in the end, has no meaning. This kind of encouragement doesn't exactly get you motivated to spring out of bed in the morning, does it?

About three-thousand years ago this was Solomon's great disillusionment. His father, David, left him a strong and wealthy kingdom to rule over. David fought all the battles of war and handed over a time of unparalleled peace and prosperity to his son Solomon. Not having to direct his money and energy to build up the war machine, Solomon used his fabulous finances and wisdom to peruse the meaning of life. After putting his mind and his bank account behind living life to the hilt, Solomon, now a weary and cynical old man, picks up his pen and records all that he learned.

Solomon tried to squeeze every drop out of life, so he tried it all. As the wisest of the wise, Solomon was a renaissance man, a man of all seasons, part scientist, part historian, part philosopher. He tells us that after all his pursuits it gained him nothing. He was like those boys walking for miles around the concentration camp only to end up back at the entrance.

In the opening lines of his journal Solomon opens with a poem to express the utter monotony and futility of life under the sun. The first half of his introductory poem gives examples from the creation and the natural world (1:4–7), while the second half of the poem draws from human experience (1:8–11). His point is that people on planet Earth may talk about progress—economic development, technological advances, evolutionary improvements—but it's all a myth. There is never any progress: life is just the same old, same old.[2] The preacher highlights three conclusions in his prologue that we shouldn't miss.

Nothing Has Really Changed (1:4–7)

Solomon begins by noticing the constancy and regularity of nature. He wants us to see that over time nothing really changes and therefore life on earth without God in focus is a predictable, boring, closed system.

First, he points to *the course of life (1:4).* "A generation goes, and a generation comes, but the earth remains forever." The Preacher contrasts the transitory nature of human generations with the permanence and apparent immutability of the creation. One commentator suggested, "We could well imagine Solomon sitting at his breakfast table with the newspaper opened, reading the birth announcements on one side and the obituaries on the next. Generations pass in a parade. In the hospital there is someone on their deathbed on the tenth floor and a baby is being born on the third

2. Ryken, *Ecclesiastes*, 25.

floor. History is a running drama of millennial length, the earth as the stage abides, but the actors play their parts and move offstage."[3]

This is true if you're rich or poor, educated or dumb, blue-collar or white collar. It's true if you live in a penthouse, the White House or the doghouse. Death overtakes us all. It comes for people that make us laugh like comedian Chris Farley. It comes for talented people that entertain and amaze us like Michael Jackson. It comes for people that give us hope and inspire us like Princess Diana. It comes for the super-wealthy like Howard Hughes.

Last time I checked the death rate is ten out of ten. Researchers estimate that over ninety million people die every year worldwide—that means about 3 people die every second, 180 every minute and nearly 11,000 every hour, 250,000 every day. Meanwhile, 4 million are born in the US every year.[4]

Rabbi Harold Kushner tells of a man who came to him for counseling. After the usual small talk, the man revealed his true purpose for coming. Kushner explains:

> "Two weeks ago," said the man, "for the first time in my life I went to the funeral of a man my own age. I didn't know him well, we worked together, talked to each other from time to time, had kids about the same age. He died suddenly over the weekend . . . It could just as easily have been me. That was two weeks ago. They have already replaced him at the office. I hear his wife is moving out of state to live with her parents. Two weeks ago he was working fifty feet away from me, and now it's as if he never existed. It's like a rock falling into a pool of water and then the water is the same as it was before, but the rock isn't there anymore. Rabbi, I've hardly slept at all since then. I can't stop thinking that it could happen to me, and a few days later I will be forgotten as if I had never lived. Shouldn't a man's life be more than that?[5]

We are born, we live, work, raise a family, pay bills, then we die and return to dust. Meanwhile, the earth mocks us because it endures while we become food for the worms.

Second, Solomon brings to our attention *the circle of the sun (1:5)*. "The sun rises, and the sun goes down, and hastens to the place where it rises." Even the sun is like a silent uncaring machine that rises and falls. The earth

---

3. Jeremiah, *Searching for Heaven on Earth*, 4.
4. Alcorn, *Heaven*, xxi.
5. Kushner, *When All You've Wanted Isn't Enough*, 20.

turns on its axis, the earth orbits around the sun, another day, another week, month, season, year . . . big deal. The sun is like a runner endlessly making his way around a racetrack. It is indifferent to the plight of humanity living out their lives on a blue orb 93 million miles away.

Actually, what astronomers tell us about the sun is quite amazing. The sun is so large that it would take a jet plane flying from the sun's surface at five-hundred miles per hour well over a month just to reach the center of our "average" star. At the same time it's blazing so violently that to produce the observed energy being emitted from the solar surface, the equivalent of a 100 billion hydrogen bombs must be exploding every second in its unfathomably hot, dense core. Or, to convey it another way, it would take the gross national product of the United States for 7 million years in order for your local power company to run the sun for a mere second.[6]

Doomsday preppers might wonder, "When will the sun run out energy and burnout?" The sun, like most stars in the universe, is in the main sequence stage of its life. Every second, 600 million tons of hydrogen are converted into helium in the Sun's core, generating 4×10^{27} Watts of energy. Astronomers tell us that this process has been going for 4.6 billion years. However, there isn't an unlimited amount of hydrogen in the core of the sun. In fact, it's only got another 7 billion years' worth of fuel left.[7]

So don't get your undies in wad! We are in no danger of a solar apocalypse ending life as we know it. This should help make Solomon's point even more lucid. The sun was here long before you or I were born, and it will remain long after we are gone. Remember that Solomon's pessimism comes from his disconnect with God. Life without God results in a universe that is an endlessly running machine, a great production line running indefinitely and producing nothing. Life is not forward progression; it's a rut, an exercise bike that goes nowhere.

Third, Solomon notes *the circuit of the winds (1:6)*. "The wind blows to the south and goes around to the north; around and around goes the wind, and on its circuits the wind returns." The wind also travels in a constant pattern blowing north to south, east to west in a big circle. The weather man has an endless job trying to predict where the next storm will arise. Sometimes they are close and sometimes they miss it totally. It's the only occupation where you can be wrong half of the time and still have a job.

Isaiah would write, "As for man, his days are like grass, he flourishes like a flower in the field, the wind blows over it and it is gone, and its place remembers it no more (40:6)." Give the wind enough time and it will erode

---

6. Dubay, *The Evidential Power of Beauty*, 133–136.
7. Cain, "The Life of the Sun."

the faces on Mt. Rushmore. Just look at the pyramids of Egypt and ruins of the Roman Coliseum. Entropy wins. Solomon's words remind me of the hit song by the rock band Kansas:

> I close my eyes only for a moment and the moment's gone.
> All my dreams pass before my eyes with curiosity.
>
> Dust in the wind, all they are is dust in the wind.
>
> Same old song, just a drop of water in an endless sea.
> All we do, crumbles to the ground, though we refuse to see.
>
> Dust in the wind, all we are is dust in the wind.
>
> Don't hang on, nothing last forever but the earth and sky.
> It slips away and all your money won't another minute buy.
>
> Dust in the wind, all we are is dust in the wind.[8]

Some of you probably had that on 8-track or vinyl back in the day! The Preacher's point is still the same. The human participants in the drama of creation—those who pass across the stage that this world provides—are relatively insignificant when considered in the context of the blowing winds. The sands of time sweep over and erase the marks they have made so that they are obliterated. Life is like the erosion of footprints on the seashore. Fourth, we must also observe *the cycle of the water (1:7)*. "All streams run to the sea, but the sea is not full; to the place where the streams flow, there they flow again." The Bible never claims to be a science text book, but Solomon has some amazing insights into the hydrologic cycle of the earth. This is an example of what many Bible scholars call "prescience"—that is scientific statements in Scripture that far exceed the general knowledge of the time.

Scientists tell us that at any given moment 97 percent of all the water is in Earth's oceans and only .0001 percent in the atmosphere is available for rain. No wonder then why the depth of the sea never seems to go up or down. The water cycle is an endless pattern of evaporation, condensation and precipitation. It rains and the water flows into the rivers and the rivers into the sea and nothing changes.

If the sun, wind and mighty rivers have nothing to show for all their constant labor, then what hope do we have of ever accomplishing anything lasting in life? Oddly enough, homemakers probably can relate to these verses better than anyone else, with the endless barrage of dirty dishes,

---

8. Livgrin, "Dust in the Wind."

soiled laundry and vacuuming up newly deposited dust and grime. James Dobson gives a perfect description of life for all those trapped in a middle-class, suburban nightmare, which he calls "the straight life."

> The straight life for a homemaker is washing dishes three hours a day; it is cleaning sinks and scouring toilets and washing floors; it is chasing toddlers and mediating fights between pre-school siblings. The straight life is driving your station wagon to school and back twenty-three times per week; it is grocery shopping and baking cupcakes for the class Halloween party. The straight life eventually means becoming the parent of an ungrateful teenager, which I assure is no job for sissies. Certainly, the straight life for the homemaker can be an exhausting experience at times. The straight life for a working man is not much simpler. It is pulling your tired frame out of bed five days a week, fifty weeks out of the year. It is earning a two-week vacation in August and choosing a trip that will please the kids. The straight life is spending your money wisely when you'd rather indulge in whatever; it is taking your son bike riding on Saturday when you want so badly to watch the baseball game; it is cleaning the garage on your day off after working sixty hours the previous week. The straight life is coping with head colds and engine tune-ups and crab grass and income tax forms; it is taking your family to church on Sunday when you've heard every idea the minister has to offer; it is giving a portion of your income to God's work when you already wonder how you make ends meet. The straight life for the ordinary, garden variety husband and father is everything I have listed and more . . . much more.[9]

Nothing Really Brings Contentment (1:8)

I think by the time Solomon writes verse eight, he does so with a sigh. "All things are wearisome, more than one can say. The eye never has enough of seeing, nor the ear its fill of hearing." What is true of the sun, wind and water is true of the temporal pursuits of man. Life under the sun is not only futile, but nothing is ever fulfilling and nothing is ever fresh. There is never enough to fill the existential void inside the human soul.

This is totally applicable to our day in which people live for the next big thing. Take a stroll through the dizzying world of consumer electronics and you'll be overwhelmed. Buy a flat screen TV and in a year they have already

---

9. Dobson, *Straight Talk to Men and their Wives*, 141.

come out with something bigger and better. Purchase a computer and in a few months the technology is outdated. First came vinyl and then in the 80s it was cassette tapes. Then in the 90s it was compact discs. Then in the 2000s the mp3 digitized and compressed all that audio into a computer file. People will wait in line for two days and practically stampede each other just to get the new smartphone or tablet. Then in a month or two a sleeker, faster, upgraded version of the same product surpasses it.

This is also true in the area of pleasure. That affair that looks so satisfying will be gratifying for a season until your spouse finds out about it. That car or boat, which is so tantalizing on the showroom floor, will eventually become burdensome once you get into making the monthly payments. That vacation that you saved up for months will be fun for a week until you get home and then it's back to work on Monday morning. You can get that promotion or that degree and then after the congratulations stop coming in you'll look around and say, "What's next?"

I read about a recent survey that was done in which people were asked the question, "What are you living for?" Not surprisingly, ninety-four percent of participants said they were waiting for something in the future. Waiting for children to grow up, waiting to retire, waiting to the next football season, waiting for a new job, waiting to get married." Pretty soon you have waited around and life is gone.

In an interview with NPR, former Beatles star Paul McCartney said:

> It seems to me that no matter how famous you are, no matter how accomplished or how many awards you get, you're always still thinking there's somebody out there who's better than you. I'm often reading a magazine and hearing about someone's new record and I think, "Oh, boy, that's gonna be better than me." It's a very common thing.

The interviewer then asked, "But, Sir Paul McCartney: You have had success in so many dimensions of music. You really feel a competitive insecurity with somebody else that's coming out with a record?" McCartney replied: "Unfortunately, yes . . . I should be able to look at my accolades and go, 'Come on, Paul. That's enough.' But there's still this little voice in the back of my brain that goes, 'No, no, no. You could do better. This person over here is excelling. Try harder!' It still can be a little bit intimidating."[10]

---

10. "What Makes Paul McCartney Nervous?," *NPR: All Things Considered*, 15 October 2013.

Nothing is Really Cutting-Edge (1:9–11)

"All new news is old news happening to new people," so said Malcom Muggeridge. Rudyard Kipling once quipped, "The craft we call modern, the crimes we call new, John Bunyan had them typed and filed in 1682." The more things change, the more they stay the same. There are no new ideas; we are all guilty of plagiarism. The ancients thought our ideas. We take old ideas and recycle them. If it appears that something new happens from time to time, it is only because our memories are short. Most of us are ignorant of history so we keep thinking we're coming up with new ideas.

This appears to be what Solomon is saying when he writes, "What has been will be again, what has been done will be done again, there is nothing new under the sun. Is there anything of which one can say, "Look! This is something new"? It was here already, long ago; it was here before our time."

I once read an interesting article about how the dimensions and standards of our modern railways and roads were determined. The article stated that the U.S. standard railroad gauge (distance between rails) is four feet, eight-and-one-half inches. Why such an odd number? Because that's the way they built them in England, and American railroads were built by British expatriates. Why did the English adopt that particular gauge? Because the people who built the pre-railroad tramways used that gauge. They in turn were locked into that gauge because the people who built tramways used the same standards and tools they had used for building wagons which were set on a gauge of four feet, eight-and-one-half inches. Why were wagons built to that scale? Because with any other size, the wheels did not match the old wheel ruts on the roads. So who built these old rutted roads? The first long-distance roads in Europe were built by the Roman Empire for the benefit of their army's legions of soldiers. The roads have been in use ever since. The ruts were first made by Roman chariots. It just happened that four feet, eight-and-one-half inches was the width a chariot needed to be to accommodate the width of two horses.[11]

I'm not an expert in the development of transportation, but the point is still the same: "nothing is new under the sun." What Solomon is describing here is a kind of historical amnesia. "No one remembers the former generations," he says. Certainly, there are new inventions and new technologies—the wheel, the telephone, the internal combustion engine, the splitting of the atom—but what Solomon is getting at here is this: don't mistake innovation for progress.

---

11. Hilton, "A History of Track Gauge," *Trains*, 1 May 2006.

These things may make life more convenient, but they don't really do much to make us happy or fix the age old problems of the human condition. The transition from spears and swords to bullets and bombs in military technology only made us more proficient at killing one another. The Internet may have turned the world into a global village, but at the same time it brought with on a new set of menaces—easily accessible pornography, identity theft and privacy infringement. Medical technology has eradicated diseases like polio, only to see other virulent strains mutate into deadlier microscopic killers. In the end the same problems still plague us: poverty, famine, sickness, shortage of resources, and moral depravity.

Solomon argues that not only are there no new experiences that can be had, there is no guarantee that you will even be remembered. Here is a sobering thought—the reality is that in one-hundred years all of us will be dead and anyone who was alive that might remember us will be dead too. Our existence will all but be forgotten. We are here today and gone tomorrow.

Just in case you think people will remember the famous and influential a recent survey done by various news magazines show that the American populace is woefully ignorant when it comes to basic facts about history. A *New York Times* article revealed that: fifty percent of US citizens could not identify when the Civil War was fought, only thirty-five percent could name one of the original signatures on the Declaration of the Independence and seventy-nine percent could not identify lines from the Gettysburg address. Most could not even recall the achievement of Neil Armstrong's moon landing. Neil who?[12]

That's life under the sun: Nothing different, nothing fulfilling, nothing new and nothing remembered. I am reminded of the genius philosopher and scientist Blaise Pascal (1623–1662). Pascal was a childhood prodigy. By age ten, Pascal was doing original experiments in mathematics and physical science. To help his father, who was a tax collector, he invented the first calculating device (some call it the first "computer"). By fifteen he had already graduated from the Academy of Science in Paris, France and was turning the heads of the intellectual elite. Later he developed the barometer, vacuum pump, air compressor, syringe, and the hydraulic press.

However, for all his achievements in science and math Pascal became very bored with life. On the verge of total disillusionment he decided to turn to spirituality. Then on November 23, 1654 he experienced what he called "the night of fire." He picked up a Bible and read John 17:3, "Now

---

12. Dillon, "Survey Finds Teenagers Ignorant on Basic History and Literature Questions."

this is eternal life: that they know you, the only true God, and Jesus Christ, whom you have sent." Pascal gave his life to Christ. He spent the rest of his days a vocal Christian and he used his intimidating intellect to argue for truth of the Scriptures. One of his most famous sayings echoes the words of Ecclesiastes, "There is a God-shaped vacuum in the heart of every man that cannot be filled with any created thing, but by God alone made known through Jesus Christ."

When Pascal died they found sewed into the lining of his coat a parchment with the Bible verse which led to his conversion, and the words of his commitment to Christ scribbled down like so:

> In the year of Grace, 1654
> On Monday, 23rd of November
>
> Fire!
> God of Abraham, God of Isaac, God of Jacob
> Not of the philosophers and scholars
> Certitude. Certitude. Feeling. Joy. Peace.
> Joy, joy, joy, tears of joy.
> This is eternal life, that they may know You, the Only true God, and Jesus Christ who You have sent.
> Jesus Christ. Let me never be separated from Him.[13]

When we can't find satisfaction under the sun, we can find satisfaction in the Son.

---

13. "Blaise Pascal: Scientific and Spiritual Prodigy," *Christianity Today*, 8 August 2008.

3

The Search for Meaning (1:12–2:11)

ONE OF THE MOST popular stories from Greek mythology is the myth of Sisyphus. According to one telling of the legend, Sisyphus was known for his cunning and trickery against the gods. Sisyphus especially angered Zeus for revealing the secrets of the divines to mortals. His greatest deception came at the end of his life when Hades, the god of the underworld, was ordered to arrest Sisyphus and take him away in chains. However, when Hades showed up to claim Sisyphus for the kingdom of the dead the wily old king was prepared. Hades brought with him a long set of chains, but clever Sisyphus expressed such an interest in the handcuffs that Hades was persuaded to demonstrate their use on himself. Thus, Hades was locked up in the palace of Sisyphus.

Finally, Sisyphus was subdued by the gods for his treachery and given a punishment far worse than death. Sisyphus was sentenced to unending labor. His eternal task was to roll a massive boulder to the top of a hill, only to watch it roll back down the hill again and repeat the exercise endlessly. His hell was in having to perform a pointless act from which nothing ever came except a vein repetition that compounded the emptiness. Not by one step, nor by a thousand, or ten thousand, was he able to expiate the sin against the gods which brought about this cursed fate. A modern rhyme expressed the same pointless existence:

> A cheerful old bear at the zoo
> He never lacked anything to do.
> When it bored him, you know,
> to walk to and fro,

He reversed it and walked fro and to.[1]

Strangely enough, Sisyphus and Solomon had a lot in common. Solomon was cursed with the same plight of a meaningless existence. Even though the famed king of wisdom had vast riches, delicacies at the snap of his fingers, beautiful women at his bedside and architectural achievements with his name etched on them, it all became banal and boring. Life for Solomon had lost all meaning and his overindulgence led to a vapid existence of rolling boulders.

In the movie and the book, *The Hitchhikers Guide to the Galaxy*, a group of pan-dimensional, hyper-intelligent creatures were so fed up with trying to understand the meaning of life that they constructed a super-computer named "Deep Thought" to calculate the answer to "life, the universe and everything." When they asked Deep Thought, "What is the meaning of life?" they are told to return in 7.5 million years—this would give the computer enough time to check and double-check its calculations. 7.5 million years go by and finally Deep Thought spits out its answer: the meaning of life, the universe and everything is "42."

"Forty-two!" some disillusioned soul yells out from the crowd, "Is that all you've got to show for 7.5 million years of work?" Deep Thought replies in its soothing monotone voice, "I checked it thoroughly, and that quite definitely is the answer. I think the problem, to be quite honest with you, is that you've never actually known what the question is."

The meaning of life is the quest of Ecclesiastes, yet in order to get the right answer we need to know the right questions. Sisyphus, Deep Thought and Solomon could not crack the code to the universe's greatest conundrum. Thus far, Solomon's focus has been totally "under the sun." He has turned over every rock in a desperate search for what will bring meaning and lasting contentment in life.

Solomon has been writing in the previous verses about the apparent futility that he observes when looking at the different cycles of the natural world. Life, he concludes, is like trying to corral the wind—frustrating, pointless and exhausting. He moves on in his journal to describe for his readers the various ways in which he tried to fill the existential vacuum in his soul. Notice that the perspective shifts from the third person to the first person beginning in verse 1:12. Solomon now draws from his reservoir of personal experience. The following passage explains the various ways that people today still try to find fulfillment in life. Solomon tried them all and, at the end of his experiment in the laboratory of life, he concludes in 2:11 that, "there was no profit under the sun."

1. Ravi Zacharias, *The Real Face of Atheism*, 75.

He Searched for Meaning in Wisdom (1:12–18)

Solomon began his journey for fulfillment down the pathway of higher learning. However, as he grew in knowledge and hung another degree on the wall, he found out that education still left him empty. 1 Kings 4:29–34 tells us of Solomon's famous wisdom:

> And God gave Solomon wisdom and understanding beyond measure, and breadth of mind like the sand on the seashore, so that Solomon's wisdom surpassed the wisdom of all the people of the east and all the wisdom of Egypt. For he was wiser than all other men, wiser than Ethan the Ezrahite, and Heman, Calcol, and Darda, the sons of Mahol, and his fame was in all the surrounding nations. He also spoke 3,000 proverbs, and his songs were 1,005. He spoke of trees, from the cedar that is in Lebanon to the hyssop that grows out of the wall. He spoke also of beasts, and of birds, and of reptiles, and of fish. And people of all nations came to hear the wisdom of Solomon, and from all the kings of the earth, who had heard of his wisdom.

As you can see, Solomon had an impressive academic resume. Yet a PhD in philosophy was not enough, so he turned his mind to other studies—biology, zoology, music, astronomy, science, political theory—his thirst for knowledge could not be quenched. However, for all his wisdom he admits in 1:15 that there were many things which remained crooked in his mind and he couldn't straighten out all the questions which vexed him. There still remained many gaps in his knowledge that he could not fill in with man's reasoning.

As someone who has spent a great deal of time in the academy I can attest to the words of 1:16–18. The more you learn, the more you become aware of how ignorant you really are. Sir Isaac Newton, the great mathematician and scientist figured this out. The genius who refined the principles of physics once said of all his learning, "I do not know what I may appear to the world, but to myself I seem to have been only like a boy playing on the sea-shore, and diverting myself in now and then finding a smoother pebble or a prettier shell than ordinary, whilst the great ocean of truth lay all undiscovered before me."

Satisfy one intellectual pursuit, and inevitably another question comes up in your mind. Finish reading one book and there is a newer one that overturns the findings of the previous book you just finished. There is always another paper to write, another topic to research, another mystery that eludes understanding.

Historians have tried to calculate and quantify the cumulative measure of human wisdom. It has been said that if we were to chart the total of human wisdom in inches from the beginning of recorded history to the year 1845 it would be one inch. Human knowledge from 1845 to 1945 would be three inches. However from 1945 to 1975 human knowledge has increased exponentially, if that amount of data were represented by distance it would be the height of the Washington monument (555 feet). Knowledge doubles every two years thus making the learner's task a never-ending pursuit.

The great irony is that we have more access to knowledge and learning today than ever before and yet we are still the most unhappy and self-destructive generation. Sadly, if you turn to the so-called "experts" you don't find much hope. Case in point: Stephen Hawking, the world-renowned Cambridge physicist. In his 2010 best-selling book, *The Grand Design*, Hawking argued that the law of gravity was the reason why there is a universe at all. He wrote, "Because there is a law like gravity, the universe can and will create itself from nothing."[2] Of course, Hawking is making some major assumptions, namely that gravity has always existed without ever explaining where it came from.

Laws don't write themselves any more than books do, yet atheists insist that a Creator need not be invoked. Moreover, laws don't create anything; they merely describe the way events occur most of the time. Gravity, inertia and quantum mechanics could never cause a car engine to assemble itself from spare parts in a junkyard, so why would the universe pull itself up by its own metaphysical bootstraps? How does the law of gravity choose to create?

So according to atheistic scientists like Hawking, we are all products of time, matter and chance. A cosmic accident brought about by the cold, uncaring laws of the universe. When asked about the meaning of life in a 2011 interview Hawking replied, "Science predicts that many different kinds of universes will be spontaneously created out of nothing. It is a matter of chance which one we are in. So we should seek the greatest value of our action."[3] In other words, Hawking was saying that since we inhabit a universe in which there is no God or prospect of life after death then we should do our very best to make every day count for the best.

That's interesting since Hawking has just told us that life is pure randomness. The atheist believes that he is an accident—a random collocation of atoms brought about by forces of intergalactic indifference. Yet at the

---

2. Hawking and Mlodinow, *The Grand Design*, 180.

3. Sample, "Stephen Hawking: 'There Is No Heaven; It's a Fairy Story,'" *The Guardian*, 15 May 2011.

same time we are told that we should try to make the best of the situation by creating our own meaning in an ultimately meaningless universe. That's under-the-sun living at its core. Sisyphus would identify with such an explanation.

Solomon is touching on a sensitive nerve that the information age needs to examine—learning is not enough. Socrates, Descartes, Newton and Hawking will never be able to scratch your deepest intellectual itch. If education were the answer to man's ills then the colleges and universities would be the treasuries of ultimate meaning. Take it from someone who has been there, if you spend some time walking around the libraries and lecture halls of higher learning you'll find out those who know the most are often the gloomiest.

Don't misunderstand me, I'm not anti-education, but knowledge without the fear of God is useless. That's why Proverbs 1:7 says, "The fear of the LORD is the beginning of knowledge." An educated man is nothing more than a smarter sinner. Learning is not enough; it leaves the student more miserable in their existential quest because they discover that even the most brilliant minds were also stumped by life's most basic questions. Unlike your high school algebra textbook, the answers to the life's questions are not found in the back of the book.

He Searched for Meaning in Wild Living (2:1-3)

Solomon did not find ultimate fulfillment in books, so he thought, "Maybe I will find it in pleasure." So he rolled up his sleeves and began doing some partying. Solomon turned his palace into an ancient version of the Las Vegas strip. Hedonism was the name of the game and if anyone could throw a party it was Solomon. He was a man with unlimited resources, unending curiosity and no accountability. In fact we get an understanding of his no-holds-barred approach when we read in Ecclesiastes 2:10 that, "Whatever my eyes desired I did not keep from them. I did not withhold from my heart any pleasure."

Consider some of the amazing facts the Bible tells us about Solomon's pursuit of pleasure. 1 Kings 4:22 tells us how much food was consumed daily in his palace, "Solomon's provision for one day was thirty cors of fine flour and sixty cors of meal, ten fat oxen, and twenty pasture-fed cattle, a hundred sheep, besides deer, gazelles, roebucks, and fattened fowl." The modern equivalent of a single cor was six bushels. In other words, Solomon had enough food every day to feed an army.

We already know from looking at 1 Kings 11:3 that he had 700 wives and 300 concubines. Solomon could have enjoyed any kind of sexual experience with any number of women at any time of the day. If Solomon were alive today he would make Hugh Hefner look like an amateur.

Solomon first tested the limits of *laughter*. According to 2:2 Solomon brought in the court jesters and comedians to see if their antics could make him happy. "I said of laughter, 'It is mad,' and of pleasure, 'What use is it?'"

I am reminded of the story of the man who made an appointment to see a psychologist. He arrived at the psychologist's office and said to him, "Doctor, I always feel depressed. No matter what I do I can't shake the blues. I just don't know what to do." The psychologist looked at him and said, "Come with me to the window." The man followed and then the psychologist pointed outside and said, "Do you see that tent over there in the distance? Well, there is a circus in town and it is really good. There are lots of acts to watch, especially the clown acts. And there is one clown in particular who is extremely funny. He will make you rock with laughter over and over again. Go and see that clown and I guarantee that you will not have reason to be depressed again!" The man turned to the psychologist with sad eyes and said, "Doctor, I am that clown." In the end, Solomon mocked laughter. It was temporary escape from a bad dream.

When the gags weren't funny anymore Solomon turned to *liquor* in 2:3. "I searched with my heart how to cheer my body with wine—my heart still guiding me with wisdom—and how to lay hold on folly, till I might see what was good for the children of man to do under heaven during the few days of their life." Many people assume Solomon was a "party animal" who got drunk as a skunk. Not so; he was too smart for that. Instead he was more like a connoisseur of fine wines and liquors. He sought to chemically alter his body in such a way that pleasure would be maximized without giving himself over to a drunken stupor. One Hebrew scholar commented this way:

> "To nourish my flesh with wine" should be taken as a reference to a consumption of wine which enables a man to get the highest possible enjoyment by a careful use of it, so that appetite is sharpened, enjoyment enhanced, and the finest banquets could be sampled and enjoyed to the highest degree. Approximating or falling into drunkenness is not under consideration. They very thought of such crude extravagance is barred by the expression, "my mind was still keeping control by means of wisdom." In other words, here was a carefully controlled experiment.[4]

---

4. Leupold, *Exposition of Ecclesiastes*, 60.

Solomon turned partying into a science, and yet it still was not enough. Does this sound like the evening entertainment news or what? You just thought the drugged-out Hollywood celebs and rock stars invented living the high life. Solomon found out that trying to find fulfillment by going after pleasure is like trying to empty the oceans with an eye dropper. The epitome of frustration is when the dopamine and endorphins don't take you as high as they once did.

Chuck Swindoll once told a story about a fictional man who had the amazing ability to make his dreams come true by merely thinking them into existence. All he had to do was think of it and—POOF—it happened! So this man imagined a mansion with fifteen bedrooms, swimming pool, and hoards of servants to wait on him hand and foot—POOF—there is was!

He imagined a huge garage filled with fleets of sports cars and trucks. Instantly he had the finest wheels that money could buy. He was free to drive any of those cars, or sit back in the black stretch limousine with mafia glass wrapped around the rear and have the chauffeur drive him wherever he wished. But there is really no place to go since he has it all, so he comes back home and imagines a sumptuous feast.

Laid out in front of him is a buffet that would make the stuff they serve on Carnival cruises look like TV dinners—lobster, t-bone steak, yeast rolls, chocolate cake—yet he sits and eats alone. After several weeks of this he grows so terribly bored and unchallenged that he whispers to one of the attendants, "I want to get out of this. I want to create something again. I'd rather be in hell than here." To which one of the servants replied, "Where do you think you are?"[5]

I think in some degree that is what hell will be like. Hell is a place where you have insatiable desires that can never be satisfied. Isn't that exactly what the rich man that Jesus talked about in Luke 16 experienced? The Bible says he was thirsty and yet Lazarus was not allowed to cool his tongue with a single drop of water (Luke 16:24). G.K. Chesterton put things into perspective when he said, "Meaninglessness does not come from being weary of pain; meaninglessness comes from being weary of pleasure." Solomon desensitized his brain to the effects of pleasure and it all became hum-drum.

He Searched for Meaning in Work (2:4–6)

Solomon next turned his energy and ingenuity towards building great monuments and pleasure palaces. He thought, "I'll etch my name in marble

---

5. Swindoll, *Living on the Ragged Edge*, 33–34.

and build something that will stand the test of time." In the words of Derek Kinder, "He creates a little world within a world: multiform, harmonious, exquisite: a secular Garden of Eden, full of civilized and agreeably uncivilized delights, with no forbidden fruits."[6] Solomon did what many men do today; he threw himself into his work and tried to make a name through industry.

The Bible tells us that Solomon spent seven years and employed 153,000 workers to build the temple, yet he spent thirteen years building his own house (1 Kings 6:38–7:1). After that the Preacher built himself a summer palace in the forest of Lebanon (1 Kings 10:17), and then a palace for one of the daughters of Pharaoh (1 Kings 9:24). His civic endeavors were epic as well; he fortified the walls of the city of Jerusalem and even built a fleet of ships to bring vast wealth into the kingdom (1 Kings 9:26).

On a much smaller scale aren't Americans doing the same thing? We think, "I'll be happy when I get that promotion. I'll be content when I get that better paying job because then I'll have more money and I can upgrade all my stuff." We covet the lifestyles of the rich and famous, thinking, "If I just had that bigger house I would be happy." So people get trapped in a mortgage they cannot afford, then they have to work their fingers to the bone just to make the monthly payment. Then one house is not enough so they look for a place down at the lake or at the beach to get away from it all. Now you have to maintain two residences and that means you have to work doubly hard. By this point you are burning the candle at both ends. Solomon is there all along saying, "Don't even go to the trouble because at the end of the day you still won't be happy."

Time magazine released a special issue in which they chronicled twenty of the most influential and important people in American history. Among those mentioned were Abraham Lincoln, Thomas Edison, the Wright Brothers and industrialist Henry Ford. The article said, "He didn't invent the automobile, but Henry Ford pretty much invented the modern world, transforming transportation and bringing manufacturing and society along for the ride."[7]

It is said that Henry Ford, like Solomon, was a work-a-holic; twelve to fourteen hour days were the norm for this man. Here is just a brief snapshot of some facts from Ford's amazing life:

- In 1888 Ford purchased an 80-acre farm in Deerborne, MI with the dream of building a business to manufacture automobiles.

---

6. Kinder, *The Message of Ecclesiastes*, 31.
7. "The Twenty Most Influential Americans of All Time," *Time*, 25 July 2012.

- In 1896 at the age of 32, Ford completed his first automobile, the quadricycle, which was basically four bicycle wheels on a simple frame, powered by a small engine. He test drove it through the streets of Detroit at top speeds of 20 mph.
- In 1907 the first affordable and practical Ford vehicles rolled out of the Michigan plant. The Model T cost $850 and it came in only one color, black. It was called, "The Everyman's Horseless Carriage."
- The Model T became so popular that Ford had difficulty reaching the demands of his buyers. Ford also became friends with another innovator, Thomas Edison. Later it was suggested that he could increase production in his factory by implementing an assembly line. This had never been done before, but once this manufacturing innovation was put into practice Ford was producing one Model T every ninety-three minutes.
- In 1915 the price dropped on the Model T to $250 and he sold one million units that first year. He was able to pay his employees the whopping salary of $5 a day.
- Later he opened the famous River Rouge plant on the farm he purchased in Deerborne, MI. This was an engineering marvel for its time. The raw materials for the cars would arrive at the entrance. Inside the Ford plant workers would manufacture their own glass, steel, paint and rubber. These materials were then assembled and finished cars would drive out the other end.
- By 1927 Ford produced 15 million cars, which was about half of the world's output. He was the richest and most successful business man alive. Historians tell us that by today's standards he was a multi-billionaire.

Yet towards the end of his life, after amassing this expansive auto-empire and changing the landscape and life in America forever, a newspaper reporter asked Ford if he was happy with his life. Ford famously replied, "I was happier when I was doing a mechanic's job." Henry Ford, Bill Gates, Donald Trump, Steve Jobs, Ted Turner and Warren Buffett at some point in their careers all end up finding out that they are kings over empires of dirt. Take it from Solomon, work, career building and achievement lead to a dead end street.

He Searched for Meaning in Wealth (2:7–11)

A 2013 survey done by *Forbes* Magazine reported that there were 1,426 billionaires in the world. If the wealth of these super-rich were combined they would reach a total income of $5.4 trillion. The United States lead the list with 442 billionaires, followed by Asia-Pacific (386), Europe (366), the Americas (129) and the Middle East & Africa (103).[8] These billionaires only make up a tiny fraction of a percent of the world's population, yet their combined total assets are greater than the GDP of many small nations.

I have a feeling that if Solomon were alive today with all of his wealth he would appear somewhere near the top of the list of the world's billionaires. If we had walked into Solomon's palace during Israel's golden age we would have seen precious stones from Egypt, spices from Arabia, almond and sandalwood from India, ivory from Africa and cedars from Lebanon.[9] Not to mention that everything would have glittered with gold.

The immensity of Solomon's wealth is really a stretch for our imaginations to handle, but these passages help us understand:

> Now the weight of gold that came to Solomon in one year was 666 talents of gold, besides that which came from the explorers and from the business of the merchants, and from all the kings of the west and from the governors of the land (1 Kings 10:14–15). (Using the price of gold in 2013, that comes to $1.06 billion in U.S. dollars every year.)

> All King Solomon's drinking vessels were of gold, and all the vessels of the House of the Forest of Lebanon were of pure gold. None were of silver; silver was not considered as anything in the days of Solomon (1 Kings 10:21)

> And Solomon gathered together chariots and horsemen. He had 1,400 chariots and 12,000 horsemen, whom he stationed in the chariot cities and with the king in Jerusalem. And the king made silver as common in Jerusalem as stone, and he made cedar as plentiful as the sycamore of the Shephelah (1 Kings 10:26–27).

Now I know what some of you are thinking, "McCarson, you're going to tell me that money doesn't make people happy, but I sure would like to give it a try." The truth is that more money does not curb your appetite for things; it just gives your appetite the ability to fully express itself. It takes the

---

8. Kroll, "Inside The 2013 Billionaires List: Facts and Figures," *Forbes*, 25 March 2013.

9. Jeremiah, *Searching for Heaven on Earth*, 31.

restrictions off the lust that is already there. Solomon had so much money and so many possessions that it became meaningless to him. In order for something to have meaning it has to have value and when you have an unlimited bank account, price tags don't mean anything anymore.

Jesus said in Mark 8:36: "For what does it profit a man to gain the whole world, and forfeit his soul?" I think Solomon would answer, "Nothing. It profits him nothing at all. It won't work. You can earn more, spend more, collect more, drink more, eat more, sin more, you name it, but none of those things will put meaning into life."

As we come to the close of this chapter I want to leave you with a few concluding remarks concerning Solomon's experience. First, we see that *intellectual pursuits always end with question marks.* The curse of learning is that it leaves us with no answers to the questions that matter the most. That's because the answers to our existential questions are not found under the sun. We need revelation—that is information from God that comes from outside our space and time to help us make sense of life.

Second, *sensual pleasures hold out promises that lack staying power.* The curse of pleasure is that it is fleeting, like trying to hold on to sand—the harder you grasp the more it slips out through our fingers. The satisfaction that comes from an achievement or an experience is fully expressed in the moment then it's gone.

Third, *materialism mistakes your body to be your soul and earth for heaven.* The human soul has a bottomless capacity for happiness. Not only that, but the human soul is immaterial. Trying to fill a soul with finite things like money and possessions is futile—that's like trying to fill up a colander with water. Because your soul is not made of matter then no material thing will be able to please it.

In the end, what we need is a Being wiser than us who can answer our toughest questions, a Being that does not change in his ability to give fulfillment and a spiritual Being that can speak to the soulish nature of man. The only answer is God.

I think that Max Lucado's story about sandcastles offers a brilliant analogy to Solomon's struggle:

> Hot Sun. Salty air. Rhythmic waves. A little boy is on the beach. On his knees he scoops and packs the sand with plastic shovels into a bright red bucket. Then he upends the bucket on the surface and lifts it. And, to the delight of the little architect, a castle tower is created. All afternoon he will work. Spooning out the mote. Packing the walls. Bottle tops will be sentries. Popsicle sticks will be bridges. A sandcastle will be built.

Big city. Busy streets. Rumbling traffic. A man is in his office. At his desk he shuffles papers into stacks and delegates assignments. He cradles the phone on his shoulder and punches the keyboard with his fingers. Numbers are juggled contracts are signed and, much to the delight of the man, a profit is made. All his life he will work. Formulating the plans. Forecasting the future. Annuities will be sentries. Capital gains will be bridges. An empire will be built.

Two builders of two castles. They have much in common. They shape granules into grandeurs. They see nothing and make something. They are diligent and determined. And for both the tide will rise and the end will come. Yet, that is where the similarities cease. For the boy sees the end while the man ignores it.

Watch the boy as the dusk approaches. Each wave slaps an inch closer to his creation. Every crest crashes closer than the one before. But the boy doesn't panic. He is not surprised. All day the pounding waves have reminded him that the end is inevitable. He knows the secret of the surging. Soon they will come and take his castle into the deep.

The man, however, doesn't know the secret. He should. He, like the boy, lives surrounded by rhythmic reminders. Days come and go. Seasons ebb and flow. Every sunrise which becomes a sunset whispers the secret, "Time will take your castles." So, one is prepared and one isn't. One is peaceful while the other panics.

As the waves near, the wise child jumps to his feet and begins to clap. There is no sorrow. No fear. No regret. He knew this would happen. He is not surprised. And when the great breaker crashes into his castle and his masterpiece is sucked into the sea, he smiles. He smiles, picks up his tools, takes his father's hand, and goes home.

The grown-up, however, is not so wise. As the wave of years collapses on his castle he is terrified. He hovers over the sandy monument to protect it. He blocks the waves from the walls he has made. Saltwater soaked and shivering he snarls at the incoming tide. "It is my castle," he defies. The ocean need not respond. Both know to whom the sand belongs . . .

And I don't know much about sandcastles. But children do. Watch them and learn. Go ahead and build, but build with a child's heart. When the sun sets and the tides take—applaud. Salute the process of life, take your father's hand, and go home."[10]

4

---

10. Lucado, *And the Angels Were Silent*, 108–111.

A Brief Glimpse above the Sun (2:12–26)

BRIAN "HEAD" WELCH WAS a rock star—long dreadlocks, tattoos, screaming guitar riffs, thousands of adoring fans, loads of cash and a platinum-selling album. By Rolling Stone's standards he had achieved success. He toured the globe as the lead guitarist for the internationally known heavy metal band, Korn. However, he still wasn't content.

"I worshipped a lot of stuff," Welch said. "Worship means love and I loved a lot of things. I loved partying. I loved music. I worshipped money." He added, "There was a high when I went onstage and saw all these people loving me and loving my music. There were all these girls after me and all these people worshipping and going nuts for me. I was puffed up on the inside. I started thinking, I'm important. That's when the drugs crept in. Cocaine, methamphetamines crept in."

After the show was over and the cheers of the crowd subsided, Welch was left with a profound sense of emptiness. He recalled one night looking over the crowd as they sang his music and thought, "If these people really knew me they would not be worshipping me. If they got up close, they would see I am just like them."

Welch's life started spinning out of control. While on the road his addiction worsened and his family life deteriorated. Eventually his wife left him and their daughter, Jennea. Welch took a hiatus from the world of rock n' roll to take care of his daughter but he could not escape the drugs. Welch admitted, "I ended up with a crippling addiction to methamphetamines . . . I sunk to the lowest gutter I could ever think of . . . I would get up in the morning and have a peanut butter and jelly sandwich and snort meth and then take her [Jennea] to school."

One evening before show time, Welch looked at Jennea and noticed she was singing. Her voice was beautiful until he realized what she was singing. Welch could not believe that she was singing the lyrics to one of Korn's songs, "A.D.I.D.A.S., All Day I Dream About Sex." It was then that Welsh realized his life was beyond fixing and he wanted to die.[1]

If anything the lifestyles of the rich and famous have taught us over the years it's that happiness cannot be earned, purchased, or injected. In fact, many pleasure-seekers find out only after exhausting every available resource that fulfillment is not found in a fat bank account, a bottle, a syringe, a wall full of degrees or a successful career. The truth is that many of the celebrities of this world live in quiet desperation. We would be shocked to see the discontent lingering just under the thin veneer of the silver screen.

Solomon, the original playboy, admitted in his tell-all memoir, "I hated life, because what is done under the sun was grievous to me, for all is vanity and a striving after wind" (Ecc. 2:17). Like Welch, Solomon lived on the pinnacle and was miserable. Solomon wrote the journal of Ecclesiastes to address a universal human question—is it possible to be happy, fulfilled and satisfied with life under the sun? So far the Preacher has told us that for all of his wealth, wisdom, and wild living it amounted to vanity and chasing after the wind. The cumulative effort of his life was a fleeting puff of smoke.

In the following passage Solomon explains why all his efforts to find meaning in the things of the world were futile. In the previous section Solomon *experienced* life under the sun; now he moves on to *evaluate* his life under the sun. Towards the end of this meditation, Solomon has a brief moment of insight as he is able to look through the misty fog and get a clear perspective.

The Folly of Wisdom (2:12–17)

Solomon sets out to discover the worth of wisdom. He wants to know if there is any advantage in the long run to being wise versus being a fool. Initially, he does say that there are benefits to wisdom in 2:13–14. Just as light is better than the darkness, so too it's better to be smart than stupid. However, after thinking about the matter Solomon concludes that wisdom has its limits and he points out two problems.

First, the Preacher deduces that *both the wise and the fool are finite* in 2:15–16, "Then I said in my heart, "What happens to the fool will happen to me also. Why then have I been so very wise?" And I said in my heart that this also is vanity. For of the wise as of the fool there is no enduring remembrance, seeing that in the days to come all will have been long forgotten. How the wise dies just like the fool!"

---

1. Bender and Sterrett, *I Am Second: Real Stories. Changed Lives*, 3–12.

The wise person may make better decisions regarding finances, career, and health which results in a temporary payoff. But, sadly once the wise man begins reaping some of the fruit of his good choices—he dies. This is Solomon's first shocker; the grim reaper stalks both the fool and the wise.

Imagine two men who go through life at nearly the same pace. Jerry is an achiever while Frank is a simpleton. Jerry goes through school with flying colors. He is top of his class, quarterback of the varsity football squad and a whiz on the debate team. After college he lands an amazing job and climbs the corporate ladder. He's knocking down a six figure income, taking his family to Disney World every summer and playing several strokes under par on the golf course. Then one day, out of the blue, he dies of a heart attack in the prime of his career.

Then there is Frank who takes an alternate pathway in life. Frank scrapes through school and is a lazy when it comes to the books. He passes by copying off others' homework and graduates by the skin of his teeth. He goes immediately into the work force after school; however he jumps from one job to the next. He doesn't apply himself and his fellow co-workers have to continually cover for his ineptitude. Frank's family is on food stamps, and their existence is a constant struggle because he likes the taste of whisky. One day, bumbling Frank has an accident on the job and he dies, ironically on the same day as Jerry.

Meanwhile, down at the funeral home both of these men are having their final arrangements carried out. Frank's casket is on one end of the parlor, while Jerry is on the other end. If you were to bring a total stranger to both of these men in the funeral home and ask them to view the corpses, chances are they will notice little difference between them. Just by looking at them laying cold and stiff in the casket you couldn't tell which one was wise and which one the fool.

This is Solomon's point. In the end, death comes for both the wise and the fool alike and none of the wise man's advantages can stay the hand of death. As Harry Ironside has said, "Death is the great leveler of all men. Whether rich or poor, wise or foolish, powerful or weak, renowned or obscure—no one can rise above it, or escape its eventual claim on the living."

Second, Solomon points out that *both the wise and the fool are forgotten*. In 2:16, he adds insult to injury, "For of the wise as of the fool there is no enduring remembrance, seeing that in the days to come all will have been long forgotten." The reality is that people suffer from acute memory loss. If death wasn't bad enough, being totally forgotten might be worse. Even if you are one of those rare, influential people who makes their mark in history there is no guarantee that people will actually take the time to pick up a book and read your biography.

Take for instance America's Founding Fathers. In 2007 the U.S. mint released the Thomas Jefferson $1 coin and in conjunction with the new money the mint also conducted a national survey with startling results. Only seven percent of those surveyed could name the first four presidents in order: George Washington, John Adams, Thomas Jefferson and James Madison. Only 30 percent knew that Thomas Jefferson was the third president.[2]

What about those who erected the engineering marvels like the Great Wall of China—5,500 miles long and so massive astronauts can see it from space—surely you know the name of emperor who commissioned that? Or what about the Roman Coliseum? Why the name of the Caesar that expended so much slave labor to deify himself on that project, he's practically a household name, right? What about the great pyramids in Egypt? The facts on those tremendous monoliths of stone are astounding—2.3 million blocks each weighing two tons a piece, enough stone to build ten foot high wall around the perimeter of France. That's a mausoleum that has stood the test of time. Practically, everyone knows the name of the Pharaoh's who erected those, right? Maybe you learned his name in history class long enough to pass the test, but now you could not remember that factoid to save your life.

Solomon seems to be saying that the best you can hope for is your name to be remembered in an encyclopedia article that some kid is forced to read for a school project. If you're fortunate you may be referenced in a footnote on Wikipedia. Thus, Solomon's first conclusion is that his wisdom could not help him escape the inevitable clutches of death and obscurity.

The Frustration of Wealth (2:18-23)

In 1922 Howard Carter made the archaeological discovery of the ages. Despite all the so-called "experts" who said there was no more treasure to be found in Egypt's Valley of the Kings, Carter unearthed the tomb of the boy-king, Tutankhamen. Carter had discovered an unknown ancient Egyptian tomb that had lain nearly undisturbed for over 3,000 years. What lay beneath the sands of time astounded the Carter and the world.

Inside the four-rooms of the tomb was a trove of unbelievable wealth and cultural history. The sepulcher was stacked to the ceiling with priceless artifacts. In his diary, Carter described the inside the tomb as a "strange and wonderful medley of extraordinary and beautiful objects heaped upon one another." It would take months to carefully document each item in the collection, the most amazing being the solid sold gold death mask of King Tut.

---

2 Longley, "Mint Survey Shows Most Americans Can't Name Founding Fathers," 21 August 2007.

The truth is all of King's Tut's wealth couldn't buy him an extra minute of life on Earth and like every other king before or after, he left it all behind in that desert tomb. Scenes like this drove Solomon into despair. Even so, Solomon's assets made King Tut's treasure look like thrift store collection of knick-knacks. What vexed the Preacher is that when he croaked he knew that his vast estate would pass on to the next guy wearing the crown.

Thus, Solomon points out the first frustration about riches in 2:18—*we cannot possess wealth*. He wrote, "I hated all my toil in which I toil under the sun, seeing that I must leave it to the man who will come after me, and who knows whether he will be wise or a fool? Yet he will be master of all for which I toiled and used my wisdom under the sun." There are no compartments in caskets, no pockets in shrouds, and there aren't any u-hauls behind hearses. David Jeremiah adds:

> You may not appreciate hearing it, but Solomon is simply saying aloud what we all know to be true. Build what you want; save what you might; put it in the bank; liquefy it into stocks and bonds; drop it into real estate; place it anywhere you choose. You control your wealth for a season and then it's out of your hands completely. As you draw your last breath, you withdraw your grip on all that you have labored to build under the sun.[3]

Did you know there is a reason why you have heard of Microsoft and IBM and not Eagle computers? In the 1980s all three were competing for their slice of the computer market in Silicon Valley and any one of them could have won out. Then tragedy struck the young CEO of Eagle Computers, Dennis Barnhart. Charles Swindoll recaps how this man lost it all:

> Dennis Barnhart was president of an aggressive, rapidly growing company, Eagle Computer Incorporated. His life is a study in tragedy. From a small beginning, his firm grew incredible fast. He finally decided they should go public. The forty-four-year-old man, as a result of this first public stock offering, became a multimillionaire virtually overnight. Then for some strange reason, while he was in his red Ferrari only blocks from the company headquarters, he drove his car through twenty feet of guardrail into a ravine and died. A Los Angeles Times account read, "Until the accident at 4:30 Wednesday afternoon, it had been the best days for Barnhart and the thriving young company, which makes small business and personal computers. Eagle netted $37 million from the initial offering of 2.75 million shares. The stock which hit the market at $13 a share quickly

---

3. Jeremiah, *Searching for Heaven on Earth*, 37.

rose as high as $27 before closing at bid price of $15.50." After describing the stock, the articles added, "That made Barnhart's ownership of 592,000 worth more than $9 million." And that same afternoon he died in an auto accident.[4]

All it takes is one brief second and everything you have worked your entire life for can be wiped out in an instant.

Secondly, *we cannot protect wealth*. In 2:19-21 Solomon says in so many words, "What's the point of working your fingers to the bone if you hand over what you worked for to someone who never lifted a finger for it?"[5] You work hard for forty years. You save every chance you get. You don't live beyond your means. You invest wisely and plan out your 401K for retirement. Yet after all that toil to amass a little pile of money, you die and pass it on to an ungrateful relative.

Can you picture the scene? They are out spending your life savings while you're six feet under. The vacation trip you always wanted to take to Europe, they are taking in your place. That motorcycle you could never legitimize buying but always lusted over is now sitting in their garage. In fact, they are waiting in anticipation for moneybags to keel over so they can start dividing up the inheritance. They are practically wringing their hands in glee while the undertaker is throwing dirt in your face.

Worse yet, there's no guarantee that the person who gets your hard-earned money will steward it wisely. Did you catch the frustration in 2:19? ". . . and who knows whether he will be wise or a fool? Yet he will be master of all for which I toiled and used my wisdom under the sun. This also is vanity."

A dear friend of mine told me a heartbreaking story of man he once knew who inherited half a million dollars from his grandfather and within a year he had already spent it all. The fool would buy a new truck from the Ford dealership drive it for a few weeks, get bored with it, take it back and trade it in for a new one. He went through a dozen brand new F-150s in a year. By the end of that year he was a penniless alcoholic living with his mother. When something is given without work it breeds irresponsibility.

What if the beneficiary of your inheritance was someone like party girl Paris Hilton? My guess is you would do the same thing Baron Hilton did and divert your fortune away from that black hole while you still had time. One article reported:

---

4. Swindoll, *Living on the Ragged Edge*, 45.
5. Peterson, *The Message*, Ecc. 2:20-23.

> Baron Hilton, 80, Paris Hilton's billionaire grandfather worth $2.3 billion and CEO of Hilton Hotels, has cut off his entire family from their inheritance in order to donate 97% of his fortune to charitable foundations because of Paris' wild behavior. Paris, who was set to receive $59 million, will now receive nothing: He was, and is, extremely embarrassed by how the Hilton name has been sullied by Paris. Hilton says "He doesn't want to leave unearned wealth to his family."[6]

I don't know if Solomon's fears were a self-fulfilling prophecy, but this very thing ended up happening to him after he died. Solomon turned his kingdom over to his brash and foolish son Rehoboam (1 Kings 12). Rehoboam listened to the council of his young generals rather than his father's sage advisors. He was a greedy man who taxed the people of Jerusalem to death and forced them into hard labor.

When an Egyptian army came marching up to the doors of palace in Jerusalem, Rehobaom went into the Temple that his father built, took out shields of gold and handed them over to the Egyptians as a tribute, hoping that would appease them and they would take their armies back to Cairo (1 Chron. 12). Rehoboam goes down as one of the genuine idiots of the Bible and a cowardly king.

Within a few years of Solomon's death the people were overworked, taxed to death, and the Egyptian's had plundered Israel's national treasure. Within a generation the kingdom would be divided and the nation would be worshipping false gods. It's almost as if Solomon could see all this coming down the pipe as he pens these words in his journal, yet he is helpless to avert disaster.

The third conclusion Solomon posits that *we cannot find peace in wealth*. Solomon found out that his riches caused him to lose a lot of sleep. At night he would toss and turn trying to figure out a way to keep the wealth that he had. He wrote, "What has a man from all the toil and striving of heart with which he toils beneath the sun? For all his days are full of sorrow, and his work is a vexation. Even in the night his heart does not rest. This also is vanity" (2:22–23).

D.L. Moody once said, "Getting riches brings care, keeping them brings more trouble, abusing them brings guilt and losing them brings sorrow. It is a great mistake to make such a big deal about scraps of paper that bring us so much unhappiness."

---

6. Nichols, "Paris Loses Out: Hilton Fortune Pledged to Charity," *Reuters*, 26 December 2007.

How many successful entrepreneurs do you know who can really kick back in the evening without turning on MSNBC to obsess over the stock market? Are there any business men or women who can leave their work at the office? Instead they lay in bed at night, with their mind racing 100 mph. trying to figure out ways to maintain their current economic status. If you're not worried about keeping money, you're worried about where you are going to get it.

Or perhaps you are on the other end of the spectrum. You're financially strapped and wondering how you are going to pay the bills, fix the car, buy a sack of groceries and, by the way, the kids need clothes for school. Such is the money trap—those who have it fret about how to keep a tight fist around what they've got and those that don't have it are worried how they are going to make ends meet.

In Billy Graham's autobiography, he tells a story about a vacation he and Ruth took. On that trip they met a very rich man who although rich had no peace in his heart:

> Ruth and I had a vivid illustration of this on an island in the Caribbean. One of the wealthiest men in the world had asked us to come to his lavish home for lunch. He was 75 years old, and throughout the entire meal he seemed close to tears. "I am the most miserable man in the world," he said. "Out there is my yacht. I can go anywhere I want to. I have my private plane, my helicopters. I have everything I want to make my life happy, yet I am as miserable as hell." We talked to him and prayed with him, trying to point him to Christ, who alone gives lasting meaning to life. Then we went down the hill to a small cottage where we were staying. That afternoon the pastor of the local Baptist church came to call. He was an Englishman, and he too was 75; a widower who spent most of his time taking care of his two invalid sisters. He was full of enthusiasm and love for Christ and others. "I don't have two pounds to my name," he said with a smile, "but I am the happiest man on this island."[7]

After they left, Graham he asked his wife Ruth, "Who do you think is the richer man?"

The Fulfillment of Walking with God (2:24-26)

It's been a maddening pursuit for fulfillment and Solomon almost lost his mind over it, that is, until he had a brief moment of insight. Notice a flash

7. Graham, *Just As I Am*, 821–822.

of brilliance in last few verses of this chapter. There is a clearing in the haze of disillusionment. The Preacher is able to raise his gaze above the clouds. He has a glimpse through the malaise. For the first time in this journal God enters the picture. A divine foot has slipped through the door.

Solomon realizes that only *God brings contentment*. "There is nothing better for a person than that he should eat and drink and find enjoyment in his toil. This also, I saw, is from the hand of God, for apart from him who can eat or who can have enjoyment?" (2:24–25). He has finally put his finger source on the of all joy and happiness—it's not in degrees, it's in the Divine; it's not it gold, it's in God; it's not in things, but in the Maker of all things. Unless God is at the center of life then lasting enjoyment is impossible.

Solomon had forgotten the words of his father, David, "You make known to me the path of life; in your presence there is fullness of joy; at your right hand are pleasures forevermore" (Ps. 16:11). If you are looking for fun without the hangover, if you are looking for fulfillment without the drag of disappointment, then center your life's pursuits on God because He has an unending supply of goodness to pour into the depths of your soul.

When you know the Lord then the existential vacuum at the core of your being is filled. It is only then that you can find joy in the simplicities of life. When was the last time you went to church and let out a hearty belly laugh? Have you recently sat outside in the cool of the day and listened to the birds sing a symphony of praise? What about taking a bite out of a ripe peach and letting the juice roll down your chin? Or have you watched a baby toddle around on his pudgy legs? God alone gives us the ability to see these things anew as wonders from His hand.

A few years ago a Boston newspaper ran an article about a woman who retired from working forty years in office building as a cleaning lady. The reporter asked her, "Did you ever get bored doing the same monotonous activity every day for 40 years?" The cleaning lady said, "Oh I never got bored. I use cleaning materials that God made. I clean objects that belong to people that God made. I make life better and easier for hundreds of people. My mop is the hand of God!"[8]

Are you looking for God in the unexpected places? He's there, but do we see Him in the mundane? Paul, in one of his last letters to Timothy, wrote as he was in a Roman prison on death row, "Godliness with contentment is great gain" (1 Tim. 6:6). Under the sun living can be a breeding ground for discontent, or it can be the training ground for the development of godliness and contentment. It all depends on whether we can see God in the ordinary.

---

8. DeHann, "Relevant Routine," *Our Daily Bread*, 24 April 2006.

A Brief Glimpse above the Sun (2:12-26)

Solomon also noticed that *God brings compensation*. The final verse in 2:26 seems a bit strange upon a first read, but it drips of irony, "For to the one who pleases him God has given wisdom and knowledge and joy, but to the sinner he has given the business of gathering and collecting, only to give to one who pleases God. This also is vanity and a striving after wind."

Solomon is saying that in the end all the work of the sinner of in trying to amass goods and wealth is going to be confiscated and redistributed by God. So the unbeliever does all the toil of working for God, and in long run the believer ends up being the beneficiary.

There is a great example of this principle from the Old Testament. In the book of Exodus, when the children of Israel were leaving Egypt, the Bible says that Israelites plundered the Egyptians of their gold and silver (Ex. 12:35–36).

What good is gold when you are going out in the desert wilderness of Sinai? What were they going to do, barter with some camels out in desert? But God had a greater purpose in mind. He owned all the gold anyway. God put it in the ground when He created the earth, then he let the Egyptians do all the hard work of mining it out of the ground and fashioning it into jewelry so that it could be handed over to His people.

When you get a little further on in the book of Exodus God commands Moses to build a container, a box to hold the Ten Commandments, which will sit in tabernacle as the center of worship—what you and I know as the Ark of the Covenant (Ex. 25). God gave Moses very specific instructions. He said, "I want you to make the box so long and so high, out of acacia wood, and then I want you to overlay the ark with pure gold." Where do you think Moses got the gold to complete the Ark? Turns out the Egyptians were working for God all along, so that the Israelites could be the recipients of a blessing.

This verse also reminds me of the eighteenth century skeptic French Voltaire, who used his pen like a wrecking ball, intent on destroying Christianity. Voltaire predicted than within a generation of his influence that the Bible would a relic of history and Christ a footnote of antiquity. Voltaire died in 1778. Ironically in 1828, fifty years later, the Geneva Bible society purchased Voltaire's house and used his printing press to produce thousands of Bible to distribute all over the globe.[9] God has an incredible sense of humor.

During the millennial reign of Christ the implements of war will be beat into plowshares (Is. 2:4). In New Jerusalem the caches of gold, which have changed hands from one corrupt kingdom to another, will be turned

---

9. McDowell, *Evidence for Christianity*, 29.

into pavement (Rev. 21:21). In a stunning reversal, the meek will inherit the kingdom of God (Matt. 5:5). Those who seek first the Kingdom of God will have all things added unto them (Matt. 6:33).

Remember our despondent rock-star Brian Welch? He finally found the fulfillment that Solomon wrote about when a Christian friend recommended a verse of Scripture, "Come to me, all you who are weary and burdened and I will give you rest" (Matt. 11:28). That verse seemed to be the cry of his soul. Welch desperately wanted the peace and contentment that Jesus offered.

Welch was invited to church where he heard the message of Jesus. Yet he was still unable to break free of his addiction. After church he went home, neglected his daughter and went back to drugs. In the fog of another high Welch cried out to God, "Jesus, you got to take the drugs from me. Search me right now. Search my heart. You know I want to stop. Take them away. I cannot do it on my own."

Welch had a powerful conversion. He felt the love of God enter his heart and instantly free him. The next day, he threw away all his drugs, quit Korn and pledged to be a father to Jennea. Welch later confessed:

> My dream came true more than I ever dreamed about. I made more money. I played bigger shows. I had houses, cars. I tried drugs. I tried sex. I tried everything to get pleasure out of this life . . . I thought I could fulfill my life with all this stuff. I used to think if my dreams just came true—well they came true, but they didn't fulfill me. I got so down I just wanted to die . . . But when Christ came in, the feeling that He gives is the feeling of understanding life. Everything was created by Christ and for Christ. We are created to be with him. Being with Christ is the most incredible feeling because you're where you belong. And contentment is given to you in life because you don't have to look anywhere else and you're exactly where you need to be. And the question about life is answered.[10]

---

10. Bender & Sterrett, *I Am Second: Real Stories. Changed Lives*, 10–11.

5

The Mystery of Time and Eternity (3:1–15)

In J.R.R Tolkien's classic fantasy story, *The Hobbit*, Bilbo Baggins becomes a reluctant participant in an adventure with a rag-tag group of thirteen dwarves and Gandalf the wizard. At one point in the journey Bilbo is lost in a dark, smelly cave where he is confronted by a strange creature named Gollum. The impish creature threatens to eat Bilbo unless he can beat Gollum in a game of riddles. One of Gollum's riddles that bakes Bilbo's noodle goes like this:

> *This thing all things devours:*
> *Birds, beasts, trees, flowers;*
> *Gnaws iron, bites steel;*
> *Grinds hard stones to meal;*
> *Slays kings, ruins town,*
> *And beats high mountains down.*[1]

Are you stumped? The answer, of course, is time. Time is as old as the universe and our ever-present taskmaster. Whether we like it or not we are mastered by minutes and slaves to seconds. Time is a familiar stranger. We intuitively know what it is, but as familiar as the notion of time may be have you ever tried to define it?

Ben Franklin tried his best to define it when he said, "Time is the stuff life is made of." Henry David Thoreau once mused, "Time is but the stream that I go a-fishing in. I drink at it; but while I drink I see the sandy bottom and detect how shallow it is." I prefer the way one man defined time by saying, "Time is what keeps everything from happening at once."

---

1. Tolkien, *The Hobbit*, 77.

Chuck Swindoll wrote about time as the currency of life:

> Lets' play pretend for a moment shall we? Let's pretend that your banker phoned you late last Friday night and said he had some very good news. He told you that an anonymous donor who loves you very much has decided to deposit 86,400 pennies into your account each morning, starting the following Monday morning. That's $864 a day, seven days a week, fifty-two weeks a year. He adds, "But there is one stipulation . . . you must spend all the money that same day. No balance will be carried over to the next day. Each evening the bank must cancel whatever sum you failed to use. With a big smile on your face, you thank your banker and hang up. Over that weekend you have time to plan. You grab a pencil and start figuring: $864 times seven equal over $6,000 a week . . . times fifty-two. That's almost $315,000 a year that you have available to you *if you are diligent to spend it all each day*. Remember, whatever you don't spend is forfeited. So much for "Let's Pretend." Now let's play, "Let's Get Serious." Every morning someone who loves you very much deposits into your bank of time 86,400 second of time which represent, 1,440 minutes—which of course, equal twenty-four hours each day. Now you've got to remember the same stipulation applies, because God gives you this amount of time for you to use each day. Nothing is ever carried over on credit to the next day . . . As someone has put it, "Life is like a coin, you can spend it any way you want, but you can only spend it once."[2]

Time is so important to each one of us because it is a limited commodity. Time is irretrievable, irreversible and invaluable. Lost wealth may be replaced by hard work, lost knowledge by study, lost health by medicine and exercise, but lost time is gone forever. The day we are born God turns our hourglass upside down and the falling sand marks the passing of our days. We can say about time what real estate agents are saying about land, "They're not making any more of it."

Solomon pondered the mystery of time and eternity and he tells us that life is really a matter of timing. In the beginning of this journal, the Preacher began by noting the circularity of life—the planet spins, the wind blows, the rain falls and evaporates, one generation replaces another. Everything in nature seemed to operate on a cycle devoid of meaning. We might expect the same treatment to the concept of time; that time is like one big karmic wheel that endlessly rotates with no real point in mind.

---

2. Swindoll, *Living on the Ragged Edge*, 53–54.

However, Solomon points out in this reflection that time is not circular but linear. Time is progressively moving towards God's desired end. Not only is time beautiful in the grand scheme of things (3:11), but we will see that it is balanced. Everything in time is ordered. Each action has a specific season allotted to it by a sovereign God. In this passage, Solomon looks in three different directions to understand time and eternity.

A Look Backwards: The Beauty of Time (3:1–11)

Everything in God's universe happens not by accident but by divine appointment. God is the time-keeper and He is never late, nor early. To illustrate this Solomon offers us one of the world's most famous poems. Each pair in this poem forms a *mereism*, which is a feature of ancient prose where two polarities comprise a whole. For example, if I were to say, "The doctor looked me over from head to toe" I would be using a mereism which you would understand to mean that I got an extensive physical examination. Birth and death, laughing and weeping, peace and war summarize the whole of human experience. Thus, Solomon poses fourteen opposites of contrasting parallelism to show how God has every event in life happening at just the right time. Let's examine these statements carefully.

"*A time to be born and a time to die;*" The two most important moments in human life are your birthday and your death day, and yet we are not in control of either one. Someone has said that on your tombstone are two dates, the year you were born and year you died and in between is a dash. The dash is your life.

On Veteran's Day, November, 11, 1963, President Kennedy visited Arlington Cemetery to pay his respects to American's fallen heroes. Gazing over the rolling Virginia hillside he remarked, "It is so beautiful that I could stay here forever." Two weeks later he returned there in a flag-draped coffin to be laid to rest under the eternal flame.[3] Ironically, in that same year, folk singer Pete Seegar adapted the words of Solomon's poem into a hit song, "Turn, Turn, Turn."

Here's a sobering statistic: Dr. Leslie Weatherhead in his book, *Time for God*, has mathematically calculated 70 years and compressed it into one day. If your age is 15 the time is 10:25 am, 20 is 11:34 am, 25 is 12:42 pm, 35 is 3 pm, 40 is 4:08 pm, 45 is 5:16 pm, 50 is 6:25 pm, 55 is 7:34 pm, 60 is 8:42 pm, 65 is 9:51, and 70 plus is 11 pm. No doubt, some of us are closer to midnight than we might think.

---

3. Jeremiah, *Searching for Heaven on Earth*, 45.

"*A time to plant and to pluck up what is planted;*" God has ordered the seasons so that we plant in the spring and harvest in the fall. A good farmer understands when it's time to drop the seed in the ground and when to prune the vines. Growing up in the country I was taught that when you put the corn kernels in the ground around mid-May, about seventy days later you'll have a full ear. When the beans and corn comes in everything has to stop, because you have to get it all harvested and canned or else it will rot or the critters will steal your hard work.

This agricultural imagery is also true of life. God has a way of uprooting us and planting us somewhere else. God is in control of moving you and me where He wants to. You may not be here but for a season until you are uprooted by God and asked to bloom elsewhere.

"*A time to kill and a time to heal;*" Life happens between a battlefield and a hospital. Solomon is merely stating a difficult fact of life. We live in a world where there is a Mother Teresa in one corner and an Osama Ben Laden in another. You can open the newspaper and read about both of them side-by-side.

"*A time to tear down and a time to build up;*" Everything is subject to the Second Law of Thermodynamics. Stuff breaks down and moves from order to disorder. The stars eventually burn out, the cells in your body break down and are replaced by news ones every seven years, your house needs a new roof every twenty years, you change the tires on your car when the tread wears thin.

"*A time to weep and a time to laugh;*" Solomon is pointing out that both sorrow and joy are part of life; without one the other is unrecognizable. Have you noticed that some of the funniest moments in life come at the times when it's not appropriate to laugh? When I was a kid I remember moments of gut-busting laughter came while sitting in church. I can remember once that the pastor had a difficult time during a baptism. The woman being baptized was a bigger lady and she went down in the water real easy but didn't come up with the same grace. Of course laughter is turned to weeping when you get the death look from your mother across the pews of the church.

I once heard Ravi Zacharias say in a sermon, "This is to me the problem with modern man, he no longer knows what to laugh at and no longer knows what to weep at. What you laugh at tells God who you are, just as equally what you cry at tells God who you are."

"*A time to mourn and a time to dance;*" I thought about families at funerals and weddings when I read this one. A family mourns the loss of loved one and in the same year celebrates a marriage. The strange thing is sometimes you can go to funerals in which there is joy and laughter because

The Mystery of Time and Eternity (3:1-15)

a saint has finished well and gone on to be with the Lord, and then you can go to a wedding where everyone is bawling their eyes out.

"*A time to cast away stones and a time to gather stones;*" This can be difficult to interpret unless you understand Solomon's culture. Before the ancients could use a field for cultivation they had to first clear away the stones. On the other hand if they wanted to harm an enemy they could throw stones on the field to make it unusable. Warren Weirsbe made this comment, "Palestine is indeed rocky land and farmers must clear their fields before they can plow and plant. If you wanted to hurt an enemy, you filled up his field with stones (2 Kings 3:19, 25). People also gathered stones for building walls and houses. Stones are neither good nor bad; it all depends on what you do with them. If your enemy fills your land with rocks, don't throw them back. Build something out of them!"[4]

"*A time to embrace and a time to refrain from embracing*" Have you ever seen how people from Eastern cultures meet and greet each other? They kiss on the cheek when they meet and part ways. This verse also could refer to sexual relations between a husband and wife. Men, we have all messed up and had to sleep on the couch. This is also applicable in other relationships as well. There are times in life when someone needs consolation after going through a trial; all they need is shoulder to cry on. Then there are times when a strong rebuke is in order when we must stand up to and confront others over tough issues.

"*A time to gain and a time to lose, a time to keep and to throw away;*" Anyone who has ever had a yard sale knows about this. Think about your closet at home or maybe your car is a disaster area. Everyone has that one drawer in their house that gets filled to the brim with junk. There is a time when we must rid our lives of things that cause clutter. The point of contention arises because men and women have different ideas of what is worn out and what is still useful. I look at a shirt and think that is perfectly fine, however, Caitlin, my wife, looks at it and says "It's time to throw it out, there is no way you are going out in public with that on."

"*A time to tear and a time to sew;*" In Jewish culture the way they expressed grief and bereavement it was to tear their outer garments, but eventually after they had to gone through the grieving process the cloak had be sewn up again.

"*A time to keep silent and a time to speak;*" This is connected to the previous statement because after the Old Testament people mourned the death of a loved one they kept silent. When the period of mourning was over, ordinary conversations of the day could continue.

---

4. Wiersbe, *The Wiersbe Bible Commentary: Old Testament*, 1118.

The problem is we speak when we should be silent and when it's time for silence we speak. Proverbs 17:28 says the "Even a fool who keeps silent is considered wise; when he closes his lips, he is deemed intelligent." A foolish person doesn't know when to shut up. This reminds me of the incessant blabbing that goes on during the morning talk shows. The hosts are forever speaking yet never coming to a knowledge of the truth. Moreover, James 3:1–2 argues that the more we talk the more likely we are to sin. However, Proverbs 25:11 says that "A word fitly spoken is more precious than gold." There are times when the right words said in the right way have a profound impact.

"*A time to love and hate, a time of war and a time of peace;*" There are times when we are justified in going to war and times for laying down our weapons. There are times when hate is the right emotion to feel in a moment of injustice. Jesus hated sin, but loved the sinner. I remember reading about an experience that Abraham Lincoln once had the first time he saw a slave being offered in New Orleans on the selling block. Lincoln recoiled within. He later wrote, "There was a rising hatred inside of me against slavery, and I swore if someday I could do something about it I would."[5]

Solomon's point behind writing this poem is found in the first part of 3:11, "He has made everything beautiful in its time." If we could have God's eternal perspective then we would see the big picture of life and we would recognize the good, bad and ugly as a wonderful tapestry spun by a Grand Weaver. With God life is not random but punctuated with the purpose of an overarching plan.

However, if we look at life from the humanistic, "under the sun" viewpoint then this list is made up of negating opposites—fourteen positives, and fourteen negatives. The cynic might conclude that in some way they seem to cancel out each other so that the net result is zero—all is vanity. However, when we include God in the picture, time is a dramatic narrative in which the plot includes ordained and pre-determined events.

Perhaps we can illustrate this with a piano. If I were to play "Jesus loves me" with just the white keys, it might sound pretty good, but I would be missing something crucial. However, if I were to play the same tune again, but this time add the black keys—all the sharp and flat notes—you would notice the tune would take on a whole new musical dimension. In order to make a beautiful melody, I need the major keys and the minor keys; I need the sharp notes and the flat notes. God takes the dissonance of life and blends it with the harmony of life, the triumph and the tragedies, the mountaintops and valleys and works it all out into a beautiful piece.

---

5. Swindoll, *Living on the Ragged Edge*, 62.

Simply put, life without God is series of disconnected, random events that end like a bad dream. But life with God is beautiful with all its seasons, varieties, twists and turns. Just look at the life of Christ. There was a cross on Friday, but then a resurrection on Sunday. History begins with man's fall in the Garden, but God will restore the blight of creation and reverse the curse of sin. How will He do it? By incorporating evil into His plan and rendering it for good.

A Look Inward: The Mystery of Eternity (3:11)

The human heart has a deep-seated longing to transcend our finite, earthly existence and to know the eternal God. The God-shaped vacuum at the core of our being demands to be filled. We have an itch for eternity that can only be scratched by the Divine. As Augustine said, "God has made us for Himself and our hearts are restless until they rest in Him."

The phrase "eternity in their hearts" means God has placed a big question mark deep in every man's soul. This is proven by the fact that anthropological evidence suggests that every culture has an innate sense of the eternal—that this world is not all there is. The Egyptians erected the pyramids, Native Americans labored over sacred burial mounds and the Romans built huge mausoleums. Why? They each were in their own darkened way grappling to work out the eternal longing imbedded in their heart. Their mythology told them that time was merely a dress rehearsal for eternity.

Don Richardson wrote a fascinating book entitled, *Eternity in their Hearts* based on Ecclesiastes 3:11. In this survey he presents more than twenty-five examples of missionaries all over the world who discovered cultures completely cut-off from Christianity. Yet all these tribal groups which were detached from civilization worshipped some kind of transcendent being. In an eerie way, these primitive people had a deep longing for God, even if their religious rituals were misguided.

For example, Richardson tells about his experiences with the Sawi tribes of Dutch New Guinea—the headhunters whom Richardson went to evangelize in the 1950s. Though the bloodthirsty Sawi people prized war and violence, they also had a sacred ritual for reconciling two warring tribes. The chief's own son would be offered to the other tribe as a "peace child." Richardson saw this ritual as a parable of the Gospel, in which the Chief of all chieftains made peace with the lost tribe of humanity by offering up His only Son. Richardson's thesis contended that, "Every human being has eternity in their heart and that winning people to Christ is a matter of discovering what piece or part of eternity they are familiar with and then helping them connect the dots to Christ."[6]

According to Solomon, humanity is caught between time and eternity, thus the best way to spend our time is to live it in light of eternity. As finite creatures we cannot understand the times and the seasons, the beginning from the end, until we have a personal relationship with the Timekeeper. The great mystery is that God accomplishes His purposes in time, but it will not be until we enter eternity that we will begin to comprehend His total plan. As Vance Havner has said, "The things we don't understand about life—God puts a note on them that says, 'I'll explain later.'"

The New Testament counterpart to Ecclesiastes 3:11, is Romans 8:28, "For we know that God works all things together for good to those that love Him and are called according to his purpose." In other words, from the Divine perspective there is no ugliness in the events of our lives, only light and dark brushstrokes from the paintbrush of the Master.

I once heard Dr. Erwin Lutzer, of Chicago's historic Moody Bible Church, tell the story about a trip that he took to an art museum. He said that as he was looking at a painting by the master artist Rembrandt he noticed an ant crawling across the surface of the canvas. He thought to himself, "How did that ant get up there on the painting?" Then he said, "There was no way the ant had any idea that he was walking on a priceless piece of art, to him it just looked like a muddled splotches of brown and grey." Lutzer commented "That's what life is like when you have a narrow, earth-bound perspective." We are like the ant unknowingly walking across a masterpiece. However, God's sees the total picture. When we see a muddled composition it's because we are too close to put things into perspective. Eternity is the only correct vantage point to judge time.

A Look Upward: The Sovereignty of God (3:12–15)

Solomon ends with a couple of conclusions in relationship to God's control over all things. In light of the fact that God is sovereign over time and eternity how do we live in the here and now? The wise sage leaves us with two simple applications.

First, we should *be joyful for God's gifts*. "I perceived that there is nothing better for them than to be joyful and to do good as long as they live; also that everyone should eat and drink and take pleasure in all his toil—this is God's gift to man" (3:12–13). Solomon isn't talking about extravagant pleasure-seeking but simply enjoying the gifts of God. In other words, lighten

---

6. Richardson, *Eternity in Their Hearts*.

up a little bit! Get an extra scoop of ice cream for dessert. Tell your kids or grandkids stories around a campfire. Take a Friday off from work and go fishing. Listen to a symphony and let the chill bumps go up your spine. Solomon is giving us the license to enjoy a balanced life while we have it.

I was reminded of this when I read a fascinating news article on the tenth anniversary of 9/11. The article was entitled, "Small Choices, Saved Lives: Near Misses of 9/11" and it chronicled how the lives of people were changed by seemingly innocuous decisions. For example, one lady whose office was on the 67th floor of the North Tower just happened to step outside for a cigarette break seconds before one of the planes exploded into the towers.

United Airlines flight attendant Elise O'Kane wanted to work her usual trip from Boston to Los Angeles that month. But in August 2001, when scheduling her flights for September on the airline's computer system, she accidentally inverted two code numbers and wound up with the wrong schedule. She tried to correct this scheduling mistake and managed to trade flights with other attendants for all her trips—except for Flight 175 on 9/11, so a scheduling error kept O'Kane from getting on Flight 175 which crashed into the World Trade Center. Later on a friend told her, "God has a plan for you."[7]

Stories like this abound. There is nothing like a near brush with death to help you understand that life is a gift meant to be enjoyed. We should understand how short our lives really are in the span of eternity and acknowledge each day as an opportunity to live for God. That is why in Psalm 90:12 Moses says, "Teach us to number our days that we may get a heart of wisdom."

Second, *we should be fearful of God's judgment*. Solomon closes this passage with these words: "I know that everything God does will remain forever; there is nothing to add to it and there is nothing to take from it, for God has so worked that men should fear Him. That which is has been already and that which will be has already been, for God seeks what has passed by" (3:14–15). The fear of God is a recurring theme through Ecclesiastes. This doesn't refer to a paralyzing fear of God but a reverential awe that leads to worship and obedience.

I used to think that living in "the fear of the Lord" was like driving down the street while watching a policeman in your rearview mirror, just waiting for the blue lights and a ticket. But actually there's a better picture for the fear of the Lord. It's like a teenage driver who suddenly spots his father's

---

7. Park, "Small Choices, Saved Lives: Near Misses of 9/11," *CNN News*, 5 September 2011.

car in her rearview mirror. Seeing him back there puts him on notice to be on his best behavior—to use the blinkers, to slow down at the yellow light, and abide by the speed limit. But it also tells him that his father cares enough to follow him. It tells him that he's safe. His father isn't trying to trap or trick him. He's trying to help him develop good habits; not just to be careful on this trip, but to obey the laws and stay safe until he gets home. He's driving on his own but not completely on his own.

So it is for the people of God. The fear of the Lord means we live life with our Heavenly Father always in our rearview mirror. We glance up and see His brilliant holiness but also His care and love. Our response, the fear of the Lord, is a mix of reverence, trust, love and submission.

6

Crooked Justice (3:16–4:3)

THE EIGHTEENTH CENTURY PHILOSOPHER David Hume was known as "The Scottish Skeptic" because of his often bleak outlook on life. Hume was not sympathetic to the Christian message to say the least. In Hume's universe God was distant and aloof, if He existed at all. Miracles were impossible and the Scriptures, because they were laden with miracles, were nothing more than quaint stories of mythology. Part of Hume's skepticism and anti-supernatural bias stemmed from the fact that all around him he saw a world of injustice and suffering. If a God of supreme love and power were alive and well, then he reasoned there would be less suffering. Hume asserted:

> Were a stranger to drop on a sudden into this world, I would show him, as a specimen of its ills, a hospital full of diseases, a prison crowded with malefactors and debtors, a field of battle strewn with carcasses, a fleet floundering in the ocean, a nation languishing under tyranny, famine and pestilence. To turn the gay side of life to him, and give him a notion of its pleasures; wither should I conduct him? To a ball, to an opera, to court? He might think that I was only showing him a diversity of distress and sorrow.[1]

It seems like the Preacher of Ecclesiastes and Hume shared the same anguish when it comes to mystery of evil and suffering. Yet if either of these men were transported into the modern world, I'm not sure they would see much progress. Turn on the television or log on to the Internet and you will

1. Hume, *Dialogues Concerning Natural Religion*, 64.

be bombarded with stories of natural disaster, corrupt politicians, pandemics, warfare, sex trafficking and extortion.

In 2006 two students from Taylor University suffered a terrible car accident. A truck hit a van carrying students head-on, killing five people. At the accident scene, someone found Laura Van Ryn's purse next to Whitney Cerak. Workers at the scene mistook the students, both blondes, for each other. Laura misidentified as Whitney, was pronounced dead at the scene, while Whitney misidentified as Laura, fought for her life on the way to the hospital.

Some fourteen hundred people attended "Whitney's" funeral, and her father spoke at the service. No one suspected that the body they buried that day actually belonged to Laura Van Ryn. When the monumental error finally came to light, both families expressed tremendous grief again. For five weeks the Ceraks believed their daughter had died, while the Van Ryns thought their daughter lived. In one conversation, the Ceraks told the Van Ryns, "We're so sorry that we have the happy ending."[2]

We live in a world of twisted justice. The scales are supposed to be balanced, but often we find that they are stacked to one side. Evil seems to prosper. The bad guy doesn't always get caught. Those who least deserve to suffer are often the ones who have been dealt the worst pain. The innocent are trodden under foot by the rich and powerful. Why is it that our cries for justice seem to fall on deaf ears? How did the Preacher deal with these depressing facts? The same way you and I do today. He asked the question, "Why God?" and waited for a response.

The Reality of Injustice (3:16, 4:1)

The Bible never sugarcoats reality. It never glosses over the dark underbelly of life. Its pages are filled with flesh-and-blood people who wrestled with evil and often received the short-end of the stick. Joseph was sold into slavery by his brothers and then wrongfully accused of rape. Job lost his entire fortune, family and fitness all in a matter of hours. Jeremiah was thrown into a cistern and Daniel into a lion's den, both for simply serving God. The ultimate injustice occurred when Jesus, the sinless Son of God, was nailed to cross by the hands of sinful men. No one is exempt from injustice, not even God who made himself vulnerable.

This was the kind of tangle that Solomon tried to sludge through in the following passage. As he looked down from his kingly perch he noted that life was unfair. In 3:16 he noted *the extortion of justice*. "Moreover, I saw

---

2. Alcorn, *If God Is Good*, 204–205.

under the sun that in the place of justice, even there was wickedness, and in the place of righteousness, even there was wickedness." Injustice was rampant. The government officials were in the pocket of the mafia. The judge's bench went to the highest bidder. If you are looking to be vindicated by the legal system then you are sadly mistaken. Even the best courtrooms are flawed on some level.

Here's just one example. In 1983, amateur boxer Dewey Bozella was charged with the killing of a 92-year-old Poughkeepsie, New York woman. There was no physical evidence to ever link him to the crime, but he was convicted based on the statements of two convicts who won their own freedom in return for testifying against him. Bozella spent the next 26 years of his life locked away in the notorious Sing Sing prison. Bozella maintained his innocence over the course of those two decades. Eventually his case was reopened and investigators found that crucial evidence proving his innocence was withheld. In 2009 he was exonerated of all crimes and released from prison. Bozella eventually went on to fight his first and last bout as a professional boxer. At the age of 52, Bozella won by unanimous decision against a man twenty years his junior.[3] A happy ending? Yes, but it makes you wonder what could Bozella have done if he hadn't been deprived of a boxing career during his prime years?

In the spring of 2013 America was shocked to learn that Amanda Berry, Gina DeJesus and Michelle Knight were still alive. These three women had gone missing ten years earlier from their Cleveland, Ohio homes. Almost everyone in the community where they lived, including family members, had all but given up hope. Then amazingly one of them escaped and called the police. The country was dazed and disgusted to find out that these three girls had been tied up and imprisoned for a decade just a few miles across town. It was later revealed that the abductor, Ariel Castro, actually attended a candlelight vigil for the girls when they first went missing. Imagine—a rapist and kidnapper on the loose for ten years. Where's the justice in that? And how did the authorities miss this atrocity for so long?

The Preacher continued his lament in 4:1 when he noted *the exploitation of power*. "Again I saw all the oppressions that are done under the sun. And behold, the tears of the oppressed, and they had no one to comfort them! On the side of their oppressors there was power, and there was no one to comfort them." The oppressed were just a tool for the wealthy to perpetuate their prosperity. The minority in power were fat and happy while the majority lived in poverty. He is describing life under the golden rule—the

---

3. Siegel, "Dewey Bozella: Wrongfully Convicted Man Wins Pro Boxing Debut Match," *ABC News*, 16 October 2011.

one with the gold rules. Those at the top of the pyramid scheme didn't mind stepping on the back of others to get there. It seemed like God was asleep at the wheel.

Simon Wiesenthal was a holocaust survivor, but his faith in God died somewhere in a Nazi concentration camp. He told the story of watching a Nazi commander shackle two Jewish prisoners back to back. The commander pushed his gun into the mouth of one of the victims and pulled the trigger. One bullet killed both men. The Nazi turned to his corporals and said, "See I told you, there's no need to waste bullets. You can kill two with one." Wiesenthal concluded, "When I saw the oppression and wickedness and injustice of that act, I could not comprehend it and I turned from God."[4]

Do you get the sense that Solomon is exasperated by the whole mess of crooked justice? Even though he's the king, his hands are tied by red tape. It's almost as if Solomon is saying, "I don't have any answers either. I'm looking at the same social problems you are. I don't understand how we can solve them or how one human could treat another like an animal. Is there anyone out there who is hearing me?"

The Reaction to Injustice (4:2–3)

If you live with injustice long enough skepticism can begin to creep in and before you know it, agnosticism can turn into hard-core atheism. Those who cannot salvage faith in the midst of life's wreckage begin to wonder, "Is there really an all-loving, all-powerful God in control of things?" Living "under the sun" causes us to agree with the infamous words of Thomas Hobbs when he said that life was "nasty, brutish and short."

Charles Templeton, who was one of America's prominent evangelists alongside Billy Graham during the late 1950s and early 1950s, drew this same conclusion. Unable to reconcile the God of the Bible with the problem of pain, Templeton found himself in the disillusionment of atheism. Plagued by unanswered doubts and the plight of a suffering world Templeton told reporter Lee Strobel:

> A loving God could not possibly be the author of the horrors that continue every day and have continued since time began and will continue as long as life exists. It is an inconceivable tale of suffering, injustice and death and because the tale is fact—is, in truth, the history of the world—it is obvious there cannot be a loving God.[5]

---

4. Tommy Nelson, *The Problem of Life with God*, 59–60.
5. Strobel, *The Case for Faith*, 29.

While some resort to a funeral for God, others resign to despair. In the face of terrible atrocities, some wish they had never been born at all. In fact that seems to be the thrust of Solomon's statement in 4:2–3. "And I thought the dead who are already dead more fortunate than the living who are still alive. But better than both is he who has not yet been and has not seen the evil deeds that are done under the sun." The Preacher congratulated the unborn, for they would never get a glimpse of a cancer victim struggling for the next breath, or a third-world genocide, or the bloated bellies of children dying of starvation.

Solomon is touching on a raw nerve. It's difficult to fathom that a verse like this could be in the Bible, but there it sits begging for an explanation. He seems to be indicating that the conclusion to life where there is no God in sight is destined for gloomy fatalism, despair and nihilism. Remember his viewpoint is totally horizontal. If we can never get above the sun then Nietzsche, Camus and Sartre had it right. In a world where there is no objective standard then injustice is merely a by-product of the survival of the fittest. Moreover, if there is no objective standard then we lose the right to call things "just" or "unjust." Morality is reduced to opinion.

In case you think that's a little extreme just listen to the musings of evolutionary biologist Richard Dawkins:

> In a universe of blind physical forces and genetic replication some people are going to get hurt, other people are going to get lucky, and you won't find any rhyme or reason in it, nor any justice. The universe we observe has precisely the properties we should expect if there is, at bottom, no design, no purpose, no evil and no good, nothing but blind pitiless indifference. DNA neither knows nor cares. DNA just is. And we dance to its music.[6]

How's that for brutal honesty? Dawkins and others of his ilk say we are merely biological machines at the mercy of our genetic programming. Good and evil are really an illusion. Does that sound like a livable worldview to you? In the end the atheist doesn't have a leg to stand on. They want to eradicate God which trashes any notion they might have for a transcendent standard of good and evil. Yet when they look at the world of suffering they claim that the evils of natural disasters, slavery and murder point to the fact God doesn't exist. My simple question is where did they get the notion of evil if God is dead and we are merely evolved primates? In short, the skeptic

---

6. Dawkins, *Out of Eden*, 133.

cannot explain evil by denying an objective moral law, and they cannot deny evil without losing their challenge for the existence of God.

If that worldview gives you a sinking feeling in the bottom of your stomach then hold on, Solomon is done yet.

The Reasons for Injustice (3:18–21)

The late radio announcer Paul Harvey once visited a young man dying of terminal cancer. Despite the fact that this vibrant life and bright future were being tragically interrupted by what seemed to be a premature death, he said to Paul, "I do not believe that the Divine Architect of the universe builds a staircase that leads to nowhere."[7]

So it is with our suffering. God has a design and purpose behind our pain even if we can't see it through the tears. In fact Solomon notes one reason in 3:18, "I said in my heart with regard to the children of man that God is testing them that they may see that they themselves are but beasts." In other words, injustice is allowed by God to teach us something about the human condition.

First, through injustice *man learns about his morality problem (3:18)*. Solomon notices that the injustice so prevalent in our world is a natural outworking of man's inward spiritual depravity. Man is not only at war with others, but he is at war with himself. His behavior is no better than the animal kingdom. In the Preacher's words we are "beasts." If you disagree, all you have to do is listen to headlines of the six o'clock news.

G.K. Chesterton was Christian who lived in London during the first part of the twentieth century. His writings consistently displayed wit and a sense of humor. He employed paradox, while making serious comments on the world, government, politics, economics, philosophy, theology and many other topics. The London Times invited several eminent authors to write essays on the theme "What's wrong with the world?" Chesterton's contribution took the form of two sentences, "Dear Sirs, in response to question, "What is wrong with the world?" I am. Sincerely Yours, G. K. Chesterton."

If we find ourselves crying out, "God, why don't you do something about all the evil and injustice in the world?" then are we willing to admit that if God were going to undertake such an eradication that he would have to begin in our own heart?

Second, *injustice teaches man about his mortality problem (3:19–21)*. Another injustice that Solomon sees is that death ultimately overtakes us all. The criminal might escape the reach of the law, but he cannot outrun

7. Geisler, *If God, Why Evil?*, 51.

death because death wears excellent running shoes and it always catches up with everyone.

"For what happens to the children of man and what happens to the beasts is the same; as one dies, so dies the other. They all have the same breath, and man has no advantage over the beasts, for all is vanity. All go to one place. All are from the dust, and to dust all return."

Don't misunderstand what Solomon is saying here. The tendency is to come away with the erroneous and heretical conclusion that there is no intrinsic difference between the animals and humanity vis-à-vis naturalistic evolution which says that man is merely a highly evolved primate with a rational brain and an opposable thumb.

What Solomon is saying is this—man has no special advantage over the animals in that we die just like they die. Man, although made in the image of God, is fallen into sin. Decay will eventually return us to the dust of earth, just like every other carbon-based life form on the planet. This is a result of living under the curse of sin (Rom. 5:12). According to Solomon that is the ultimate injustice. How can mankind with all of his intellect, creativity, and engineering ability to conquer the elements end up in the cold ground just like the dumb ox who chews his cud?

Haddon Robinson, wrote a parable that explains the cruel hand of death:

> A man opens a newspaper and discovers it is dated six months in advance from the time in which he lives. Reading through the newspaper, he discovers stories about events that have not yet taken place. He turns to the sports page and sees scores of games not yet played. He turns to the financial page and discovers the rise and fall of different stocks and bonds. He realizes that this information can make him fabulously wealthy. A few large bets on an underdog team, a simple phone call to his broker to buy and sell stocks and he's got millions coming his way. He is delighted. He turns to the back page and comes to the obituary column and notices his picture and story."[8]

Injustice or a simple fact of life? Then to add insult to injury, if dying wasn't scary enough, he adds in 3:21 that on this side of the grave no one really knows what awaits on the other side. "Who knows whether the spirit of man goes upward and the spirit of the beast goes down into the earth?" Solomon is wrestling with the age-old question of, "What really happens when we die?" He considers the question empirically with only his five senses and his three-pound brain to guide him. If we are standing on the

---

8. Larson and Elshof, *1001 Illustrations That Connect*, 248.

shores of eternity with no divine revelation to guide us then any guess is a viable option.

There is a humorous illustration of this quandary. I am told than on an Indiana cemetery tombstone over 100 years old the following epitaph has been inscribed, "Pause stranger when you pass me by, as you are now so once was I, as I am now so you will be, prepare yourself to follow me." Someone came by later and wrote beside it "To follow you I'm not content, until I know which way you went."

After the first sin, God cursed man and said, "By the sweat of your face you shall eat bread till you return to the ground, for out of it you were taken for you are dust and to dust you shall return" (Gen. 3:19). This deeply perplexed Solomon. If you aren't ready to die, then you aren't ready to live. Death is philosophy's biggest question and only God can answer it. If you don't have God in your worldview then the injustice of death cannot be fully understood. Without revelation we can know that we die, but we cannot know what happens after we die. The nagging questions which come from injustice are supposed to point us in the direction of God so that we can find real answers. Life is supposed to be vexing, vapid and vain without God.

The Resolution to Injustice (3:17, 22)

Solomon already concluded that since there is a time and season for everything under the sun, then God must also have a specific time in which He is going to exact judgment and set the record straight (3:1–15). He ends this journey through the malaise of life's darker questions with two hopeful conclusions.

We must remember that *judgment is inevitable (3:17)*. "I said in my heart, God will judge the righteous and the wicked, for there is a time for every matter and for every work." The man who ripped you off last year in that business deal gone south isn't going to get away with it. The murderer who was acquitted by a jury of fallible men will give an account to God. The phony preacher who was in the ministry for the Almighty dollar and snookered the masses will have to stand before the Judge of the quick and the dead someday. When the Judge who cannot do wrong sits behind the bench the rulings will be according to the secrets of men's hearts. Furthermore, there will be no partiality, no favoritism and no influence peddling. The date has been set and each of us will have his or her day in court. This is as comforting as it is terrifying.

But what about that skeptic who sees injustice and evil all around and concludes atheism is true? I think he makes at least two fundamental mistakes. First, the existence of evil actually demonstrates that there is a God. Think about it—if there is real evil and injustice, then there must be good, and if there is a qualitative difference between the two then there must be a moral law that helps us adjudicate between good and evil. If there is a moral law then there must be a moral Law-Giver. Thus, there must be God or else we couldn't tell the difference between a crooked stick and a straight one. Crying out "Injustice" actually acknowledges that things ought to be a certain way and are not.

Second, just because God has not defeated evil does not mean that He never will. Since God is just and wants to defeat evil and is all-powerful and can defeat evil, then it is a certainty that injustice and evil will one day be resolved by God. The apostle Peter preached in one of his sermons, "And he [Jesus] commanded us to preach to the people and to testify that he [Jesus] is the one appointed by God to be judge of the living and the dead" (Acts 10:42). Additionally, the apostle Paul told the Epicurean and Stoic philosophers in Athens, "The times of ignorance God overlooked, but now he commands all people everywhere to repent, because he has fixed a day on which he will judge the world in righteousness by a man whom he has appointed; and of this he has given assurance to all by raising him from the dead" (Acts. 17:30–31).

We all love dumb criminal stories. Did you hear the one about Gary Tindle, the man charged with robbery? While standing in the California courtroom of Judge Armando Rodriguez, Tindle asked for permission to go to the bathroom. He was escorted upstairs to the bathroom and the door was guarded by a bailiff while he was inside. But Tindle, determined to escape, climbed up the plumbing, opened a panel in the drop-ceiling and started slithering through the crawl space to freedom. He only go about 30 or 40 feet when the ceiling panels broke under him, and he dropped right to the floor—right back in Judge Rodriguez's courtroom.[9]

God's justice may be slow, but it's sure. There is a payday someday. Sometimes He judges people in this life; sometimes He puts off their sentencing until after death. Either way God gets the last laugh. While we may not see it in time, justice will be carried out in eternity. Sooner or later, the wheels of God's righteousness will right every wrong, balance every scale, and correct every injustice in the world.

Finally, we must remember that *joy is optional (3:22)*. So how are we to live in light of all this? Solomon's conclusion is pretty straightforward and in my estimation it's so frank that on the surface it's almost a bit of a

---

9. Harvey, *Paul Harvey's For What It's Worth*, 129.

disappointment. It like something you would get from your high school ball coach, "Walk it off. Put some dirt on it and get back in the game!"

If you have been a victim of injustice then how should you keep from growing bitter and cynical? The natural reaction is to get even at those who have wronged you. Or you could start a campaign of complaining, assuming that anyone will actually listen. You might brood over injustice and write about it in your blog, or pray that God will strike your enemies with a case of explosive hemorrhoids.

No. The biblical advice is to avoid living with self-pity at all costs. Solomon says just leave it in God's hands, enjoy the life you do have and move on. Eugene Peterson paraphrases 3:22 like this, "So I made up my mind that there's nothing better for us men and women than to have a good time in whatever we do—that's our lot. Who knows if there's anything else to life?"[10]

So you've been dealt a bad hand in life? Join the club. Take that disadvantage and turn it into an advantage. Recognize your life as a gift from God and turn it all over to him and let Him make something beautiful out of a tragedy.

Philip Yancey, in his book, *Disappointment with God*, writes about how the Gospel puts injustice into perspective:

> Author Henri Nouwen tells the story of a family he knew in Paraguay. The father, a doctor, spoke out against the military regime there and its human rights abuses. Local police took their revenge on him by arresting his teenage son and torturing him to death. Enraged townsfolk wanted to turn the boy's funeral into a huge protest march, but the doctor chose another means of protest. At the funeral, the father displayed his son's body as he had found it in the jail—naked, scarred from electric shocks and cigarette burns, and beatings. All the villagers filed past the corpse, which lay not in a coffin but on the blood-soaked mattress from the prison. It was the strongest protest imaginable, for it put injustice on grotesque display.

Yancey goes on to write, "Isn't that what God did at Calvary? The cross that held Jesus' body, naked and marked with scars, exposed all the violence and injustice of this world. At once, the cross revealed what kind of world we have and what kind of God we have: a world of gross unfairness, a God of sacrificial love."[11]

---

10. Peterson, *The Message*, Ecc. 3:22.
11. Yancey, *Disappointment with God*, 216.

God has entered into our evil. He knows injustice firsthand and cares enough to do something about it. In the meantime, let God handle the big stuff, while you get busy living for Him.

7

Overcoming Loneliness (4:4–16)

In the movie *Cast Away*, Tom Hanks plays the role of a highly demanding, time-obsessed systems analyst for Federal Express. Hanks' character, Chuck Noland, travels the world resolving productivity problems in an attempt to make package delivery more efficient. The movie takes pains to show how his relentless work schedule interferes with his relationships. The audience gets the idea very quickly that he is married to his work.

However, the film takes a sharp plot twist when a Fed Ex plane crashes and Noland finds himself marooned on a deserted island somewhere in the Pacific. Noland is surrounded by nothing but palm trees, sand and the constant lap of ocean on the shore. Ironically, he must now adjust to a world where time doesn't matter.

Noland learns how to survive by improvising with the rudimentary elements of the island and with the Fed Ex packages that continue to wash up on shore from the downed plane. He is able to construct a tent out of an old survival raft. He converts the blades off some ice skates into a makeshift cutting tool. The film even chronicles his struggle in learning how to make fire the old fashioned way without matches.

As the story progresses, the days turn into months and the search crews are nowhere in sight. Having conquered everything the elements could throw at him, Noland is surviving pretty well, except there is still one big problem. He is lonely. There is no one there he can talk to, no one to help in the search for food, no one to sit around the campfire with him at night and tell stories of the good ole' days. Then serendipity strikes and Nolan discovers a volleyball that washes up on the shore.

This volleyball would be the spontaneous cure for the agonizing ache of loneliness. As the movie goes on Noland paints a face on the volleyball, creatively names him Wilson, then has full-blown conversations, and even arguments, with this silent companion.

As the viewer you get the sense that Wilson is a very important character in the story, for without him Noland would really go off the edge of sanity. For those of you who have not seen the movie I won't ruin the rest of the plot for you, but Wilson serves an illustration for the universal void created by loneliness.

Loneliness has been defined by one its victims as "malnutrition of the soul which comes from living on substitutes." In *Cast Away* Chuck Nolan has to resort to a make-believe relationship with a volleyball in order to satisfy the desire for companionship. The idea of talking to an inanimate object sounds ridiculous until you realize that so-called "well-adjusted" people deal with loneliness by substituting relationships for riches, success, substances or a digital avatar in cyberspace.

It is well known that Sigmund Freud died at the age of 83, a bitter and disillusioned man. Tragically, the Viennese physician, one of the most influential thinkers of his time, had little compassion for the common person. Freud wrote in 1918, "I have found little that is good about human beings on the whole. In my experience most of them are trash, no matter whether they publicly subscribe to this or that ethical doctrine or to none at all." Not surprisingly, Freud died friendless.[1]

The list of the lonely goes on and on and includes people you would never think would have any shortage of friends. Albert Einstein, the world renowned physicist said, "It is strange to be known universally, and yet be so lonely." Star of the silver screen and Playboy centerfold Marilyn Monroe admitted, "Sometimes I think the only people who stay with me and really listen are people I hire and people I pay." The classic novelist Earnest Hemingway said, "I live in a vacuum that is as lonely as a radio tube when the batteries are dead and there is no current to plug into."

People today will admit any problem—drugs, divorce, depression—but there's one admission that people loath to make whether they're a star on television or someone who crawls under cars. It's just too embarrassing. It penetrates too deeply to the core of who they are. People don't want to admit that they are lonely. Loneliness is such a humiliating malady that it ought to have its own politically correct euphemism. Maybe we should call it being "relationally challenged." Anything to make it safer to confess this embarrassing truth that afflicts every respectable person.

---

1. "Sigmund Freud," *Discoveries*.

Flip on the radio and what do you hear? Tunes such as "Eleanor Rigby," "Heartbreak Hotel," "I'm So Lonely I Could Die," and "Message in a Bottle," all resonate from the cry of a lonely heart. One writer described man's malady like this: "In a society where people live in impersonal cities or suburbs, where electronic entertainment often replaces one-to-one conversation, where people move from job to job, and state to state, and marriage to marriage, loneliness has become an epidemic."[2]

The following entry in Solomon's journal deals with the root causes of a lonely, depressed world. Solomon is perceptive enough to know that once you get below the surface, people are basically broken, hurting and alienated from each other. Most of these wounds are self-inflicted. Competition in the workplace makes us enemies scrambling for the penthouse office. Envy of our neighbor's stuff causes us to keep our noses to the grindstone instead of building relationships. The drive for prestige and power may lead to the top, but who will we share the summit with?

The Preacher is in the business of making comparisons in this section. In fact, this passage hinges on three comparative statements beginning with the phrase, "Better than" (4:6, 4:9, 4:13). Solomon is contrasting different ways of living—the worldly model (which leads to loneliness) and the biblical model (which leads to contentment). By using this method, Solomon advises us to make three importance choices.

Choose Contentment over Competition (4:4–6)

The Preacher turns his gaze to the business world and what he finds there is an exhausting rat race. Off with the rose colored glasses of optimism and now with another ragged-edged look at reality. Solomon gives us his appraisal of Wall Street and the marketplace as he encounters three different kinds of workers, each one with a different outlook on life.

First, we encounter *the industrious man (4:4)*. "Then I saw that all toil and all skill in work come from a man's envy of his neighbor. This also is vanity and a striving after wind." This guy is climbing the corporate ladder. He reads the Wall Street Journal every day and is a ferocious contender in the dog-eat-dog battle to be alpha male. His bloodstream pumps caffeine and capitalism. He's definitely a work-a-holic because he has to keep up with his neighbor who has a BMW and a Mercedes, a 60 inch flat screen television, pool, boat and a timeshare in Palm Springs. He's working hard to buy things he doesn't need, with money he doesn't have, to impress people he

---

2. Barrett, "An Epidemic Called Loneliness."

doesn't like. Ask him what his philosophy on life is and he'll tell you, "Get all you can. Can all you get. Sit on the can. Poison the rest."

Second is *the idle man (4:5)*. "The fool folds his hands and eats his own flesh." On the complete opposite end of the spectrum there is the lazy sluggard who took the path of least resistance. He dropped out of the rat race a long time ago. This is the guy who refuses to get a real job and opts to lives off the welfare system. He thinks, "I've got food stamps and 900 channels of cable, who needs to work?" This dude's skin hasn't seen the sunlight in ages. He's doing well to get up by noon and his biggest decision of the day is if he's going to waste hours watching re-runs of Sports Center or play video games.

Third, we see *the insightful man (4:6)*. "Better is a handful of quietness than two hands full of toil and a striving after wind." This character has achieved balance and moderation in his life—he's married wisdom to his work. He's not killing himself trying to have everything that his neighbor has got, nor is he slothful and unproductive. Solomon is saying that it's better to work hard and be content with what you have rather than obtaining fistfuls of money that bring all kinds of extra burdens. Better to live within your means, to sell that expensive home and downsize, drive a used car, and cut up some of your credit cards than the alternative of burning the candle at both ends to keep up appearances. Its better enjoying your family and watching your kids grow up than being stuck in an office on nights and weekends trying to get one up on the cubicle next door.

Several years ago a story came to light that highlighted a growing problem in our fast-paced society—overwork. In 2006, a forty-five year old engineer for Toyota literally worked himself to death. The Japanese man who died had been under severe pressure as the lead engineer in developing a hybrid version of Toyota's blockbuster Camry line which we know as the Prius. In the two months up to his death, the man averaged more than eighty hours of overtime per month. He regularly worked nights and weekends and was frequently sent abroad. Eventually he expired of ischemic heart disease. The Japanese have a term for this phenomenon—*karoshi*, meaning "death from overwork."[3]

Blessed are the balanced! The wise person realizes that a career is not the measure of your self-worth and that having more money can't replace the joy of spending time with people you love. As one commentator said, "Our problem is not the high cost of living; it is the cost of high living. We want far too much. The cure is contentment, being willing to settle for

---

3. Alabaster, "Japanese Man Dies of Overworking," *The Huffington Post*, 9 July 2008.

less materially if it means we can have some rest."[4] As Solomon has showed contentment is not freedom from desire but finding our desires in God.

Choose Relationships over Riches (4:7–12)

The Preacher writes, "Again, I saw vanity under the sun: one person who has no other, either son or brother, yet there is no end to all his toil, and his eyes are never satisfied with riches, so that he never asks, "For whom am I toiling and depriving myself of pleasure?" This also is vanity and an unhappy business" (4:7–8).

The man in the Preacher's second example reminds me of Ebenezer Scrooge. He is materially wealthy but relationally poor. While he was at work, the kids grew up, his wife went back to college and found a career of her own, his children moved out, and now the house is empty. He can't believe it. The Board of Directors just named him CEO. Now there's no one to share the good news with because he made it to the top—alone. He's got money and he loves it, but money doesn't love him back. He eats alone in front of the TV, goes to sleep in a king-size bed all to himself, and when he dies who knows what will come of his fortunes. Will he bequeath his money to a long distance relative or will his stocks be sold to shareholders?

A few years ago I came across the following story of one such wealthy spinster by the name of Grace Groner:

> She lived alone in a tiny one-bedroom cottage in Lake Forest, Illinois. She had no husband and no family to speak of. She bought her clothes at rummage sales, didn't own a car and worked 43 years of her life as a secretary for a pharmaceutical company. Yet after her death at age 100, Grace Groner left Lake Forest College a gift of $7 million to be used for scholarships. The money came from three $60 shares of stock she bought in 1935—and held on to. She never sold a share, even after repeated stock splits. She also kept reinvesting the dividends. By the time of her death, she owned more than 100,000 shares in the company and she was literally a secret millionaire.[5]

Solomon is not impressed with such stories. He seems to imply that those who put riches in front of relationships never stop to ask themselves a very basic question, "Why am I doing this?" What good is it if you don't

---

4. Krell, "Alone at the Top (Ecclesiastes 4:4–16)."

5. Frank, "How A Secretary Made and Gave Away $7 Million," *The Wall Street Journal*, 8 March 2010.

have the capacity to enjoy your wealth and you don't live to see anyone benefit from it either?

It is said that in a churchyard in the village of Leamington, England, there stands a tombstone with the following epitaph: "Here lies a miser who lived for himself and cared for nothing but gathering wealth; now where he is or how he fares nobody knows and nobody cares." A stark reminder of the truth the Preacher is trying to prove.

Solomon now shifts from an unhealthy example to a more balanced and enjoyable lifestyle centered on friends and family. The cure for loneliness is not more stuff or a better job but pouring ourselves into others. If you wanted to boil Solomon's advice down to its essence it seems to be, "Spend more time developing people than your wealth portfolio because in the end relationships are your greatest assets." Through the use of pithy examples, Solomon shows how we cannot assign a monetary value to a good relationship.

First, notice that *two are better than one in working (4:9)*. "Two are better than one, because they have a good reward for their toil." When I read this, I thought of the great business ventures that were born out of friendship. Two out-of-the-box thinking geniuses, Steve Jobs and Steve Wozniak, started Apple Computers out of their California garage. Ben and Jerry started selling ice cream out of a Vermont gas station and now "Chunky Monkey" is a household name. Orville and Wilbur Wright were brothers and bicycle mechanics with dreams of flying. Despite naysayers they did the unthinkable by successfully building and piloting the first heavier-than-air craft. Needless to say, the world was changed by these friendships.

Work is more productive and more enjoyable when you have someone there to share it with. Remember in the Garden of Eden when Adam was all alone? The Bible says that Adam looked around after naming the animals and realized that there was no helper suitable for him. God said, "It is not good that the man should be alone, I will make him a helper suitable for him" (Gen. 2:18). Because of the way God has wired us, no man is an island. I once heard a teacher quote Leonardo Da Vinci in saying, "An arch consists of two weaknesses, which leaning against one another make a strength!" So it is with friends as well.

Second, *two are better than one in walking (4:10)*. "For if they fall, one will lift up his fellow. But woe to him who is alone when he falls and has not another to lift him up!" When I read this I thought of Frodo and Sam from the Lord of the Rings trilogy. Frodo would have never made it to Mt. Doom to destroy the ring if Sam had not shared the burden. There are numerous biblical examples of dynamic duos: David and Jonathan locked shields and fought off the Philistines. After spending some time sulking in a cave and wishing he was dead, Elijah met up with Elisha one day, threw his cloak over him and said, "We're in this together." Paul needed a man like Barnabas to come alongside him and encourage him in the ministry.

The Christian life is difficult and downright impossible to live in seclusion. God has given us each other as a source of perspective, accountability and encouragement. A good friend warns us of the pitfalls of sin and helps us up when we have fallen in a trial. I once heard a good piece of advice, "The time to make friends is before you need them."

Third, *two are better than one in warmth (4:11)*. "Again, if two lie together, they keep warm, but how can one keep warm alone?" My wife's feet are like ice cubes. I know because every night as we crawl into bed, she places those polar ice caps on me! This verse also reminded of the phrase "three-dog night." That's when it's so cold outside that you have to sleep with three dogs on the bed to ward off the cold.

Really what this passage is talking about is warmth that is created because of the mutual love companions have for one another. Solitude is like a frozen tundra, but companionship is like a warm blanket of affection and affirmation. Here's an experiment: take two coals from the fire place and separate them, then take two more coals and place them close together. Which pair do you think will stay warmer longer? It's obvious right—the ones that stay close. This is why it's so important for the church to stay connected through regular worship (Heb. 10:24–25).

Fourth, *two are better than one in watchcare (4:12)*. "And though a man might prevail against one who is alone, two will withstand him—a threefold cord is not quickly broken." Did you notice that Solomon began by talking about one (4:8), then he moved to two in (4:9) and now he made it to three (4:12)? The immediate application pertains to attacks from thieves as a pilgrim travels along a dangerous road. "A cord of three strands is not quickly torn apart" was a proverbial way of saying "there is strength in numbers."

Out of the furnaces of war come many true stories of sacrificial friendship. In 2011 Sergeant First Class Leroy Petry was awarded the military's most distinguished award—the Medal of Honor. Petry was recognized for his selfless and heroic actions on May 26, 2008 when his Ranger battalion came under heavy fire in Afghanistan. Though already wounded in both legs, he grabbed a live grenade that landed amidst his team and attempted to throw it away. The grenade exploded before he could release it, destroying his right hand and forearm. The medics improvised a makeshift tourniquet on his arm to stop the bleeding. Amazingly, Petry continued to direct his men until the fight was over. Petry's sacrifice saved his fellow soldiers from certain death or injury.[6]

This is an illustration of the three-fold chord that Solomon envisioned. Jesus said to his disciples on the eve of his crucifixion, "Greater love has no one than this, that someone lay down his life for his friends (John 15:13)." The world has many misconceptions about what love is. According to the Bible, love is not just an emotion or a warm feeling we have, but love is displayed by willing the good of another no matter the cost. In short, love is rooted in sacrifice. So before you head into a battle be sure to dig a foxhole big enough for you and a friend.

Choose People Over Popularity (4:13-16)

The miserly millionaire cannot escape the haunting specter of loneliness and neither can the king on his throne. Solomon tells a parable in the last few verses to illustrate that the applause of the masses and the approval of glowing fans is not enough to assuage the demon of loneliness. The reason is because popularity is fleeting. The view from the peak is good for a while, but people are fickle and as the king they will love you one day and hate you the next.

Notice there are two characters in this story: the old foolish king and a poor wise youth. The old king is soon eclipsed by the poor youth who rises to prominence. He goes from zero to hero. Then within just a few years, the poor youth that everybody loved is now replaced by another youth. Today's hero becomes tomorrow's forgotten name.

Personally, I think that Solomon is writing from his family's personal experience, except he has kept the names anonymous. Think of Saul as the old, foolish king. The people wanted Saul to be king because he was head and shoulders above the crowd, but really he was a terrible leader. He ascended to glory, but his career ended with suicide and ignominy.

Saul was eclipsed by the youth David—the poor, wise youth who was a shepherd boy from Bethlehem. He was the man after God's own heart. He slew the Philistine colossus, Goliath, and the people cried out, "Saul has killed his thousands, but David his ten-thousands." David was on top for many years until he too became his own worst enemy. David's double sin of adultery and murder destroyed his household and tainted the throne.

David was then replaced by his son Solomon who achieved worldwide fame. People everywhere knew about the wealth and wisdom of Solomon,

---

6. Martinez, "Medal of Honor Awarded to Ranger Leroy Petry," *ABC News*, 12 July 2011.

yet even as he was writing this verse Solomon knew that his fame would soon fade away into obscurity (2:16).

Public opinion is a strange bird. It's never a good barometer of character; just think of the beloved phonies that have been exposed only to feel the bludgeoning sting of unpopularity when days before they were riding high on a wave of fanfare. Moreover, those who end up in the halls of fame rarely garner the affection of their contemporaries. Just think of a few examples—Jesus, Martin Luther King Jr. and Abraham Lincoln were all killed for their revolutionary views, yet in hindsight their influence was incalculable.

Speaking of Lincoln, there is a story associated with his assassination that is a reminder of how fickle popular opinion can be. During a PBS documentary Dr. Daniel Boorstin, the Librarian of Congress at the time of filming, brought out a little blue box from a small closet that once held the library's rarities. The label on the box read: "Contents of the president's pockets on the night of April 14, 1865"—which you know was the day of his assassination. There were five things in the box: a handkerchief, with "A. Lincoln," embroidered on it, a country boy's pen knife, a spectacles case repaired with string, a purse containing a $5 bill and some old and worn newspaper clippings.

The clippings were concerned with the political career of Lincoln and one of them was an article in which the headline read, "Abraham Lincoln is one of the greatest men of all time." One writer commented on this news clipping by saying:

> The world now knows Lincoln was a great president, but in 1865 millions of people shared quite a contrary opinion. The President's critics were fierce and many. His was a lonely agony that reflected the suffering and turmoil of his country ripped to shreds by hatred and a cruel, costly war. There is something touchingly pathetic in the mental picture of this great leader seeking solace and self-assurance from a few old newspaper clippings as he reads them under the flickering flame of a candle all alone in the Oval Office. Remember loneliness stalks where the buck stops.[7]

I like Walt Disney's final appraisal of fame, "As far as I can remember, being a celebrity has never helped me make a good picture . . . or commanded the obedience of my daughter, or impressed my wife. It doesn't even seem to help keep fleas off our dog, and if being a celebrity won't give

---

7. Swindoll, *The Quest for Character*, 62–63.

one an advantage over a couple fleas, then I guess there can't be that much in being a celebrity after all."[8]

Solomon's lesson is simple and direct—those who seek popularity and fame are going after a futile object that won't matter a hill of beans when it's all said and done. To those trying to achieve fame they might as well try to write their name in sand while the tide is coming in because that's how long their ride will last. In the end it is better be faithful in the eyes of God than famous in the eyes of men.

---

8. Disney, quoted by Arterburn and Farrel, *The One Year Devotions for Men on the Go*, 162.

8

Wise Words for Worshippers (5:1–7)

In 2012 a 19-year-old man from Washington State, Dakoda Garren, was charged with stealing a rare coin collection worth at least $100,000. After Garren completed some part-time work for a woman living north of Portland, she reported that her family coin collection was missing. Her collection included a variety of rare and valuable coins, including "Liberty Head" quarters, "Morgan" dollars, and other coins dating back to the early 1800s.

Initially, Garren denied any involvement claiming that the police didn't have any evidence against him. But then he started spending the coins at face value, apparently unaware of the coins' worth. He and his girlfriend paid for movie tickets using quarters worth between $5 and $68. Later on the same day, they bought some pizza with rare coins, including a Liberty quarter with an appraised value of $18,500.

The news article reported, "Garren has been charged with first-degree theft and is being held in jail on $40,000 bond. Which, technically, is an amount he could easily afford if the valuable coin collection were actually his."[1]

I think that man's ignorance towards the value of those coins is a good picture of how we often treat God in worship. We dishonor the Lord in our worship when we treat God like an ordinary or even a cheap object. When we show up to church on two wheels running late we tacitly send the message that we are squeezing God into our schedule. When we doze off during the message or the mind wanders while the praise music is going we

---

1. Pfeiffer, "Man Allegedly Steals $100K Coin Collection, Then Spends at Face Value on Pizza and a Movie," *Yahoo! News*, 21 September 2012.

show that God really doesn't capture our attention. When our prayers are empty and repetitious it's evident that we've forgotten who we are talking to. Worship is cheap because we don't value the God we are supposed to be worshipping.

So let's face it—some of us stink at worship. We find it difficult to get excited about Sunday morning but easy to be fanatics about a favorite sports team. We know the hymns by memory; we can sing the first, second and last stanzas by heart, yet we rarely reflect on the meaning of the words. Whether it's a suit and tie, casual dress, or jeans and t-shirt, we spend more time getting ready on the outside than we do on the inside.

Truth is, we are better at nit-picking than genuine adoration of the Lord. First off, we don't want to sit close to someone, so please make sure there is ample room for movement. If the sermon is too long, we start folding up our Bibles (if we actually brought one) and rattling our keys. Music too loud? We'll be sure to let someone on staff know to turn the volume down. Child care is a sensitive issue as well. We expect an army of chipper babysitters on call to do face-painting, crafts and engaging flannel board lessons. Also, we shouldn't have to wait in line to pick up the kids. Instead we need a fingerprint scanner that instantly identifies us and releases our child on a slide, dumping them gently at our feet. That's consumer Christianity at its finest.

Someone has said that there are two kinds of Christians, those who are more like cats and those who are more like dogs. If you pet a dog and feed a dog they think your God, but if you pet a cat and feed a cat they think they're God. Many Christians still think God exists to serve them instead of the reverse. David Platt puts his pulse on the issue when he writes:

> We are giving in to the dangerous temptation to take the Jesus of the Bible and twist him into a version of Jesus we are more comfortable with. A nice, middle-class, American Jesus. A Jesus who doesn't mind materialism and who would never call us to give away everything we have. A Jesus who would not expect us to forsake our closest relationships so that he receives our affection. A Jesus who is fine with nominal devotion that does not infringe on our comforts, because, after all, he loves us just the way we are. A Jesus who wants us to be balanced, who wants us to avoid dangerous extremes, and who, for that matter, wants us to avoid danger all together. A Jesus who brings us comfort and prosperity as we live out our Christian spin of the American dream. But do you and I realize what we are doing at this point? We are molding Jesus into our image. He is beginning to look a lot like us, because, after all, that is whom we are most

comfortable with. And the danger now is that when we gather in our church buildings to sing and lift up our hands in worship, we may not be worshiping the Jesus of the Bible. Instead we may be worshiping ourselves.[2]

When men stop worshipping God, they promptly start worshipping man with disastrous results. This was also a problem in Solomon's day. His palace was just a stone's throw away from the temple and no doubt he could have sat on his balcony and watched as the people went in and out of worship services. However, as he observed the people going to the temple for worship he noticed some things that troubled him. Much of the praying and singing that went on was an empty and vain routine. You could even argue that the people in Solomon's day, much like today, came out of the temple in no better condition than when they went in. Much of their worship was wooden, hypocritical, insincere and to put it bluntly—a waste of time.

Tucked away in the middle of his reflective journal, Solomon has some wise words for worshippers. In the first seven verses of chapter five he gives a few pitfalls that every church goer should avoid. I would submit that not only are his insights applicable today, but his comments teach us something on how *not* to approach God.

Avoid Walking Irreverently into the House of God (5:1)

In the opening line of 5:1 Solomon deals with our preparation for worship and our participation in worship. The phrase "guard your steps" warns us of potential danger just ahead. I think about what the bus driver or flight attendant says as we exit the vehicle, "Watch your step!" In the same way, Solomon is telling us that when we walk into worship we should tread lightly. The Preacher noticed that most people who went into the temple for worship were not prepared in their heart to meet with God.

The first pitfall *is approaching God with iniquity.* Psalm 24:3-4 says, "Who shall ascend the hill of the Lord? And who shall stand in his holy place? He who has clean hands and a pure heart, who does not lift up his soul to what is false and does not swear deceitfully." How many times have you barged into the worship service with a week's worth of unconfessed sinning under your belt? From Monday through Saturday we have spoken harshly to our spouse, swore under our breath five or six times in rush hour

---

2. Platt, *Radical*, 13.

traffic, lusted in our heart and fell asleep during our devotional time. As we enter church with a big grin we say, "Here I am Lord. Bless me!"

The flooring in my childhood home was wall-to-wall white carpet. My mama had very strict rules about her white carpet. It was an unthinkable sin for us to go outside play in the creek, ride bicycles up and down the road, bounce on the trampoline and then come strolling inside with our mud-caked shoes on. There were clear boundaries that we understood and if those were broken we would feel the pain of a hickory switch. All it took was one muddy footprint on the white carpet to incur the wrath of Mama. Before we entered the house our shoes came off on the front stoop, maybe even the socks as well depending on the level of soiling.

Entering the house of God stained with sin would be like asking my mom to ignore muddy shoes on her carpet. When we go into God's presence He makes the rules, not us. His holiness should not be trifled with and we need to do a self-evaluation before we enter into His presence. Perhaps that's why God told Moses to take off his sandals at the burning bush because he was unwittingly standing on holy ground (Ex. 3:5).

Another pitfall we must consider is *approaching God indifferently*. Solomon also admonishes us to "...draw near to listen rather than to offer the sacrifice of fools, for they do not know that they do evil." It seems that the Preacher is warning against apathetic worship which substitutes a life of obedience and holiness with pious platitudes. Warren Wiersbe adds:

> Sacrifices are not substitutes for obedience as King Saul found out when he tried to cover up his disobedience with pious promises (1 Sam. 15:12–23). Offerings in the hands without obedient faith in the heart becomes "the sacrifice of fools," because only a fool thinks he can deceive God. The fool thinks he is doing good, when he or she is really doing evil. And God knows it.[3]

Notice also the emphasis that is placed on hearing. When we draw near to God we should be ready to hear His word and obey it (James 1:19, 1:22). Hearing and listening are two different actions. You can hear a message that pricks the heart and stings the conscious, but not heed its warning. If you hear a message long enough and neglect to appropriate its truth to life then the heart becomes calloused. Listening on the other hand, allows the truth of God and the Holy Spirit to trickle deep into the soul.

I read a news clip about some creative thieves. A hurricane ravaged Florida and left thousands without electrical power. One man who used a portable generator to supply power until the electrical lines could be repaired, reported a strange indecent to the police. Some daring thieves found

---

3. Wiersbe, *The Wiersbe Bible Commentary: Old Testament*, 1123.

the generator in full operation outside the man's house and stole it. The homeowner didn't discover the theft until he went outside to put gasoline in the generator. How did the thieves cover up such an obvious crime? They started another gasoline engine and left it running right beside the generator. The robbers took off with their prize, while the owner was lulled into a false sense of security created by the sound of his own riding lawnmower.

I think that anecdote serves as an illustration of hollow worship. We can go through the motions, listen to sermons, offer prayers and mouth the words to praise songs, all the while thinking that we are hearing the voice of God, when in actuality, true worship has been drowned out by religious noise that sounds "churchy." The sounds of religion subtly cover over the fact that Satan has carried true worship out the back door while we are content with a substitute.

These pitfalls can be avoided if we adequately prepare for worship. The experience we have on Sunday morning actually begins on Saturday night. What kinds of preparation should be made? Go to bed early and wake up early. Meditate on Scripture. Pray and ask God to clear your heart and mind so you can hear His voice. If you have walked out of church not hearing from God then you have not worshipped. You have attended church but you have not actually had fellowship with the Living God. You can check off your obligation card "I did it," but you did not worship.

Avoid Talking Flippantly to God (5:2-3)

Gregory of Nyssa commented on these verses like this, "Knowing how widely the divine nature differs from our own, let us quietly remain within our proper limits." The God we worship—or pretend to worship—is the sovereign and Mighty King who rules the universe. Solomon wants us to understand that God is not the "big man upstairs." He's the infinite, eternal, unchangeable God who is full of wisdom, power, holiness, justice, goodness, and truth. We inhabit the fishbowl of time and space with all the limitations imposed by that habitation. God, however, is outside the fishbowl entirely and He sees past, present and future with equal clarity. We cannot wrap our minds around that any more than a goldfish can understand a map of the land.[4] So there is a fast difference between the finite and the infinite, our ignorance and His omniscience.

The Preacher even offers an analogy, "For a dream comes with much business, and a fool's voice with many words." Just as hard work produces sleep and dreams, so a fool produces many words and mind-numbing

---

4. Jeremiah, *Searching for Heaven on Earth*, 110.

babbling. Thus, we should manage our mouth when asking for an audience with God. Certainly, we can be honest with God and He can handle any emotion that we throw at Him. Yet, we should still remember that advising God on how to run the cosmos is about as ridiculous and irreverent as a finger-painter giving tips to Michelangelo.

Have you ever noticed that when tragedy strikes is when people are most prepared to give God a piece of their mind? God gets a black-eye from suffering people who demand explanations for their plight. Why has God singled us out and picked on us? When Job was covered from head-to-toe in painful sores he demanded answers from God, and the Lord responded with a whirlwind of fury, "Who is this that darkens counsel by words without knowledge?" (Job 38:2). At end of God's interrogation we find Job repenting in dust and ashes and admitting, "I have uttered what I did not understand" (Job 42:3). God's questioning took Job to a vast ocean, and from the shores of ignorance he looked out into the endless sea of God's inscrutable wisdom. I think philosopher Peter Kreeft offers a good analogy to help put humanity in its place:

> How can a mere finite human be sure that infinite wisdom would not tolerate certain short-range evils in order for more long-range goods that we couldn't foresee . . . Imagine a bear in a trap and a hunter, who out of sympathy, wants to liberate him. He tries to win the bear's confidence, but he can't do it so he has to shoot the bear full of drugs. The bear, however, thinks this is an attack and that the hunter is trying to kill him. He doesn't realize that it's being done out of compassion. Then in order to get the bear out of the trap, the hunter has to push him further into the trap to release the tension on the spring. If the bear were semiconscious at that point, he would be even more convinced that the hunter was his enemy who was out to cause him suffering and pain. But the bear would be wrong. He reaches this incorrect conclusion because he's not a human being. How can anyone be certain that's not an analogy between us and God? I believe God does the same to us sometimes, and we can't comprehend why he does it any more than the bear can understand the motivations of the hunter. As the bear could have trusted the hunter, we can trust God.[5]

---

5. Kreeft quoted by Lee Strobel, *The Case for Faith*, 32.

Avoid Vowing Recklessly before God (5:4–7)

I once heard a story of a pilot and his navigator. Their aircraft had been shot down and they were adrift at sea in a tiny lifeboat. After several days without food, water and any hope of rescue the pilot began to pray. He said, "God, you know I haven't lived a very good life. I've been a miserable husband and a terrible father. I've cheated. I've stole, got drunk and cussed. I admit I haven't had much use for the church either. But God if you'll save us from dying out here, I promise, I'll never . . ." The navigator interrupted, *"Don't say another word!* I think I see land!"

If we wanted to summarize Solomon's exhortation into a simple command it would be, "Don't bribe God." We all know it's much easier to make a promise than to keep it. If you think you been shafted over the years by empty promises then think of how many times God has been on the bad end of a raw deal. A man and woman stand before God and say, "Till death do us part." A few years later they have divorced on account of irreconcilable differences. A young man stands in front of a congregation and says, "I'm going into the ministry." Years later he has yet to even teach a Sunday school class. Two parents dedicate a baby and commit to raising the child in the fear of the Lord but only show up for Easter and Christmas services. David Jeremiah has written:

> As a troubled young man walked through a field in Germany, a terrible electrical storm filled the sky. A lightning bolt struck a nearby tree and he instantly took it as a sign from God. "Help me!" cried the young man, "and I will become a monk." That sudden vow changed the life of Martin Luther. Another young man, a despicable character named John Newton, made a similar promise to God in the middle of deadly storm at sea. "Help me," he prayed "and I will change my life." Out of that prayer came a gradual transformation that led Newton into ministry and made him a world class hymnist, the author of *Amazing Grace* . . . We sometimes call this "foxhole Christianity." It's the ultimate expression of using God. Bargaining with God is an extremely questionable activity, generally one to be avoided. But if you put yourself on the line, do not even think about not making good, for God is not mocked.[6]

If every person kept the promises they made to God in a pinch, then Africa and Asia would be swarming with missionaries, church coffers would be filled with tithe money and the church would not be in short supply of

---

6. Jeremiah, *Searching for Heaven on Earth*, 111–112.

volunteers. God does not forget our vows and He holds us to them. When we fail to make good on our vows the Lord has some creative ways of making us pay what we promised.

Remember wily ole' Jacob? He was the master manipulator and con-artist who stole the blessing from his brother Esau. If you study Genesis 28, Jacob is running from his brother Esau who wants to kill him for staling the blessing. In his flight from home he spends the night at Bethel and during his sleep he gets a revelation from God in the form of a ladder descending from heaven. In that dream God promises Jacob a number of things, namely that the blessing which he gave to his Grandfather, Abraham, would pass through him.

After Jacob woke up he made a vow to God, in effect, saying "Alright God if you come through on your end of the promises, then I will make you my God and I will even give a tenth of all my belongings" (Gen. 28:20-22). Years roll off the calendar and the promise is lost in a flurry of activity. In the meantime, Jacob gets conned by Laban and he has to give up fourteen years of life working for Laban in order to get Rachel. Then there is the episode in Genesis 32 beside the Jabbok stream, where the Lord and Jacob have a knock-down-drag-out wrestling match. God eventually made Jacob tap out with a divine touch on the hip. Jacob walked away with a limp and a bruised ego. Finally, thirty years after his original vow, in Genesis 35 Jacob takes his family back to Bethel and completes his end of the vow but this time as a cripple.

The example of Jacob teaches a couple of truths. First, we are prone to forget our vows when God has fulfilled His side of them. God blessed Jacob with riches, a family and special place in His nation building program as one of the founders. Yet, Jacob never seemed to find the opportunity to keep his vow. Second, when things are going well in life it makes it even easier to forget that promise. Jacob was rich in possessions, but somehow his prosperity made it more difficult to give his tenth. Thirdly, the overriding principle is this—if you make a vow before God you had better keep your end of the covenant. There is fine-print on that contract which says, "I am the Lord, I will not be mocked." That is legal terminology which is better translated, "God reserves the right to use any means necessary to enforce the binding terms of the contract."

A believer can suffer the judgment of God for not fulfilling their vow. That judgment may not come in the form of physical ailments like a gimp leg, but by means of God destroying the work of our hands. God may take our goals, aspirations and efforts to succeed and turn those things into dust, or He may allow us to prosper but make us miserable in our prosperity. Like locusts that eat up the crops before they are harvested, God can make the fruit of our hands wither if we test Him.

In light of the gravity of making a vow to God, Solomon concludes in 5:7 with the simple command, "Fear God." In short, he says, "It's time to take God seriously." Think about the fact that the God you are worshipping is an unimaginably holy being who allows you to breathe His oxygen molecules. We should reverently fall on our face before Him, trust His purposes and not make eleventh hour deals. It's best to approach God with a closed mouth and an open heart.

Perhaps, C.S. Lewis summarized the concept of fearing God best in a passage from the *Chronicles of Narnia*. Susan, one of the children who haphazardly discovered the enchanted land of Narina, is talking to Mr. and Mrs. Beaver about meeting Aslan the lion (who in the book represents Jesus Christ).

> "Who is Aslan?" Susan asked. Mr. Beaver replied, "Aslan is a lion—the Lion, the great Lion." "Ooh!" said Susan, "I'd thought he was a man. Is he—quite safe? I shall feel rather nervous about meeting a lion." "That you will, dearie, and no mistake," said Mrs. Beaver, "if there's anyone who can appear before Aslan without their knees knocking, they're either braver than most or else just silly." "Then he isn't safe?" said Lucy. "Safe?" said Mr. Beaver. "Don't you hear what Mrs. Beaver tells you? Who said anything about safe? Course he isn't safe. But he's good. He's the King I tell you."[7]

---

7. Lewis, *The Complete Chronicles of Narania*, 99.

9

Beware of the Money Trap (5:8–20)

A SATCHEL OF MONEY may look like a fortune to you and me, but to a beaver it's just building material. Case in point—the amazing discovery made by some Louisiana lawmen of a beaver's dam that was worth a pretty penny. A news article explains this bizarre account:

> A bag of bills stolen from a casino was snatched up by a family of beavers who wove thousands of dollars in soggy currency into the sticks and brush of their dam on a creek in eastern Louisiana. The money was part of $70,000 stolen from the Lucky Dollar Casino in Greensburg, LA. Deputies searched for the money for days until a lawyer, hoping to make a deal with prosecutors for a client, called and said the money had been discarded by the thieves in a nearby creek... Officers searched the creek, finding one money bag right away and spotting a second downstream against the beaver's dam ... Altogether, deputies found about $40,000 stuffed inside the beaver dam.[1]

As I read that story the inevitable question popped into my mind, "What would you have done with the money had the beaver's not gotten to it first?" Some of us would have squirreled it away in a saving account. Perhaps some of you would have splurged for a European vacation or a new sports car. Maybe you would have done the prudent thing and paid off some outstanding bills. Or would you have been an Honest Abe and turned it in to the authorities?

---

1. "Beaver's Make Big-Bucks Dam," *Associated Press*, 15 November 2004.

Whether for good or evil, money is a necessity. Some have eschewed riches all together in a pursuit to rid themselves of the temptations that come along with it. Some spend their whole lives pinching every penny, while others have squandered fortunes on good times and possessions. In reality money is neither good, nor evil it is merely a tool to achieve a desired end. Money is merely slips of paper. Coins are just pieces of metal. However, this benign substance does one thing very well—it reveals the heart condition of the one who holds it. Look at a person's monthly bank statement and you can tell a lot about their heart.

The Bible has tremendous insights on the right and wrong uses of money. Consider this: sixteen out of thirty-eight of Christ's parables deal with money; more is said in the New Testament about money than heaven and hell combined; five times more is said about money than prayer; and where there are five-hundred-plus verses on both prayer and faith, there are over two-thousand verses dealing with money and possessions. Why all this talk about money? Jesus said it best, "For where your treasure is, there your heart will be also" (Matt 6:21). God understands that our use of money and possessions may be the single greatest indicator of our spirituality.[2]

In fact, you might argue that Solomon is the Bible's Chief Financial Officer. Without a doubt, Solomon was the wealthiest person in the Scriptures. Based on the information recorded in 1 Kings, scholars have estimated that his base annual income in gold alone was in the neighborhood of $20 million. 1 Kings 10:27 says that he "made silver as common in Jerusalem as stone." Solomon's throne was carved out of solid ivory and overlaid with gold (1 Kings 10:18). His pleasure palace, complete with garden parks, thousands of servants, and a fleet of ships would have made the Taj Mahal look like run-down 7–11 by comparison.

So when a man like Solomon speaks about money matters it's time to pay attention and take notes. The Preacher wants to demolish several of the popular myths that people hold about wealth. He is going to talk about four different kinds of people: the unrighteous rich, the righteous rich, the unrighteous poor and the righteous poor. The overall theme of this passage is that money affects every one of us living under the sun—we can own it or it can own us.

Money Will Not Solve Political Problems (5:8–9)

Solomon takes a long look down the corridors of government and sees corruption in city hall. He doesn't see rich philanthropists giving for

---

2. Krell, "The Naked Truth (Ecclesiastes 5:10–20)."

humanitarian causes; instead he sees the rich using their wealth to oppress the poor (James 2:6). "Face it," the Preacher explains, "it's the wealthy who can afford to run for office and it's the rich who end up becoming the primary policy makers." Ever notice how the ones making the laws always end up voting themselves a raise at the end of every year? Solomon also points out the intricate web of red-tape bureaucracy. It's a system so complex that the poor cannot gain entrance into the exclusive circle of the wealthy. *The Message* paraphrases verses 5:8–9 like this: "Don't be too upset when you see the poor kicked around, and justice and right violated all over the place. Exploitation filters down from one petty official to another. There's no end to it, and nothing can be done about it."[3]

The closer you begin to look at the whole messed up political machine you realize that the love of money is at the root of the problem. In the end the elected officials don't really care about serving the best interest of the people they represent, but about lining their pockets with tax dollars and maintaining their comfortable lifestyle.

This reminds me of a joke that I heard years ago which explained political philosophy for dummies:

> Communism: You have two cows. The government takes both of them and gives you part of the milk.
>
> Socialism: You have two cows. The government takes one and gives it to your neighbor.
>
> Fascism: You have two cows. The government takes both cows and sells you the milk.
>
> Nazism: You have two cows. The government takes both cows then shoots you.
>
> Bureaucracy: You have two cows. The government takes both of them, shoots one, milks the other, then pours the milk down the drain.
>
> Capitalism: You have two cows. You sell one of them and buy a bull.
>
> Democracy: Everyone has two cows, then a vote is taken, and whatever the majority decides to do, you do, and that's no bull!

Without getting too political let's be clear that all forms of government will be imperfect because imperfect people are running them. The reason why human government is crooked is because the White House, Parliament,

---

3. Peterson, *The Message*, Ecc. 5:8–9.

Kremlin, NATO, and any other governing body is filled with sinners. In fact, it's a revolving door where one sinner is elected and serves his term only to be replaced by another sinner. The Preacher says we shouldn't be surprised by this so don't put your hope and trust in man-made government. Until Christ changes the human heart all you are going to see is sinners rotating through seats of power abusing their authority and taking advantage of the little guy.

Money Will Not Bring Lasting Pleasure (5:10)

It is important to notice the twofold repetition of the verb "loves" in this verse. "He who loves money will not be satisfied with money, nor he who loves wealth with his income; this also is vanity." Money is not the problem; rather, *the love of money* is the issue. That's why Paul warns, "For *the love of money* is the root of all kinds of evil" (1 Tim. 6:10). Wealth underachieves when it comes to bringing happiness, but it overachieves when it comes to bringing misery. Money can buy tons of comfort but not a single ounce of contentment. Money makes a lousy lover. The more you love it, the less it satisfies. The more you focus on it, the less it delivers.

The entire gambling industry is built off the addictive feeling that comes from the prospect of hitting it big. Yet, the odds are that you have a better chance of getting struck by lightning than becoming a millionaire. In fact one expert on the issue, Michael Orkin, a statistician and Dean of Business, Math and Science at Laney College in Oakland, California says that the chances of winning the jackpot in Powerball are 1 in 195,249,054. He added, "Let's say you buy fifty Powerball tickets a week, you'll win the jackpot about once every 75,000 years."[4]

Most people are tempted to think, "Well if I just had a little bit more, then I could get out of this hole, buy the dream home, obtain a certain status and then I would be happy." The reality is that more you have, the more you want and the more you want the more you spend. Have you ever noticed that the average person is not content to stay within their means? The hardworking American gets a raise that allows them the ability to adjust their lifestyle to a higher standard. Why am I driving a Camry when I could be driving a Cadillac? Why am I staying in a double-wide trailer when I could have a three bedroom home? More money now means that we upgrade our technology, eat out more and buy newer, plush furniture.

---

4. Haley, "Seduced into Spending Thousands on Lottery Tickets," *CNN News*, 4 January 2010.

Think about the rich man Jesus talked about in Luke 12. His sudden windfall profits didn't cause him to step back and say, "Alright Lord, how can I manage this money to expand Your kingdom?" Instead he tore down his barns and built bigger ones. Little did he know he would die that night and God would call him a "fool." So it is if we succumb to the money trap. As the old saying goes, "A fool and his money are quickly parted."

Instead we should take a lesson from Socrates. It is said that the Greek philosopher was known to take a daily walk through the marketplace in Athens. He would often gaze at the abundance of things that could be bought, glittering in the sun. A student asked him why he was so allured he replied, "I love to go there and discover all the things I am perfectly content without."

Money Will Not Solve Personal Problems (5:11)

The Preacher continues, "When goods increase, they increase who eat them, and what advantage has their owner but to see them with his eyes?" When I was growing up there was a hip-hop song which crystallized Solomon's warning. The chorus of the song repeated the phrase, "Mo' Money, Mo' Problems." A person who comes into wealth suddenly discovers he or she has long-lost relatives and friends that they never knew about (Pro. 19:4). With more money comes all kinds of scavengers and vultures who want to feed off those earnings. Don't forget that the IRS will come calling too to demand that Uncle Sam get a piece of the pie as well. Everyone stands with an open hand thrust out and a sob story to tell.

G.K. Chesterton has said, "To be clever enough to get a great deal of money, one must be stupid enough to want it." Commenting on this verse William MacDonald put his two cents in by saying, "When a man's possessions increase, it seems there's a corresponding increase in the number of parasites who live off him: management consultants, tax advisors, accountants, lawyers, household employees and sponging relatives."[5]

Believe it or not I personally knew a man who won the lottery. He was actually the custodian of the church I was serving at. As the story goes he topped off his gas tank with fifteen dollars and on a whim he took the remaining five dollars in change from his twenty dollar bill and bought a lottery ticket. His prize was the largest in North Carolina's history at that time, $141 million. Soon after he won I asked him how the money changed his life. He relayed to me story after story of strangers trying to track him down with sob stories of their own and how they needed his help. The begging

---

5. MacDonald, *Chasing the Wind*, 47.

got so bad that he decided to move, take his contact information out of the phone book and cut ties with many so-called "friends."

Solomon advises that if you have the unfortunate experience of coming across a large sum of money you had better be ready to fight off the parasites because with a heap of cash comes a heap of anxiety, worry, and ulcers. If you don't know how to handle money the right way it will only magnify and compound you problems. As we get more stuff there are more things to take care of that will demand more of our time and money. As a result we become even more tied down. This is what Randy Alcorn calls "the tyranny of things." Ironically, more money means paying more advisors to help make, distribute, and protect wealth. To make matters worse there is always the danger that there will be those who people who resent you for what you have. Even money comes with a high price tag and hidden fees.

As one preacher said, "Money is a lot like manure. If you pile it up it begins to stink, but if you spread it around it helps things grow." It seems that giving and generosity are the only antidotes to greed and the snare of the money trap.

Money Will Not Bring Peace of Mind (5:12)

Many people think that the more money they have, the better they will sleep at night, but Solomon says the opposite is true. "Sweet is the sleep of a laborer, whether he eats little or much, but the full stomach of the rich will not let him sleep." The more we have the more we worry about keeping it. Wealth does not give peace or rest but only promotes insomnia because the rich worry about how the wealth is to be maintained.

Take for example John D. Rockefeller, the great American industrialist and oil tycoon, who at age fifty-three became the world's first billionaire. In 1897 his income was one million dollars per week. But he was physically sick from worrying about his oil empire. Rockefeller resorted to eating nothing but crackers and milk and surviving on only a few hours of sleep every night. Eventually, he became a philanthropist and learned how to give his money away. As soon as he learned how to let go of his money his health improved and he lived to celebrate his ninety-eighth birthday.

On the other end of the spectrum is the simple, working man. Maybe he's a welder, or a construction worker, or a landscaper. His day is simple because from 8:00 a.m. until 5:00 p.m. he works hard for a measly paycheck. He drives a beat-up pick-up truck, the kind with the old hand crank windows. It's got a 255 model air conditioner—that's two windows down at fifty-five mph. After a hard day's work he goes home, kisses his wife, plays with his kids and sits down to bowl of beans and cornbread. He watches some TV, enjoys a few laughs, but by 9:30 he's sawing logs in the Lazy Boy.

According to Solomon, that's easy living. Why? His life is simple. He works, he loves his family and he is free from all the high pressure decisions of trying to keep up with finances. Perhaps, billionaire Ross Perot put it best when he said to a room full of aspiring millionaires:

> Guys, just remember, if you get lucky, if you make a lot of money, if you get out and buy a lot of stuff—it's gonna break. You got your biggest, fanciest mansion in the world. It has air conditioning. It's got a pool. Just think of all the pumps that are going to go out. Or go to a yacht basin any place in the world. Nobody is smiling, and I'll tell you why. Something broke that morning. The generator's out; the microwave oven doesn't work. Things just don't mean happiness.[6]

Money Will Not Bring Permanent Security (5:13-17)

Solomon continues to knock out the props out from our understanding of what money can and cannot do. He gives a couple of scenarios in which money could not provide the security that it was supposed to bring. We come across a miserly hoarder who has saved up for a rainy day; however, he makes a bad business investment and all his hard-earned capital goes up in smoke. "There is a grievous evil that I have seen under the sun: riches were kept by their owner to his hurt, and those riches were lost in a bad venture. And he is father of a son, but he has nothing in his hand." In a matter of just a few hours he sees everything he's worked for his entire life evaporate. To add insult to injury he has nothing left over to give to his children as an inheritance.

Money is a good servant but a poor master. All it takes is one bad day on the stock market and your investments are worthless or the conniving plot of con men to ruin your nest egg. Many of us remember how Bernie Madoff made off with millions of dollars through his elaborate Ponzi schemes. Madoff will go down as one of Wall Street's most notorious criminals. The slick operator duped celebs like Steven Spielberg, Kevin Bacon, Larry King and baseball great Sandy Koufax out of $65 billion. In 2008 one of Madoff's victims, a prominent French aristocrat, committed suicide after

---

6. Perot quoted by Craig Brian Larson, *750 Engaging Illustrations for Preachers, Teachers and Writers*, 340-341.

he lost $1.6 billion in one of Madoff's schemes.[7] Proverbs 18:11 is a sober reminder that money is a false security net, "A rich man's wealth is his strong city, and like a high wall in his imagination."

The Preacher continues in 5:15–17 by making the application that no matter how much we have, we can't take it with us. The language of these verses will be familiar to anyone who knows the story of Job, "Naked I came from my mother's womb and naked shall I return" (Job. 1:21). Solomon has voiced the naked truth that we all know—money and prosperity stop six feet under (1 Tim. 6:7). The more you have the more you have to lose.

A preacher named Ray Stedman traveled across the country for a week of meetings. The only problem was his baggage didn't make it. He needed a couple of suits so he went down to the local thrift shop. When he told the salesman, "I'd like to get a couple of suits," the man smiled, led him to a whole rack of them and said, "Good, we've got several. But you need to know they came from the local mortuary. They've all been cleaned and pressed, but they were used on stiffs. Not a thing wrong with 'em. I just didn't want that to bother you."

Stedman said, "No, that's fine." He tried a few of the suits on and finally bought two of them for about $25 dollars each. When he got back to this his room, he began to get dressed for the evening's meetings. As he put one on, he tried to put his hands in the pockets, but couldn't. Both sides were all sewn up! The suits looked as if they had pockets, but they were just flaps on the coat. He thought about that for a second. "Of course! Dead people don't carry stuff with 'em when they die." Stedman later admitted: "I spent all week trying to stick my hands in my pockets. I had to hang my keys on my belt."[8]

Conclusion

Solomon's talk on dollars and sense ends with two vital applications we must learn if we are to be good stewards of God's treasure. *First, our ability to earn money is a gift from God (5:18)*. "Behold, what I have seen to be good and fitting is to eat and drink and find enjoyment in all the toil with which one toils under the sun the few days of his life that God has given him, for this is his lot." Even though work was cursed due to the Fall of Adam (Gen. 3:18–19), it still gives man an opportunity to provide for his family and worship God. The biblical way to look at money is to remember that it's on loan, not to own (Ex. 19:5, Ps. 24:1). Every person who ever earned a dime did

---

7. "Madeoff Investor Commits Suicide," *The New York Times*, 23 November 2008.
8. Swindoll, *Swindoll's Ultimate Book of Illustrations & Quotes*, 391.

so because God gave them the ability to do it (Deut. 8:18). If you have a job which allows to you earn a wage which affords you a comfortable lifestyle then praise God everyday your feet hit the floor.

Martin Luther understood the connection between work and worship when he wrote, "The maid who sweeps her kitchen is doing the will of God just as much as the monk who prays—not because she may sing a Christian hymn as she sweeps but because God loves clean floors. The Christian shoemaker does his Christian duty not by putting little crosses on the shoes but by making good shoes because God is interested in good craftsmanship."[9] Your job is not just work, but worship to Almighty God (Col. 3:17).

Finally, *our ability to enjoy money is a gift from God (5:19-20)*. "Everyone also to whom God has given wealth and possessions and power to enjoy them, and to accept his lot and rejoice in his toil—this is the gift of God. For he will not much remember the days of his life because God keeps him occupied with joy in his heart."

These final verses tell us that the ability to enjoy food, sex, money or any other good gifts comes from God alone. Satisfaction is sold separately from our earthly possessions. That is why it's pointless to amass wealth irrespective of the Creator. What good is a can of peaches without a can opener or a string of Christmas lights without a power source? It might be fun to sit in the driver's seat of a Lamborghini but it's useless unless you have the expensive premium fuel to run it. So it is with the pleasures of life unless we know God. A blessing is nothing without knowing the Blesser; we need both. As C.S. Lewis has said:

> God made us: invented us as a man invents an engine. A car is made to run on petrol, and it would not run properly on anything else. Now God designed the human machine to run on Himself. He Himself is the fuel our spirits were designed to burn, or the food our spirits were designed to feed on. There is no other. That is why it is just no good asking God to make us happy in our own way without bothering about religion. God cannot give us a happiness and peace apart from Himself, because it is not there.[10]

There is a story told of a rich industrialist who came across a simple fisherman. The rich man was quite perturbed to see the fisherman sitting back with his feet up next to his boat on a sunny afternoon. "Why aren't you out there fishing?" he demanded. "Because I've caught enough fish for the day," replied the fisherman. "Why don't you catch more fish?" asked the rich

---

9. Luther, quoted by Mark Allan Powell, *Giving to God*, 85.
10. Lewis, *Mere Christianity*, 50.

man. "What would I do with them?" "You could earn more money," said the rich man, who was becoming more impatient, "and buy a better boat so you could go deeper and catch more fish. You could purchase nylon nets, catch even more fish and make more money. Then you could buy more boats and could hire others to help you fish. Soon you would have a fleet of boats and would be rich like me!" "Then what would I do?" "You could sit down and enjoy life" said the industrialist. "What do you think I'm doing right now?" replied the fisherman as he gazed out towards the sea.

10

Satisfaction Sold Separately (6:1–12)

I ONCE READ A humorous story that took place in New York City—home to at least half a million cats and counting. The Big Apple is basically concrete and steel, so when someone has a pet in New York City and it dies, they cannot just go out in the back yard and bury it. Instead the city charges a fee of $50 to come and take it away.

One rather enterprising lady thought, "I can render a service to people in the city and save them money." So, she placed an ad in the newspaper that said, "When your pet cat dies, I'll take care of it for you for only $25." This was half the price of the city fee. Then this lady would go to the local Salvation Army store and buy an old suitcase for two or three dollars. When someone would call about their pet, she would go to the home and carefully place the cat in the suitcase. She would then take a ride on the subway in the early evening, which was a perfect time for pickpockets and thieves. She would sit the suitcase near the door and act like she was not watching. A thief would come by when the doors opened, steal her suitcase, and run out. What a surprise for the thief!

The world is running after suitcases they think hold the contents to happiness—but it never quite delivers what it advertises. Founding Father Ben Franklin once noted that "The U.S. Constitution only gives people the right to pursue happiness. You have to catch it yourself."

Did you hear about the man who walked into a shoe store and asked for a pair of shoes, size eight? The well-trained salesman says, "But sir, you need an eleven or eleven-and-a-half." "Just bring me a size eight." The sales guy brings the shoes and the man crams his feet into them and stands up in obvious pain. He turns to the salesman and says, "I've lost my house to the

IRS, I live with my mother-in-law, my daughter ran off with my best friend, and my business has filed for bankruptcy. The only pleasure I have left is to come home at night and take my shoes off!"

Unfortunately, there are many of us who can relate to both of those stories. It seems that the game of life is rigged so that the house always wins. Pleasures that promise to be sweet ends up turning to dust in our mouth. Perhaps you find yourself living out the chorus to U2's hit song, "I still haven't found what I'm looking for."

Solomon, the despondent author of Ecclesiastes, spent a vast portion of his life trying to find happiness on Earth. I think by the time he sat down to pen the words in his reflective journal he was a man caught in the pit of a mid-life crisis. His words in chapter six are some of the most cynical. This is an honest and unapologetic appraisal of life lived under the sun without reference to God. By chapter now we have arrived at the mid-point of Solomon's journal and he seems to find this a good place to summarize some of the major problems that occur if we live life merely on the horizontal plane of existence.

In my estimation, Solomon gives us four conclusions about life under the sun in this chapter. Many of his observations touch on themes that he has already visited. His main thesis is that gratification in this life is here today and gone tomorrow. Life does not come with a 90-day money-back guarantee of satisfaction.

You Can Have Luxury without Contentment (6:1–2)

In this first section, Solomon discusses the three measuring sticks of success in Hebrew society: wealth, long life, and lots of children. While each one of these are great blessings, they aren't much good unless God gives us the ability to enjoy them. We are back to the problem of the can of peaches with no can opener again. It's like finding out that your property contains oil reserves and then learning you have only six weeks to live. Life plays those cruel injustices upon us that make us shake our fist at the sky and say, "Gimme' a break!"

In these opening verses we read of a miserable millionaire. "There is an evil that I have seen under the sun, and it lies heavy on mankind: a man to whom God gives wealth, possessions, and honor, so that he lacks nothing of all that he desires, yet God does not give him power to enjoy them, but a stranger enjoys them. This is vanity; it is a grievous evil."

Picture a guy who was a boy genius. He graduated early at age eighteen from a prestigious Ivy League school. By twenty-five he's a retired millionaire because he built and sold a lucrative tech company. His got it all—brains, Benjamins, babes and Bentleys. Yet when his head hits the pillow at night he can't kill the longing in his soul.

Notice here that a "foreigner" or a "stranger" swoops in like a vulture and steals away the enjoyment of his wealth. The predator could be an adversary, premature death, unexpected illness or some natural calamity. For some providential reason the man who had everything a man could want never really enjoyed what he had. Sadly, when he expired it all went to someone he didn't even know.

A boat and a garage full of cars won't do you any good if you are diagnosed with cancer. You might win the lottery and then die in a car wreck going to cash the check. A mansion built on the side of the Hollywood hills cannot stand up to wildfire or an earthquake. You may have wealth squirreled away, but what happens to that money when the bottom falls out of the stock market?

The story of General John Sutter perfectly illustrates this. On Jan. 24, 1848 a gold nugget was discovered on his California property. He tried to keep his gold a secret, but within a day all his ranch hands left their tasks in a mad frenzy, digging and panning and scratching for gold. Within a week, the whole countryside was in turmoil as ranches, towns and villages were abandoned, everyone rushing to Sutter's ranch in search of gold. By 1849 it seemed that half the country was camping on Sutter's ranch, soldiers were deserting the army and sailors would land in San Francisco and head directly for the hills. John Sutter could only look in a helpless rage as his ranch was ransacked, his barns burned down, his crops trampled and his cattle slaughtered. When Sutter began to proceed with legal cases to claim the gold on his land mad crowds murdered one of his sons and blew up his home with dynamite. In the spring of 1880 Sutter died alone in Washington. He didn't have a single dollar to his name, although he did possess a legal deed to the greatest fortune on earth.[1]

You Can Have Longevity without Fulfillment (6:3-6)

The man described in these verses had the best life that anyone in Old Testament times could imagine. "If a man fathers a hundred children and lives many years, so that the days of his years are many, but his soul is not satisfied with life's good things, and he also has no burial, I say that a stillborn child is better off than he." The Preacher doesn't tell us how old he was, but in a

---

1. Morgan, *More Real Stories for the Soul*, 270-271.

culture that considered children to be a blessing from the Lord, he hit the jackpot by fathering an extensive family.

Wiersbe writes, "Here is a man with abundant resources and large family . . . but his family does not love him, for when he died he was not lamented . . . His relatives stayed around him only to use his money and they wondered when the old man would die. When he finally did die, his surviving relatives could hardly wait for the reading of the will."[2] To add insult to injury, when this man died he didn't receive a proper burial, leaving many to believe that he was under the curse of God.

Solomon makes quite a shocking statement than a miscarried child is better off than this person! Don't misunderstand what the Preacher is saying here. Both a stillborn child and an unfulfilled life of longevity are tragic. However, his point here is that it is more tragic for life to be granted and a person not to enjoy the good things in life than it is for a baby to not come to term. In a nutshell his point is: "Better to miscarry at birth than to miscarry throughout life."[3] The unborn child never has to deal with the effects of sin, endure suffering, or struggle for existence. Better yet, the stillborn fetus goes straight to his heavenly home.

A man and wife enjoyed playing the "Here's How I'd Remodel That House" game as they traveled. They would take turns picking out certain houses and explain how they would remodel them. One day as they were driving, they saw an old, dilapidated house that looked like it had been abandoned. The husband stopped in front of the house and said, "I tell you what I'd do with that shack. I'd bulldoze it down and start over." At that moment, an elderly man stepped out of the house onto the front porch. With a big smile on his face, the old man waved at them as though they were long-lost friends. The couple waved back and then drove on down the road. The husband said, "Do you think he would have been that friendly if he knew what I said about his house?" After a long pause the wife replied, "Probably so!"

Solomon's point here is obvious; you can live twice as long as Methuselah, but if your life is not centered on God then growing old is a terrible fate. Growing older without God leads to an end filled with ingratitude, bitterness, dissatisfaction and regret. Medical science may be able to add years to your life, but only Jesus can add life to your years.

---

2. Wiersbe, *The Wiersbe Bible Commentary: Old Testament*, 1126–1127.

3. Eaton, *Ecclesiastes*, 106.

You Can Have Labor without Enjoyment (6:7-9)

What is your favorite food? For me it's a big, juicy steak. For you carnivores out there imagine a thick-cut ribeye sizzling to perfection on a grill. This flame-kissed delicacy is put on a plate with a buttery baked potato, warm yeast roll, sautéed green peppers and onions and fresh garden salad. Is your mouth watering yet? As you cut into the steak, you notice that it's cooked just to your liking and seasoned with just the right amount of charred goodness. There is only one problem with this whole picture. It doesn't matter how well you ate yesterday, tomorrow you will be hungry again. A man works and works to buy food, but it's never enough.

This was Solomon's problem—we all have insatiable appetites that are never filled. This is what the Preacher means when he writes, "All the toil of man is for his mouth, yet his appetite is not satisfied." We work so that we can eat, but we are always hungry a few hours after a banquet. Worse yet, according to verse 6:8 the wise seem to have no advantage over the poor in this area. Whether you're the CEO of a Fortune 500 company or a blue-collar working stiff who digs ditches, we all work to eat and try to satiate the appetites of the flesh. Like the American poet Robert Frost has said, "By working faithfully eight hours a day you may eventually get to be boss and work twelve hours a day."

Solomon pinpoints the primary problem in verse 6:9 as a "wandering appetite." He writes, "Better is the sight of the eyes than the wandering of the appetite: this also is vanity and a striving after wind." Probably the best rendering of this verse is the old adage, "A bird in the hand is worth two in the bush." Solomon is saying, "It's better to have little and really enjoy it than to dream about much and never attain it."

If your career is the determining factor in your life then you are going to be focused on getting the next promotion. If you base your life on entertainment then you are always living for the next big thrill or the next season of sports. If you draw meaning from stuff, then you'll never be happy with what you have because someone else will have something newer, faster and shinier. Most people view their career as a means to end. They work so they can make money, which in turn allows them the ability to buy stuff. But the stuff never leaves them satisfied, so they work harder to buy bigger and better houses, faster cars and fancier clothes, or upgrade their technology. After thirty years of years of running on this hamster wheel you'd think man would learn his lesson, but he still chases after the wind.

George Foreman tells the following story in his book, *God in my Corner*:

A friend told me, "George, one day you're going to have it all. You'll have money, fleets of cars. . ." I envisioned everything he was describing. "Wow," I replied, "I'm going to feel good when that happens." My childhood hero, football sensation Jim Brown, once came to my ranch to do a television interview with me. I always wanted to be just like Jim. By now, I was a successful world champion boxer and my idol actually came to my house. After gawking at my manicured lawn, beautiful home, and exquisite furniture, Jim Brown said, "George, you've got it made. I just hope one day I can get it together like you." Get it together like me? I was trying to get it together like him!"[4]

You Can Have Learning without Improvement (6:10–12)

There is an old saying that goes, "As things have been, so they still are; and as things are, so they will be." This seems to be the basic thrust of what the Preacher is getting at here when he says, "Whatever has come to be has already been named, and it is known what man is, and that he is not able to dispute with one stronger than he." The human condition hasn't changed much. We are still living in the ruin of Adam's blunder. Life is characterized by the curse of sin, the folly of wisdom, the frustration of work, fleeting pleasures and the inevitability of death. There is no sage who has really been able improve our condition by clever argumentation or posturing of words. Instead those added words only stir up and muddy the waters even more.

Moreover, if we find ourselves unhappy with our plight we could try arguing with God, but this is futile since He is "stronger" and smarter than we are. God is sovereign and man is not, thus arguing with Him and quarreling over why life is the way it is gets us nowhere. Protesting heaven with a clenched fist is like sawing off the branch on which you are sitting. Or as C.S. Lewis said, "To argue with God is to argue with the very power that makes it possible to argue at all."[5] Our arms are just too short to box with God. Job tried it and concluded, "I have uttered what I did not understand . . . therefore, I despise myself, and repent in dust and ashes" (Job 42:3, 6). So, Solomon ends this section with a sigh of disappointment, wondering about how to live a good life and what awaits us on the other side of death.

These final words point out the limitations of man's knowledge. "For who knows what is good for man while he lives the few days of his vain life, which he passes like a shadow? For who can tell man what will be after

---

4. Foreman, *God in My Corner*, 32.
5. Lewis, *Mere Christianity*, 48.

him under the sun?" We must accept that we are finite, limited creatures and God has seen fit in His wisdom to give us enough information to trust Him, but not enough information to know it all. As one of my seminary professors would say, "God is not a doctrine to be mastered, but a person to be trusted."

The secret to finding meaning in life is understanding who you are in relationship to God and acknowledging your need for Him. So if you are looking for answers to *all* of life's "why" questions you will never find them. But if you are seeking answers to life's most basic questions—origin, purpose, meaning, morality and destiny then Jesus is the key. Christ did not say, "I have come to answer all your questions," but he did say, "I have come that they may have life and have it to the full" (John 10:10).

Solomon's vexing questions at the close this chapter reminded me of something I read from Bart Ehrman, a hardened skeptic and professor of Religious Studies at the University of North Carolina at Chapel Hill. Ehrman's faith took a tumble in his mid-twenties while studying for the ministry. His wounded theism never recovered and he has done much to undermine the credibility of the Bible. I should know. I sat under his teaching for a semester as a college freshman. In his book, *God's Problem: How the Bible Fails to Answer Our Most Important Question—Why We Suffer*, Ehrman gives his philosophy for living on this crooked planet. His conclusions aren't too far from what Solomon has been wrestling with:

> I think we should work hard to make the world—the one we live in—the most pleasing place it can be for ourselves . . . We should make money and spend money. The more the better. We should enjoy good food and drink. We should eat out and order unhealthy desserts, and we should cook steaks on the grill and drink Bordeaux . . . We should drive nice cars and have nice homes. We should make love, have babies and, raise families. We should do what we can to love life—it's a gift and it will not be with us for long.[6]

When I read that passage the questions in my mind peaked. How can life be a gift if it has no giver? Then I went a little further and discovered the gaping hole in his life. Ehrman admits:

> The problem is this: I have such a fantastic life that I feel such an overwhelming sense of gratitude for it. I am fortunate beyond words. But I don't have anyone to express my gratitude to. This

---

6. Ehrman, *God's Problem*, 277.

is a void inside me, a void of wanting someone to thank, and I don't see any plausible way of filling it.[7]

Can it get any more depressing than that? All those degrees, book deals and academic prestige, yet empty inside. Perhaps, this is what Paul meant when he said that the secular man was "forever learning but never able to arrive at a knowledge of the truth" (2 Tim. 3:7).

Let me close by asking you a question, "Would you say that Einstein was a bad physicist if he couldn't explain the theory of relativity to a first grader?" Certainly, that would be an unfair judgment. The problem isn't with Einstein it's with the child's limited understanding of math and science. Just so, as finite creatures we face a similar problem in trying to understand God's infinite ways. Even if He could explain everything to us it is unlikely that we would have the capacity to understand it all (Is. 55:8-9). The supreme function of reason is to show man that some things are beyond reason. This is where the element of faith comes in. Part of being wise is trusting God with the things you cannot know, based on what you do know about Him. Faith is not the absence of reason; on the contrary it is belief that is married to our brains. As John Donne said, "Reason is our soul's left hand, faith her right." Faith is not wishful thinking, a leap in the dark or superstition. Instead, faith is more like stepping into the light which allows you to see and be seen (Is. 1:18, John 3:19-21). Moreover biblical faith is not in something, but Someone (Heb. 11:1-3). Faith takes over where reason ends and says, "I may not know what the future holds, but I know the One who holds the future."

---

7. Ibid., 128.

11

Taking the Bitter with the Better (7:1–14)

BENJAMIN FRANKLIN ONCE SAID, "The things which hurt, instruct." This is one of the most interesting paradoxes of life. The greatest lessons we learn are taken in the most unexpected classrooms and the teachers are often the most unwanted instructors. "Failure is often the backdoor to success," Erwin Lutzer has pointed out. From the ashes of a tragedy come the triumphs. Walking by a graveyard will teach us more about living than dying. It takes a conversation with a homeless man for us to learn the riches of poverty. Before we can be built up we have to be broken and before we can learn how to win we must feel the sting of loss.

Dr. Beck Weathers is a good case study. Weathers, a wealthy pathologist from Dallas, TX, was forty-nine years old when he ascended the slopes of Everest. Weathers was one of the climbers who nearly died during the now-infamous 1996 misadventure that cost twelve people their lives. Weathers was an avid mountaineer and for ten years prior to the Everest debacle he summited six of the globe's seven highest peaks. Reaching the summit of Earth is all that consumed him. He candidly admitted in an interview:

> I regret the time taken away from my family, from my wife and two children. There's a large dose of selfishness involved in such an activity . . . I realize I was defining myself by climbing and not dealing with the rest of my life. It's an excessive goal, and it never ends. You get about one day of happiness and then you're planning your next trip.[1]

---

1. "Surviving Everest Heightens Texan's Priorities about Life," *Atlanta Journal Constitution*, 14 November 1988.

Weathers and his New Zealand guide, Rob Hall, were making great progress up the mountain until they tried to ascend the peak on May 10th. Some years before, Weathers had undergone radial keratotomy surgery to correct his vision. As he went up the mountain, the change in altitude caused the lenses in his eyes to flatten out, and that made him blind. Conditions worsened when a sudden blizzard dropped the mercury to fifty degrees below zero and blew in seventy mile per hour gusts of wind.

In the panic to find shelter, Weathers was left behind by his group. All alone in unimaginable conditions, Weathers slipped into a hypothermic coma. A search party was sent out and on May 11 Weathers was found covered in ice, showing no signs of life. So his fellow climbers left him for dead, returned to base camp and radioed back to his wife that he expired in the storm.

Amazingly, Weathers was revived and found the will to live. He staggered back into camp suffering from severe frostbite to his face and extremities. He was later evacuated from Everest by helicopter and when he reached a medical clinic doctors began the grueling amputations. In the end, Weathers survived but he lost his nose, half his right arm, all the fingers on his left hand and parts of his feet. After the incident Weathers spoke about how the ill-fated Everest incident profoundly changed his life:

> One of the things that surprised me when I first got back, somebody would say, "Hey, would you do it again?" And I'm a train wreck. And I think to myself, "What a stupid question," you know? But Everest, because of what happened, turned out to be the best thing that ever happened to me. Because I know that if I hadn't been hit across the face with a 2x4 to slow me down, I would have kept going. It wouldn't have been Everest, it would have been something else the next year and the next year after that, and it was going to continue until I got just too old to do it. Things had fallen apart, and I would have lost my marriage, my family. At the end, I would have been a very lonely old guy. And I've been given a second chance, not just at rebuilding a life but to live each day. And I still have my wife; I still have my kids; I still have my parents and my brothers. And I'm a happy person.[2]

The blizzard atop Everest was a blessing in disguise. Franklin was right, "The things which hurt, instruct." Fortunately, you don't have to become a human popsicle and nearly lose your life to get that kind of wisdom. Imagine all the trouble Weathers, and scores of others trying to reach the

---

2. "Storms Over Everest: Life After Everest," *PBS: Frontline*, 13 May 2008.

top of the heap, could save themselves if they just had an ounce of Solomon's God-given wisdom.

Wisdom is the ability to see life with discernment, to view life as God perceives it. Bible teacher Tony Evans has said, "Wisdom requires knowledge and understanding. Just like it takes both a man and woman to come together and make a baby, when knowledge gets married to understanding it has a baby called, wisdom."[3] Wisdom is nothing-more than "God's holy horse-sense" applied to everyday life.

According to 1 Kings, when Solomon was given a blank check by God he didn't ask for prosperity, or longevity, or power, but wisdom. The ironic thing about Solomon was that for a man who had so much wisdom he made some really foolish mistakes. However, by now we've reached a turning point in the book. Solomon is beginning to change his perspective, and the wisdom that he was famous for comes back into the picture. He also changes his delivery method from meditative prose to short, pithy, proverbial axioms that are pregnant with insight on how to handle life. To be precise, literary experts call these sayings "comparative couplets." That is an ancient form of poetry in which two clauses are connected by the terms "better" and "than."

In this section of the journal, Solomon is going to help us turn life upside-down and inside-out to look at it from a different perspective. The main lesson he wants to drive home is that bad can be good. Blessings are often disguised as burdens. Life's most important lessons come by way of adversity, suffering, pain and hardship. Therefore, we would do well to listen up and take notes because life's tests are pass/fail.

It's Better to Define Life Backwards than Forwards (7:1)

The Preacher begins with a paradoxical statement, "A good name is better than precious ointment and the day of death than the day of birth." At first glance this verse will make you scratch your head and think, "Has Solomon gone off his rocker? How can death be better than birth?" There are two days in our lives when our name is prominent: the day we receive our name—birth, and the day our name appears in the obituary column—death. What happens between those two days determines whether our name is a lovely ointment or a foul stench.[4] The Preacher is referring to the reputation and the value of personal character. A man's funeral may be more joyous than his birthday if he has achieved a godly legacy. This is similar to the maxim

3. Evans, *Tony Evans Book of Illustrations*, 340.
4. Jeremiah, *Searching for Heaven on Earth*, 163.

which goes, "When you were born, you cried and the world rejoiced. Live your life so that when you die, the world cries and you rejoice."

Alfred Nobel is known today for his philanthropy and the prestigious awards that are given every year in science, literature, economics and politics which carry his namesake. However, in his day Alfred Nobel was not known for peace, but as "the merchant of death." That title was given to him because he made most of his vast fortune from the invention of dynamite and other types of explosives. The story is told that in 1888 Alfred's brother, Ludvig, died and he opened the newspaper to discover that the editor who wrote Ludvig's obituary made a mistake. The newspaper published the obituary under the title: "The merchant of death is dead. Dr. Alfred Nobel, who became rich by finding ways to kill more people faster than ever before, died yesterday." When Nobel saw the reputation that came from his name in that obituary it changed everything. He spent the rest of his life trying to improve his public image and thus he decided to leave his fortune to those who made the greatest contributions to humanity.

Solomon's point is that if we could hear what people would say about our name on the day of our funeral we might live totally different. The truth is that every person has already preached their own eulogy by the time they are in the casket. So here's a helpful exercise: If you could have one sentence which summarizes your entire life and you could write it, what would it say? That's why it's better to define life from the perspective of your funeral. Solomon's suggestion is that if you die with a good name, then you can do nothing to tarnish it, but on your birthday the value of your name has not yet been determined. Therefore, you need to define your legacy and start living it today.

It's Better to Learn from Heartache than Happiness (7:2–4)

One again it seems as if the Preacher has got things mixed up for he says, "It is better to go to the house of mourning than to go to the house of feasting, for this is the end of all mankind, and the living will lay it to heart." A blunt paraphrase of this proverb might go like this, "You will gain more wisdom and perspective in life by walking through a hospital than spending a weekend in Vegas." Spend your vacation in a nursing home, orphanage, soup kitchen, or a mission field and you will have a better handle on what is really important in life than you will if you go to Disney World. According to Solomon going to a funeral is good medicine for the soul. Death allows sober contemplation of our own mortality and teaches us to "number our days" (Ps. 90:2). It is standing on death's door that we can peer into eternity and plan accordingly. Haddon Robinson wrote in a devotional:

> If you were to visit old churches in New England, you would notice that many of them have a cemetery in the churchyard. The windows in the sanctuary are filled with clear rather than stained glass so that the pastor would see the graveyard as he preached. As he communicated his message to the congregation, a very serious message was being communicated to them. Two hundred fifty years ago, Christians believed that the central mission of the church was to bring men and women into a right relationship with God. That's why they constructed their church buildings with see-through windows. They wanted their pastors to be continually reminded of the seriousness of their calling. Everyone who sat in the pews before them each Sunday would eventually fill a place in the cemetery and ultimately stand before God to be judged . . . You're not ready to live until you are ready to die.[5]

Death is not the only good teacher but so is suffering and struggle. Sorrow can bring one to God, while pleasure seldom does. Suffering causes us to dig into the deep questions of life, while happiness keeps us in the comfort zone of superficiality.

Foolish people go through trials and tribulations and get mad at God. They feel as if they are getting picked on by a cosmic bully. They become cynical and bitter, and they don't grow from their experience. Many cannot cope with pain so they try to deaden it with alcohol, entertainment and other diversions.

Wise people go through the same experiences and see it as God's development program. In the end they come out more graceful, humble, seasoned and they are closer to Jesus than ever before. If Job were sitting across the table from you, he would probably say that the best thing that ever happened in his life was when he lost everything. Paul would tell us that those times when he was in prison, alone and suffering, was when he did his best writing. Likewise, Joseph wouldn't trade the lessons he learned about trusting God from being tossed into a pit and sold into slavery.

Robert Browning Hamilton, said it like this in poem entitled "Along the Road":

> I walked a mile with Pleasure;
> She chatted all the way;
> But left me none the wiser.

5. Robinson, "Funeral or Birthday?" *Our Daily Bread*, 15 July 1994.

> For all she had to say.
> I walked a mile with Sorrow;
> And ne'er a word said she;
> But, oh! The things I learned from her,
> When Sorrow walked with me."

It's Better to Hear Words of Frankness than Flattery (7:5-6)

Have you ever taken a bundle of brush and piled it on to a fire? The result is a quick burst of light, heat and sound. The act of those nettles catching fire is followed by a concert of pops, hisses and crackles. Solomon is making an analogy by comparing the words of a fool to that of a thorn bush put on a campfire. "It is better for a man to hear the rebuke of the wise than to hear the song of fools. For as the crackling of thorns under a pot, so is the laughter of the fools; this also is vanity." In other words, the praise of a fool is temporary and showy. It flames up with lots of heat and noise but quickly dies down. Thorns and brambles won't stoke a fire that will burn long into the night and neither will flattering words strengthen a soul.

However, the rebuke of a wise friend can burn for years to come—it's like throwing a massive oak log on the fire. The rebuke of a wise person will do a lot more for us in the long run than the flattery of a fool. The sting of correction from a wise man can be life changing. The truth hurts, but we need people to tell us what we need to hear, not what we want to hear. Ultimately, people that never tell you the truth don't really care about you and don't love you.

Wise people pick good mentors, cultivate valuable friends and have high-quality relationships. Solomon is telling us, "Don't have friends who will always pat you on the back. Look for some honesty in your relationships." The best friends you can have are the ones who are willing to hurt your ego and correct you from going down the wrong path. Consider some of these parallel verses:

> "A rebuke goes deeper into a man of understanding than a hundred blows into a fool" (Pro. 17:10).

> "A word fitly spoken is like apples of gold in a setting of silver" (Pro. 25:11).

> "Whoever rebukes a man will afterward find more favor than he who flatters with his tongue" (Pro. 28:23).

Have you ever had a teacher, coach, or preacher who was really tough on you and had some hard words for you? They may have even made you mad, but deep inside you knew they were right. I think about David who needed the boney finger of the prophet Nathan stuck in his face to tell him he was wrong (2 Sam. 12). Likewise, Peter was corrected by the Lord, even called "Satan," (Matt. 16:23) but eventually he did become "the rock" Jesus saw in him.

There are few people who know the name Fred Lynch, but I guarantee that Michael Jordan will never forget his name. Fred Lynch was the high school basketball coach at Laney High in Wilmington, NC. He is the infamous coach who cut Jordan from the varsity team as a sophomore. Crazy, right? Who would cut the greatest player ever to lace up sneakers? Yet it was probably that moment of rebuke that made Jordan into the great basketball player that we know today. That rebuke spurred him to practice harder for varsity the next year.

Likewise, famous New York Yankee slugger Mickey Mantle tells how as a teenager playing in the minor leagues, he began playing poorly. Growing discouraged, he gave into homesickness and self-pity and tearfully called his father to come and take him home. But when Charles Mantle arrived, he didn't give the expected sympathy and reassurance. Instead, he looked at his son and said, "Okay, if that's all the guts you've got, you might as well come home with me right now and work in the mines." It was a stinging slap in the face, but the young man got the message, stuck it out, and went on to make baseball history.[6]

A good word of rebuke is like the proverbial "rock in the shoe." It's unpleasant, but we are forced to stop and deal with it. If we take it to heart it, we can allow it make us better in the end.

It's Better to Choose the Way of Character than Convenience (7:7–8)

Solomon warns of the dangers of compromise when he says, "Surely oppression drives the wise into madness, and a bribe corrupts the heart." There are many easy and convenient paths one can take in life—bribery, dishonesty, cheating, lying—however, in the end all those choices end up selling you short on the things that really matter. In essence, Solomon is saying, "The long-haul is better than the short-cut." Notice that the one who is disciplined and patient is really the winner in life, "Better is the end of a thing than its

---

6. Jeremiah, *Searching for Heaven on Earth*, 173.

beginning, and the patient in spirit is better than the proud in spirit." David Jeremiah has commented on this passage:

> One man climbs a mountain. He struggles up the path, taking frequent stops to catch his breath before continuing the slow trek to the top. He reaches the crest just as his friend steps off a helicopter. Which one enjoys the view the most? The one from the helicopter says, 'It's a nice view but probably not worth the price of a copter ride.' His friend looks at him for a moment and says, 'It's the most beautiful view I've ever seen. Every aching muscle in my body makes it look that much better.[7]

The best way out of adversity is always through. Patience tests our resolve to trust God when life doesn't move at the speed we desire. Richard Hendrix once said, "Second only to suffering, waiting may be the greatest teacher and trainer in godliness, maturity, and genuine spirituality most of us ever encounter."

Think about the temptation of Jesus in the wilderness. At the outset of His ministry the Devil tempted him for forty days, each time giving Him the easy way out (Matt. 4:1–11). Satan said to Jesus, "You can have bread now, you have the kingdoms of the world now and you can have worldwide fame now." The testing of Jesus was all about convenience verses the cross. Satan always tempts us to trade short-term good for God's long-term best.

In school it's easy to cheat on the big test, but when you walk across the stage and get your diploma in the back of your mind there is going to be that nagging voice which says, "You really didn't earn this." In the business world the way to a quick buck is to cut corners and give the customer less than what they paid for, but remember that all those people you cheat are the people you have to live with every day. In parenting, it's easy to let the computers and televisions raise the kids rather than sitting down with them teaching them the Bible and getting them to church. But when that kid hits those rocky teenage years with no fear of God then he will become a terror for Mom and Dad.

The story is told of an old carpenter who was ready to retire. He told his employer-contractor of his plans to leave the construction business for a more leisurely life with his wife and grandchildren. He would miss the paycheck, but he needed to retire. The contractor was sorry to see his good worker go and asked if he could build just one more house as a personal favor. The carpenter said "Yes," but in time it was easy to see that his heart was not in his work. He resorted to shoddy workmanship and used inferior materials. It was an unfortunate way to end his career. When the carpenter

---

7. Ibid., 178.

finished his work and the contractor came to inspect the house, the contractor handed the front door key to the carpenter. "This is your house," he said, "My gift to you."

The truth is, you're only as good as your last project and who you are will show in what you do. Every day the choices we make determines what kind of life we build, we have the choice to take the way of character or the way of convenience. The fruit of our labor (or lack thereof) will show up when God evaluates our works (1 Cor. 3:11–15).

It's Better to Deal with Anger Sooner Rather than Later (7:9)

Related to the theme of patience, Solomon also touches on the collateral damage that can be caused by a sudden outburst of anger. "Be not quick in your spirit to become angry, for anger lodges in the heart of fools." If not dealt with properly anger can boil beneath the surface and violently explode on an unsuspecting victim causing untold damage to a relationship. Anger can make us do some really stupid things as Proverbs 14:17 says, "A quick-tempered man acts foolishly."

The Arizona Republic once reported that when Steve Tran of Westminster, California, closed the door on 25 activated bug bombs, he thought he had seen the last of the cockroaches that shared his apartment. However, when the spray reached the pilot light of the stove, it ignited, blasting his screen door across the street, breaking all his windows, and setting his furniture ablaze. "I really wanted to kill all of them," he said. "I thought if I used a lot more, it would last longer." According to the label, just two canisters of the fumigant would have solved Tran's pest problem. The blast caused over $10,000 damage to his apartment building. And the cockroaches? Tran reported, "By Sunday, I saw them walking around."[8]

It's been noted that anger is just one letter short of danger. The Bible says a lot about anger, in fact it's one of the seven deadly sins (Pro. 6:16–19). It mostly speaks of two types of anger, the anger that quickly blazes up and just as quickly subsides and the type of anger which is the slow burn, revenge-seeking kind of anger. In either case, explosions of anger can be avoided. Proverbs 17:14 reads, "Starting a quarrel is like breaching a dam; so drop the matter before a dispute breaks out." Anger can be controlled. Before we reach the boiling point we need to back up, take a breather and count to ten. The tone of our voice and the words we choose can also control

---

8. Rowell, *1001 Quotes, Illustrations, and Humorous Stories for Preachers, Teachers and Writers*, 201.

anger, "A soft answer turns away wrath, but a harsh word stirs up anger" (Pro. 15:1). Usually, if we would be honest with ourselves, most of the things we may become angry about are not all that important in the long run and we would be wise to ask ourselves, "Is this really worth hurting someone and losing my testimony?"

It's Better to Live in the Present than to Dwell on the Past (7:10)

There is an old saying which goes, "The Good ole' days are nothing more than the combination of bad memory and a good imagination." This is what Solomon is dealing with in 7:10, a preoccupation with past to the detriment of the present. He writes, "Say not, 'Why were the former days better than these?' For it is not from wisdom that you ask this." Yet, every small town has a diner where old men gather every day to sip on coffee, tell the same stories from the "glory days" and decry the present state of affairs. The past is a rudder to guide you, not an anchor to drag you. We must learn from the past but not live in the past. Nostalgia, sentimentality and tradition can hold the future hostage to the past.

This is exactly what the children of Israel did when the Lord delivered them from Egyptian bondage. While struggling for survival in the desert wilderness they complained and moaned to Moses for the leeks and onions of Egypt (Num. 11:5). It seems unthinkable to us. Who would want to go back to slavery? However, this happens more often than we would like to admit. When we nurse old grudges and hurts from the past, when we are unwilling to change, when we tremble at the thought of an uncertain future we choose the safety of the past. Too many churches are living in the past; unwilling to make the necessary changes to stay relevant. Solomon's warning reminds us that we should not live in the past, because God's focus is on the future. Heaven reminds us that the best is yet to come and we should be looking forward more than backward.

It's Better to Have Wisdom than Wealth (7:11-12)

The NLT paraphrases these verses, "Wisdom is even better when you have money. Both are a benefit as you go through life. Wisdom and money can get you almost anything, but only wisdom can save your life." In essence Solomon is saying, "In life you will need two things: money to pay your bills and wisdom to get you through the decision making process. However, if you don't have wealth coupled with wisdom then all the money in the world won't help you."

Money can lose its value or it can be stolen, but true wisdom doesn't depreciate and it cannot be taken away. Moreover, wealth does you no good if you don't have the wisdom to steward it correctly. What good is money if you have no common sense?

I was reminded of this when I saw the controversial documentary *Reversal of Fortune,* in which cameras follow Ted Rodriguez, a 45-year-old who has been periodically homeless for most of his adult life. The documentary chronicles Ted's up-and-down journey from rags to riches and then back to rags again. Director Wayne Powers conducted a social experiment to see how $100,000 would change the life of one homeless man, Ted, who at the film's outset lived under a bridge.

A scene is staged where Ted is filmed discovering a suitcase of cash while rummaging in a garbage bin for cans and bottles. Ted actually cried in shock when he found the money. At first Ted got himself an apartment and then he bought a $34,000 truck. Ted announced to his family and friends that he was set for life. He then bought his friends cars by taking them to a car dealership and having them purchase the car that they wanted. It's painful to watch as Ted kept on buying more and more useless stuff. The film maker even gave Ted the opportunity to use a financial advisor and counselor for free. Ted did not take him up on his offer. Not surprisingly, Ted lost everything and in the course of six months he was back on the streets again.

It is safe to say that from the example of Ted, that money is best when it is earned and not given to you. Especially not in a lump sum; which is exactly what the Bible teaches, "Wealth gained hastily will dwindle, but whoever gathers little by little will increase it" (Pro. 13:11). In 7:12, Solomon explains that money is a security net for all kinds of situations, but wisdom is a greater kind of protection that prevents us from the pitfalls of life.

It's Better to Trust God's Plan than Man's Predictions (7:13-14)

Solomon ends this section with a cryptic conclusion, "Consider the work of God: who can make straight what He has made crooked?" The first temptation upon reading these final verses is to assume that the Preacher has resorted to straight-up fatalism. However, this is not what he has mind when he talks of life being irreparably crooked. When the Preacher is talking about the things that are "crooked" in life he's referring to the limitations of our universe. There are things we would like to change about life, but we simply cannot. We look for an escape hatch from tribulation, but there is none to be found. Our heart yearns for an end to war, but another conflict has erupted in the Middle East. We save our money for a vacation, but alas a board with protruding nails has deflated our tires. This is the frustration of living on a fallen planet.

Why has God made life crooked? Simply put, it's so that we will trust in His sovereignty. God has ordered the events in life to be too complicated for us so that we will learn to depend on Him. Adversity and prosperity are both ordered by God. Wisdom allows us to navigate through both stormy and placid seas of life. This is the meaning of the 7:14, "In the day of prosperity be joyful, and in the day of adversity consider: God has made the one as well as the other, so that man may not find out anything that will be after him." A wise person realizes that God is in control and accepts whatever He allows into their life—despite it's perceived as good or bad. In fact, Ecclesiastes 7:14 carries the same thought as that of Job 2:10, "Shall we not receive good from God and shall we not receive evil also?" Wiersbe adds:

> God balances our lives by giving us enough blessing to keep us happy and enough burdens to keep us humble. If all we had were blessings in our hands, we would fall right over, so the Lord balances the blessings in our hands, with the burdens on our backs . . . Why does God constitute out lives this way? The answer is simple: to keep us from thinking we know it all and that we can manage our lives by ourselves.[9]

We must cooperate with the inevitable and play the cards that we have been dealt, remembering all the while that God is the dealer.

The story is told of a wise old Chinese woodcutter who lived on the troubled Mongolian border. One day his favorite horse, a beautiful white mare, jumped the fence and was seized on the other side by the enemy. His friends came to comfort him. "We're so sorry about your horse," they said. "That's bad news." "How do you know it's bad news?" he asked. "It might be good news."

A week later, the man looked out his window to see his mare returning at breakneck speed—beside a beautiful stallion. He put both horses into the enclosure, and his friends came to admire the new addition. "What a beautiful horse," they said. "That's good news." "How do you know it's good news?" replied the man. "It might be bad news."

The next day, the man's only son decided to try the stallion. It threw him, and he landed painfully, breaking his leg. The friends made another visit, all of them sympathetic, saying, "We're so sorry about this. It's such

---

9. Wiersbe, *The Wiersbe Bible Commentary: Old Testament*, 1131.

bad news." "How do you know it's bad news?" replied the man. "It might be good news." Within a month, war erupted between China and Mongolia. Chinese recruiters came through the area, pressing all the young men into the army. All of them perished, except for the woodcutter's son, who couldn't go off to war because of his broken leg. "You see," said the woodcutter. "The things you considered good were actually bad, and the things that seemed bad were actually good."[10]

God has engineered life to be complicated, with a balance of good days and bad days, so that you and I will continually need Him for perspective and guidance in every situation.

---

10. Morgan, *Nelson's Completes Book of Stories, Illustrations, and Quotes*, 653–654.

12

The Balancing Act of Wisdom (7:15–29)

ONE OF THE FIRST guitars I owned was an Ibanez acoustic that I bought in a pawn shop with some birthday money. It had several dents and dings in it, but it was a good guitar for a beginner like me. One thing I remember about that guitar was the smell. It had a musty odor like it had stayed locked up in a garage or an attic somewhere for years before its previous owner got tired of it collecting dust and finally decided to pawn it. I loved that guitar and I can remember playing it so much that my tender fingertips begged for mercy until I developed calluses on them. I would play that guitar late into the night until my mom would come in my room and tell me to stop playing because I was keeping everyone up.

As proud as I was of that first guitar, there was one recurring problem with it—keeping the strings in tune. It seemed like I had to tune that guitar almost every day. I would play it for little while and then the strings would fall out of tune and sometimes it felt like I spent more time tuning it than playing it. At first I thought the problem was with the strings, so I bought better quality strings, but despite the new strings it still would not stay in tune.

Finally, I had a friend of mine, who was an expert in instruments, take a look at it. As I explained the problem to him, he examined the neck of the guitar and quickly found the problem. He said the reason why the guitar didn't stay in tune was because the tuning keys on the neck of the guitar were warped. In other words, the guitar couldn't hold a tune because it couldn't handle the stress of keeping the strings taught and under the correct pressure. He said, "A guitar is a precision instrument, if something is wrong with at the neck, then it interferes with the tension of the strings and instead of beautiful music what you get is dissonance."

What was true of that cheap guitar is true about life. In order to have a well-tuned guitar you must achieve a perfect tension in all parts of the instrument. Life is like that as well. Part of being skilled at living involves mastering the ability to balance the tension and pressure of life under the sun. Marriage, church, finances, family, work, recreation—must all be in their proper alignment and spinning in their proper orbits. The tool which helps us keep everything at an even keel and prevents things from spinning out of control is wisdom.

In the last half of Ecclesiastes chapter seven, Solomon gives us council on the benefits of wisdom. Wisdom is what I would call "nuts and bolts" theology. It involves not only knowing God's principles for living but also applying those principles to your finances, marriage, work, spiritual life, etc. When we do this we find out that life achieves the correct balance, as Jesus said, "Seek first the kingdom of God and his righteousness, and all these things will be added to you" (Matt. 6:33). Amazingly, when we place the principles of God at the top spot we discover that everything else seems to fall into place.

As the Preacher closes out his discourse on wisdom, he lays out for us four ways that wisdom produces virtue in life.

Wisdom Gives Us Balance for Spiritual Living (7:15–18)

This section opens with one of the mystifying perplexities of under the sun living—pious, God-fearing, people seem to die young, while the wicked seem to prosper and outlive everyone. Solomon says, in 7:15 "In my vain life I have seen everything. There is a righteous man who perishes in his righteousness, and there is a wicked man who prolongs his life in his evildoing." Missionary Jim Eliot was martyred at age twenty-eight by the Auca Indians he was trying to minister to, yet Hugh Hefner is still living it large with a vixen on each arm. Missionary Eric Liddell was just forty-three when he expired in a Japanese concentration camp, yet the ruthless communist dictator Joseph Stalin lived to be seventy-four. Where is the justice in that?

I saw this happen on in my own family. On one side of the extended family, my grandmother was the sweetest, godliest woman you could ever meet. She loved her family and she single-handedly took my dad and his three siblings to church every Sunday. Her favorite hymn was "I'd Rather Have Jesus." Yet, she died a slow, painful death with colon cancer. She was just fifty-seven when she went to be with the Lord.

On the other side of the family was my grandfather who smoked and drank his entire life away. He suffered from the advanced stages of emphysema and other ailments. He had no spiritual life that I knew of and yet he lived to be seventy-nine. He died when I was in my twenties and I can remember feeling nothing at his funeral. I'll never know why God allowed him to linger for so long, while a saint was cut short in her prime. Perhaps, it was because God was giving him more time to repent of his sins and come to Christ (2 Peter 2:8–9).

I think that Charles Colson was on to something when we wrote, "Life is not like a book. Life isn't logical, or sensible or orderly. No. Life is a mess most of the time and our theology must be lived out in the midst of that mess."[1] Solomon has put his finger on this incongruity to raise a question in our minds. In light of the injustice that the good seem to die young and the evil prosper in their years, does it really matter how we live?

The Preacher answers with some sage advice in 7:16–18. Eugene Peterson has paraphrased these verses:

> I've seen it all in my brief and pointless life—here a good person cut down in the middle of doing good, there a bad person living a long life of sheer evil. So don't knock yourself out being good, and don't go overboard being wise. Believe me, you won't get anything out of it. But don't press your luck by being bad, either. And don't be reckless. Why die needlessly? It's best to stay in touch with both sides of an issue. A person who fears God deals responsibly with all of reality, not just a piece of it.[2]

Verses like this can become fodder for misinterpretation. Some commentators have dubbed these verses "the golden mean," which suggests we should not be too righteous or too wicked. Rather, we should strike a balance and achieve a happy medium. But this is not what the Preacher is getting at here. He is not advocating that we sin to a moderate degree, nor is he saying "Don't take your devotion to God too seriously."

His point is that we should not depend on our righteousness or wisdom to guarantee God's blessing in our lives. In other words, if you are a particularly righteous person don't be too confident that you will live to see your one-hundredth birthday. Solomon is saying, "Don't assume that God owes you anything for your righteousness." If you do, you might be confounded or disappointed like the righteous person who dies at a young age.[3]

---

1. Colson, *Loving God*, 218.
2. Peterson, *The Message*, Ecc. 7:15–18.
3. Glenn, "Ecclesiastes" in *The Bible Knowledge Commentary: Old Testament*, 994.

God doesn't grant his "super-saints" a free pass from suffering, injustice or untimely death.

On the flipside, the Preacher is also saying, "Don't live like a rebel either." Don't test the limits of God's grace by intentionally getting into sin. Don't remove the guardrails from life and expect that there will be no consequences. In the end, it does no good to become a Pharisee or a pagan. Neither lifestyle is balanced or beneficial.

How then should we live? The solution is found in 7:18, ". . . for the one who fears God shall come out from both of them." The believer who fears God finds a balance in the Christian life, they don't become legalistic and they don't backslide into a life of sin either. A wise person keeps short accounts with God's character and doesn't go to either extreme. The one who fears God finds a way to live with discernment, avoiding the dangers of a destructive lifestyle. Having a true and proper view of God will help us not to be self-righteous. We will realize that God sees through our attempts to be overly religious and we will not pretend to be someone we aren't. On the other hand, the one who fears God will have a safeguard against wickedness, because we understand His holiness and we tremble at the thought of falling under His judgment.[4]

In his work, *The Pleasures of God*, John Piper explains how the fear of God can lead us to both reverence and protection:

> Suppose you were exploring an unknown glacier in the north of Greenland in the dead of winter. Just as you reach a sheer cliff with a spectacular view of miles and miles of jagged ice and mountains of snow, a terrible storm breaks in. The wind is so strong that the fear rises in your heart that it might blow you over the cliff. But in the midst of the storm you discover a cleft in the ice where you can hide. Here you feel secure. But, even though secure, the awesome might of the storm rages on, and you watch it with a kind of trembling pleasure as it surges out across the distant glaciers. At first there was the fear that this terrible storm and awesome terrain might claim your life. But then you found a refuge and gained the hope that you would be safe. But not everything in the feeling called fear vanished from your heart. Only the life-threatening part. There remained the trembling, the awe, the wonder, the feeling that you would never want to tangle with such a storm or be the adversary of such a power. And so it is with God.[5]

---

4. Ryken, *Ecclesiastes*, 168.
5. Piper, *The Pleasures of God*, 205–206.

Wisdom Gives Us Strength for Skillful Living (7:19–20)

Solomon argues that wisdom is the greatest ally in this crooked world. The Hebrew word for "wisdom" (*hokmah*) refers to "the skill of living." This involves both a godly perspective and a godly power to live life. Perspective and power are like the two wings on a bird, the two blades of a pair of scissors, or the two sides of a coin. The whole of wisdom doesn't exist without both perspective and power.[6]

The Preacher's point is that one ounce of God's wisdom is better than the strength of ten strong men, "Wisdom gives strength to the wise man more than ten rulers who are in a city." Why is this? Physical strength and vigor will leave us with time, but wisdom will serve us faithfully through our years. Wisdom doesn't deprecate with age, while strength diminishes as the second law of thermodynamics does its dirty work on our mortal frame. We should get a hold of wisdom because it will govern our wills, thoughts and desires, thus setting the course of our lives.

However, this truth is presented in tension. Did you notice Solomon's strong denunciation of the human condition in 7:20? "Indeed, there is not a righteous man on earth who continually does good and who never sins." It seems that Solomon puts this in there as a reminder to us that even the wisest man is still fallen and his heart bent towards evil. Alas, wisdom alone will not be enough to save us. We may become very wise, yet we should remember that no one ever arrives at a state of perfection in this life. We are still sinners in need of a Savior.

One of the great preaching heroes of nineteenth century Scotland, Alexander Whyte, was approached one day by a woman who showered him with words of flattery and praise. She was sincere, and Whyte knew that. But he also knew that the applause she was heaping upon him was not his to receive, nor was it an accurate perception of what he knew himself to be. In a response that is more typical of the nineteenth century than the twenty-first, he said to her, "Madam, if you knew the man I really was, you would spit in my face."[7]

This reveals an important aspect to wisdom—humility and a self-awareness of our fallen condition. Our wisdom should be tethered to an understanding of how rotten our hearts really are. This reality should make us cry out to God not only for more wisdom but also for daily forgiveness and strength to avoid temptation. In fact, I would say that those who are truly wise recognize their moral weakness and work doubly-hard to shore

---

6. Jeremiah, *Searching for Heaven on Earth*, 204.
7. MacDonald, *The Life God Blesses*, 59.

up their lives in those areas where they know they are susceptible to moral failure.

According to Greek mythology, sirens (mermaid-like creatures) inhabited certain Mediterranean coastal areas. As ships passed by the sirens sang such enchanting songs that the sailors, drawn by the music, would jump overboard and drown. Homer's epic poem, *The Odyssey*, follows the hero of the story, Odysseus, on his decade long trip home from fighting in the Trojan Wars. During one memorable scene Odysseus and his men were sailing through the treacherous waters rumored to be inhabited by the seductive sirens. Aware of the powerful allurement of those songs, he ordered that he be bound with ropes to the mast and that the crewmen's ears be sealed with wax to block out the tantalizing music of the sirens. Having taken such precautions, Odysseus and the rest of the crew were able to sail past without yielding to the lure of the sirens.

As wise Christians we should be prepared to do the same in our own lives. Drastic measures must be taken. Safeguards and precautions should be implemented. You must keep away from any enticements that you know would play into your weakness. The best protection against temptation is to heed the warning Paul gave to Timothy: "Flee also youthful lusts; but pursue righteousness" (2 Tim. 2:22). That was good counsel then and it's still good today. The strength of wisdom is to keep the walls of your life sealed up against possible points of invasion.

Wisdom Gives Us Discernment for Sensible Living (7:21-24)

I have read that researchers have figured out that a single issue of *The New York Times* contains about twice as much information as the average citizen of Shakespeare's London would have come across in an entire lifetime. Any one of us has instantaneous access to more information than Shakespeare could have expected to see in several lifetimes. But it is certainly not obvious that we have more wisdom than Shakespeare, Socrates or Solomon. It stands to reason that there's a clear difference between access to information and acquisition of wisdom.

This is where discernment comes into play. Discernment is a byproduct of wisdom. It is the unique skill that allows us to differentiate between what has value and what doesn't, what is good from what is best, what is profitable from what is corrupt. Those who have discernment are able to look at the blurring array of options in our world today and extract from it exactly what is needed. They can look at the grey areas of life and parse out the black from the white. Solomon notes at least two additional areas in life where discernment helps us look through the murky areas and make the best choices.

First he points out that we need *discernment in how we listen*. "Do not take to heart all the things that people say, lest you hear your servant cursing you. Your heart knows that many times you yourself have cursed others." The Preacher reminds us that we shouldn't make it a point to eavesdrop on every conversation because sooner or later we will be disappointed with what we hear. Listening in on conversations through thin walls can reveal who our true friends really are. Everyone knows the sting of betrayal when they hear damning words from a so-called friend driving a verbal dagger into the heart. Like one man told me, "Gossip is the art of confessing other people's sins."

Solomon's advice is that we not take the criticism and slander of others too seriously. If you are totally honest, you know in your heart you have said unkind things about others behind closed doors. So if we get upset when people talk about us, we are holding them to a higher standard than we hold ourselves to, because we are prone to do the same thing.

The truth is that listening to gossip is just as damaging as telling it. Proverbs 18:8 reads, "The words of a whisperer are like delicious morsels; they go down into the inner parts of the body." In other words, listening to gossip is like eating junk food all the time. If you eat nothing but candy and chips, it might taste good but it will destroy your health. In the same way, a gossiping tongue may be entertaining to listen to, but in the end it's disastrous for your spiritual life. Listening to gossip does to your soul what second-hand smoke does to the lungs.

I once heard a story about how Winston Churchill exemplified integrity and respect in the face of wagging tongues. During his last year in office, he attended an official ceremony. Several rows behind him two gentlemen began whispering. "That's Winston Churchill." "They say he is getting senile," one man said. Another threw in his two cents, "Yes and they say he should step aside and leave the running of the nation to more dynamic and capable men." When the ceremony was over, Churchill turned to the men and said, "Gentlemen, they also say he is deaf!"

Charles Spurgeon once told a group of young pastors training for the ministry, "Every minister should have one blind eye and one deaf ear. You cannot stop people's tongues and therefore the best thing to do is to stop your own ears and never mind what is spoken. There is a world of idle chit-chat abroad and he who takes note of it will have enough to do."[8]

---

8. Spurgeon, *Lectures to My Students*, 321.

Second, we also need *discernment in what we can learn*. Solomon reached the edge of human reason and said, "I tested all this with wisdom, and I said, 'I will be wise,' but it was far from me. What has been is remote and exceedingly mysterious. Who can discover it?" As creatures made in God's image we have the intrinsic desire for knowledge and understanding, yet there are many mysteries where we must throw up our hands in ignorance. The fact is we are limited, finite creatures and there is some information that is beyond our security clearance and above our pay grade.

Derek Kinder describes these verses as "the epitaph of every philosopher."[9] Solomon, the wisest man besides the Lord Jesus Christ, did not understand everything there was about God and life. Therefore, the Preacher had to be comfortable with what he couldn't know. A wise man acknowledges the limits of human understanding and admits that that are gaps in his theology.

Just because I went to seminary and had four years of theological training doesn't mean that I have all the answers. In fact, it's more like the opposite; the more I study theology and dig into the Bible, the more questions I have that will not be answered until I see Jesus face-to-face. My mind is too small to get it wrapped around the incomprehensible ways of God. I don't have an airtight argument which can explain the problem of evil. I can't tell you where God's sovereignty ends and man's free will begins—I just know that the Bible says both are true. I can give you clever analogies to explain the mystery of the Trinity, but sooner or later they will break down because our language is limited. I don't think I'll ever fully grasp the virgin birth or the incarnation of Christ.

Fortunately, I don't have to. This is where faith comes into the picture. What Solomon is getting at it this—wisdom gives us as limited, finite creatures the ability to release things we cannot know into the hands of a faithful God. He's almost saying this: "I have learned two things in life—God exists and I'm not Him." Moreover, it's really liberating when you finally figure out how small and ignorant you really are because it just makes God that much greater.

The only fitting illustration that the Bible uses to describe the immensity of God is the vast expanse of the universe. Is. 40:26, "Lift your eyes and look to the heavens: Who created all these? He who brings out the starry host one by one, and calls them each by name. Because of his great power and mighty strength, not one of them is missing." If you could travel the speed of light (186,000 miles per second) it would take you 100,000 years to travel from one end of the Milky Way Galaxy to the other. Scientists estimate that just the Milky Way alone contains about 300 billion stars. Yet, astronomers

---

9. Kinder, *The Message of Ecclesiastes*, 71.

say there are trillions upon trillion of galaxies, many of them larger than our own, with billions of stars in each galaxy. The best guesstimate to the number of stars are in the universe is something akin to the number of sand grains on all the beaches of Earth. If we have difficulty coming to terms with the size and scope of our universe how can we ever expect to wrap our minds around the God who made all the stars and knows everyone by name?

Knowing the limits of reason is part of wisdom. The more we know the more we should realize how little we know, and that whatever wisdom we gain comes as a gift from God.[10]

Wisdom Gives Us Power for Sanctified Living (7:25-29)

Interpreting the last verses of Solomon's meandering mediation is quite challenging. The identity of the woman in question is not so easy to settle. "And I find something more bitter than death: the woman whose heart is snares and nets, and whose hands are fetters. He who pleases God escapes her, but the sinner is taken by her." Was Solomon referring to a flesh-and-blood seductress or was he personifying folly as a prostitute like he did in Proverbs 2? If his intent is to refer to an adulteress then the application is quite simple: avoid sexual immorality at all costs. Similarly, if he is referring to folly then the point is that foolishness is like a seductive woman so beware for she will lead you to your demise. Be a wise person who refuses to be captured by her. Use discretion as you travel this life.

Either way, wisdom will help us steer clear of the pitfalls in life. Again we return to the skill of Eugene Peterson's paraphrase of these final verses:

> One discovery: A woman can be a bitter pill to swallow, full of seductive scheming and grasping. The lucky escape her; the undiscerning get caught. At least this is my experience—what I, the Quester, have pieced together as I've tried to make sense of life. But the wisdom I've looked for I haven't found. I didn't find one man or woman in a thousand worth my while. Yet I did spot one ray of light in this murk: God made men and women true and upright; we're the ones who've made a mess of things."[11]

Please don't take Solomon's comments about women to be misogynistic. Solomon is not down on women. Remember he also extolled the virtues of a godly woman in Proverbs 31. Instead what the Preacher appears

---

10. Ryken, *Ecclesiastes*, 175.
11. Peterson, *The Message*, Ecc. 7:25-29.

to be pointing out is that in all his searching he only found one man and no women whose true desire was to please the Lord. Solomon's words are a general indictment against the depravity of the whole human race.

This is confirmed by his final words in 7:29, "God made man, but they have sought out many schemes." This verse contains two important foundations to the Christian message: creation and fall. This is the biblical doctrine of original sin. Adam and Eve, our first parents, were created sinless, yet they chose to disobey God's only command. Their blunder threw the entire universe off balance. Sin has blighted the creation and cursed the creature. As a result the human heart is bent towards evil, work is drudgery, life is a vapid search for meaning and death is mandatory. As C.S. Lewis eloquently said, "To come from the Lord Adam and the Lady Eve is both honor enough to erect the head of the poorest beggar, and shame enough to bow the shoulders of the greatest emperor on Earth."[12]

If Solomon were here today he might remind us of this following story. During the Middles Ages there lived a blacksmith who boasted that he could break any chains, except those forged on his anvil. Through a series of trial and error, the blacksmith patiently developed a metal which made his chains unbreakable. One day this blacksmith neglected to pay his taxes and the nobleman punished him by condemning him to be locked away in the castle dungeon. On the way to the dungeon, the blacksmith boasted that he would soon be out again as he was sure he could break any chain put upon him. When he was chained, he immediately started to look for the flaw in the links which would set him free, but he found his own brand on the links, and knew he was hopelessly bound by his own handiwork and could not escape because of his own chains.

Man's worst enemy is himself. We forge the chains which hold us in bondage. Wisdom should reveal to us that only Christ can break the shackles of sin and set us free (John 8:32). Jesus is the only man who remained upright and never fell into sin. By faith in His atoning work on the Cross we can be set free from our schemes. Even if we do not have the wisdom to solve all the deep mysteries of the universe, we should at least be wise enough to see the sin in our own hearts and as Jesus to be our Savior.[13]

---

12. Lewis, *Prince Caspian*, 233.
13. Ryken, *Ecclesiastes*, 179.

13

Wisdom for a Warped World (8:1–17)

IT HAS BEEN CALLED the "little cube that changed the world." Since its invention in 1974, the Rubik's Cube has become the world's most popular toy. It's estimated that 350 million cubes have been sold since 1980 and about 1/5 of the world's population has been confounded by its seemingly endless permutations. There's just one solution out of 43 quintillion possible combinations, and even the man who invented it, Erno Rubik, spent a month of solid research trying to figure it out before he cracked the code. Amazingly, cube experts claim that any 3x3x3 cube can be solved in just twenty moves. Try doing that in 5.66 seconds and your name will be in the Guinness Book of World Records as a cube speedster.[1]

A few winters ago my wife was rummaging around in some old boxes and found her Rubik's Cube. We spent the next several weeks in a tag-team effort trying to get all the colored blocks to match up without resorting to the cheat guides on the internet. If you have ever played with a Rubik's Cube then you know how infuriating it can be. The more you twist and turn the more complicated it becomes. Just when you have a face of all green or all yellow, the next turn ruins all your progress. The cube's inventor once said of his puzzle, "The key to its solution is that you must have a connection with its chaos and order." He wasn't kidding.

I think the Rubik's cube offers a good metaphor for Solomon's underlying theme in Ecclesiastes. The Preacher has been wrestling with the puzzle of life. Life under the sun, like the cube, is a perplexing mess in the hands

---

1. Webster, "The Little Cube that Changed the World," *CNN News*, 11 October 2012.

of novice. In fact, the more we try to make it work in our own skill and intellect, the more messed up and disorderly it becomes. Just when it looks like we have a mystery solved, another challenge presents itself and we are back to the drawing board. Perhaps you can identify with the words of G.K. Chesterton who said, "My problem with life is not that it is rational, nor that it is irrational, but that it is almost rational."

Solomon has already made known our need from wisdom in this off-kilter world. He restates this again in 8:1, "Who is like the wise? And who knows the interpretation of a thing? A man's wisdom makes his face shine, and the hardness of his face is changed." Wisdom is the game-changer for those living under the sun. Wisdom helps us answer the big questions—Who am I? Where did I come from? What happens when we die? Wisdom also sets the parameters for what we can know and what is outside our knowledge base. Wisdom takes us so far, while faith allows us to trust that God is in control of those things we don't understand.

This seems to be one of the main points of chapter eight. The Preacher takes a realistic appraisal of a warped world filled with inequity, iniquity and injustice. Finding God's purpose in this mess can be more frustrating than a blind man trying to solve a Rubik's Cube. Solomon ends up telling us that wisdom can take us so far, but for the rest we must fear God and trust in His unseen sovereign plan to bring order out of the chaos.

Wisdom to Obey Those in Control of the World (8:2-7)

Solomon begins by teaching the importance of respecting human authorities. According to 8:2, Solomon explains that our responsibility to obey the rulers of the land is not for the sake of the king; it's for the sake of God who allowed those people to gain positions of authority, "I say, 'Keep the command of the king *because of the oath before God*." Part of our commitment to God is directly related to our submission to human government even if the man in the Oval Office is wicked. Thus, for the believer being a good citizen is theological not political.

Paul reinforces this in Rom. 13:1-2, "Let every person be subject to the governing authorities. For there is no authority except from God, and those that exist have been instituted by God. Therefore whoever resists the authorities resists what God has appointed, and those who resist will incur judgment." Keep in mind that when Paul wrote those words, the Emperor of Rome was massacring Christians by the droves.

Notice what Jesus said to Pilate at His trial in John 19:10-11, "So Pilate said to him, "You will not speak to me? Do you not know that I have authority to release you and authority to crucify you?" Jesus answered him, "You would have no authority over me at all *unless it had been given you from above.*" Even Jesus, the Son of God, submitted to human authority while he was on Earth. Why? Because He recognized that the One who He was submitting to was not Pilate, but His Heavenly Father. There is no ruler, despot, president, or king who is outside the sovereignty of God. Proverbs 21:1 reminds us, "The king's heart is a stream of water in the hand of the LORD; he turns it wherever he will."

We ought to remember that any authority under which we find ourselves is a God-ordained authority and should be obeyed. The only exception to this rule is when such an authority commands us to do something that is in opposition to God's Word. A good rule of thumb is the one Peter gave when the rulers of Jerusalem told him to stop preaching the Gospel, "We must obey God rather than men" (Acts 5:29). When it comes to a conflict between God and man we must obey the higher authority.

The remaining verses in this section, 8:3–7, indicate to us in a general sense how the wise person finds a way to operate justly within an evil and unfair political system. A wise person gives the governing authority respect for their office and if they are evil he doesn't try to fight evil with evil (8:3). Moreover, the wise person realizes that obeying the authority, even though they may not like the rules, makes life easier in the long run (8:4–5). In other words, when you drive the speed limit, you don't have to worry about speed traps. When you pay your taxes, you aren't particularly worried about an IRS audit. When you do your work faithfully on the job, it doesn't concern you that the boss is watching.

Finally, the wise person has impeccable timing and knows how to act at the right time in the right manner (8:6–7). There is a time to submit to authority and a time to stand up to oppression and corruption. Wisdom helps us discern as it did the case of Daniel and his three Hebrew comrades. When Daniel was commanded to defile himself with king Nebuchadnezzar's meat, he wisely found an alternative solution and God honored him (Dan. 1). When Shadrach, Meshach and Abednego refused to bow to the golden statue of the king, God spared them through the fire (Dan. 2). Christians should resist a government that commands or compels evil, and should work nonviolently within the laws of the land to change a government that permits evil.

Vice President, George H. Bush once represented the U.S. at the funeral of former Soviet leader Leonid Brezhnev. Bush was deeply moved by a silent protest carried out by Brezhnev's widow. She stood motionless by the coffin until seconds before it was closed. Then, just as the soldiers touched the lid, Brezhnev's wife performed an act of great courage and hope, a gesture that must surely rank as one of the most profound acts of civil disobedience ever committed: she reached down and made the sign of the cross on her husband's chest. There in the citadel of secular, atheistic power, the wife of the man who had run it all hoped that her husband was wrong. She hoped that there was another life, and that that life was best represented by Jesus who died on the cross, and that the same Jesus might yet have mercy on her husband.[2]

Francis Schaeffer said in the *Christian Manifesto* that, "We must not confuse the Kingdom of God with our country. To say it another way: We should not wrap Christianity in our national flag . . . If there is never a case in which a Christian would practice civil disobedience, then the state has become Lord."[3] One either confesses that God is the final authority, or one confesses that Caesar is Lord. The Bible clearly teaches that there are times when a believer must disobey civil law so that he or she can obey God's higher law. Wisdom helps us differentiate when we should submit and when we should stand.

If we are to translate Solomon's words into a modern context he would be saying to us, "You're going to have to work for a boss that isn't a Christian. You're going to have to take college classes from atheistic professors. The Supreme Court is going to make policy that you strongly disagree with. So how are you going to uphold your Christian convictions while at the same time being obedient to the authority?"

Here's what we should do. That boss that treats you unfairly and is an incompetent manager—you should show up on time and work hard all day (1 Thess. 4:11). Don't complain or gossip about him around other co-workers. Give him forty hours a week, smile and remember that your real boss is Jesus (Col. 3:23). If you're a Christian college student then attend class, study hard, filter out what's truth from what's lies, take the test, and leave the rest to God. When election season comes around, don't just pray for God's will, but get out and vote. You can't complain about bad government if you don't get involved.

---

2. Thomas, "Wise Christians Clip Obituaries." *Christianity Today,* 3 October 1994.
3. Schaeffer, *A Christian Manifesto,* 121, 130.

Wisdom to Accept What We Cannot Change about the World (8:8-9)

Bible teacher Herbert Vander Lught once told the following story:

> During the Great Depression my father moved to a farm as a tenant. He signed a contract stating that he hand the owner would share equally in the proceeds from milk and crops. In the fall, however, the landlord wouldn't give us our share of the money from the wheat crop. Dad's appeals to him accomplished nothing, so he consulted a Christian lawyer. Reading the fine print in the contract, the lawyer advised my father that he could take no legal action. The landowner was unethical and he had been clever in the fine print of the contract. Rather humorously, the lawyer said, "Sir you have three choices. You can kill the crook and get yourself in deep trouble with the law. You can cheat him and become like him. Or you can take the wrong and let God take care of you and him."[4]

When you get down to the brass tacks of life, the truth is there is very little we are in control of. As Charles Swindoll has said, "Life is ten percent what happens to me and ninety percent how I react to it." We have no control over the weather that affects us daily, we have no control over the family we were born into, and we cannot pick when we die or even the events that might hasten our death. According to Solomon, we cannot avoid our death any more than a good soldier can avoid danger on the battlefield. "No man has power to retain the spirit, or power over the day of death. There is no discharge from war, nor will wickedness deliver those who are given to it."

I saw a bumper sticker the other day which said, "Exercise, eat right, die anyway." This is a sad reality. As we all take the slow march towards the grave we should be constantly trusting in God to take care of the areas that only He can. Death is not an accident, but an appointment (Heb. 9:27). The wise person does not fear death, but they make preparations for eternity. Thankfully, because of the resurrection of Christ death is not final (John 14:19).

Wisdom to Make Sense of the Chaos in the World (8:10-14)

A tornado touches down and leaves a swath of destruction across five states, taking lives and leaving thousands homeless. Meanwhile on the other side

---

4. Vander Lught quoted by Roy B. Zuck, *The Speaker's Quote Book*, 278.

of the world, a soldier from one of those mid-western states protects his buddies by jumping on a hand grenade thrown by a terrorist. In a downtown courtroom a slick-tongued lawyer spins a web of lies and convinces a jury of a murderer's innocence. A doctor looks into the eyes of young lady and gives her the grim news, "Because of the extensive chemotherapy, you will never be able to conceive a child."

Life under the sun is one brutal injustice after another it seems. Solomon doesn't deny the existence of real, palpable evil at work in the world. In fact, as you read these verses you can feel him wrestling with some of the unexplainable mysteries of suffering and iniquity. The Bible never shies away from presenting the ragged-edge reality of life. It always gives an honest appraisal of our fallen state.

The Preacher's next bellyache is *the praise of the wicked (8:10)*. "Then I saw the wicked buried. They used to go in and out of the holy place and were praised in the city where they had done such things. This also is vanity." "Why is it," Solomon asks, "that the wicked are made out to be saints?" Good question. How can the corrupt people at the top be venerated as idols of goodness and virtue, while the godly are forgotten and trampled underfoot? Solomon wasn't the only one who chaffed under this absurdity. Asaph lamented in Psalm 73:11–14, "What's going on here? Is God out to lunch? Nobody's tending the store. The wicked get by with everything; they have it made, piling up riches. I've been stupid to play by the rules; what has it gotten me? A long run of bad luck, that's what—a slap in the face every time I walk out the door."[5] Moreover, David Jeremiah has written:

> Television shows us a godless celebrity whose death is mourned by the entire world. A successful millionaire is ushered to his grave with great fanfare. But the simple, humble, godly man or man isn't even afforded an inch on the obituary page. The memory of all their deeds of love and kindness appears to be swiftly forgotten, blown away like the particles of the wind.[6]

Vladimir Lenin was a bloody tyrant in his own right. He personally approved the murder of thousands of political opponents on his way to becoming the leader of USSR. His mausoleum is in Moscow's Red Square. Since 1924 his body has been in a glass covered casket available for public viewing. On his casket are these words, "He was the greatest leader of all peoples of all countries of all times, he was the Lord of the new humanity and the Savior of the world."

---

5. Peterson, *The Message*, Psalm 73:11–14.
6. Jeremiah, *Searching for Heaven on Earth*, 220.

Solomon shakes his head and turns to another problem—*the perversity of justice (8:11–14)*. "Because the sentence against an evil deed is not executed quickly, therefore the hearts of the sons of men among them are given fully to do evil" (8:11). Solomon explains that one of the primary reasons the wicked continue in their evil is because justice is delayed. God's mercy in not executing judgment immediately against those who sin is interpreted by those who do not openly fear God as being either a sign of weakness or a sign of a laissez-faire attitude on God's part.[7] Because punishment isn't immediate and swift, the wicked keep sinning, thinking they can always get away with it.

In 2013 the government of Hungary filed charges against a 98-year-old former police officer, Laszlo Csatary, for beating Jews and assisting their deportation to Nazi death camps. Prosecutors said that, "Csatary beat, brutalized and sent 16,000 Jews to their deaths in the Ukraine and Auschwitz while operating in Kosice, Slovakia, between 1941 and 1944, when the city was ruled by a pro-Nazi Hungarian regime."[8] Csatary spent decades running from the long arm of the law under false identities but now it looks like he will pay, if he doesn't keel over of old age first. Yes, we are glad that this criminal was finally caught, but still something doesn't seem right that he had the opportunity to enjoy his years of relative freedom.

Drop down to 8:14 and we read more injustice, "There is a vanity that takes place on earth, that there are righteous people to whom it happens according to the deeds of the wicked, and there are wicked people to whom it happens according to the deeds of the righteous. I said that this also is vanity."

If you're a person who walks around with your eyes open, keeping score, then it looks like the bad guys are winning. The justice system is backwards—evil people don't always get what's coming to them and righteous people seem to always suffer. A thief breaks into someone's house and gets shot by the homeowner and sues the homeowner trying to protect his family. A Christian family is killed by an irresponsible drunk driver. Orphans that fall through the cracks of society are abducted and forced into sex-trafficking.

In 2013 the world was stunned to learn what happened to one baby in China. A five-pound infant was discovered by residents in Jinhua, China when they heard cries coming out of a fourth floor toilet in a local apartment building. When the firefighters arrived on the scene they discovered

---

7. Krell, "Living Under the Thumb (Ecclesiastes 8:1–17)."

8. Ames, "Hungary Interdicts 98-Year-Old for Nazi War Crimes," *Global Post*, 18 June 2013.

a two-day old baby lodged in the piping below the toilet. After attempts to pull the baby out of the toilet failed, the rescuers resorted to sawing off a whole section of piping containing the baby and brought it to the neighboring hospital. On the operating table, firefighters and doctors worked meticulously to remove the baby from the plastic pipe. Amazingly, the baby lived![9] But still the appalling fact remains that this child was not wanted by the parents and they simply discarded him as trash.

Why does God allow things like this to happen? Why does He delay judgment? For some this is all the evidence they need to become a card-carrying atheist. For others who are willing to wrestle with the problem they may come to the conclusion that these are deep mysteries of life that can never be resolved with certainly because of our limited "under the sun" perspective.

I believe that God is able to allow short-term evil to accomplish His long-term good (Gen. 50:20). I also know that what we view as long delays, are actually not applicable to God's standard of reckoning because He views things from the perspective of eternity. It's also true that God's patience in postponing judgment grants the wicked more time to repent and respond to the gospel (2 Peter 3:9). Moreover, we must acknowledge that these mysteries may have been allowed by God so that humans would have to trust Him for ultimate justice and guidance. In fact, if we resign to atheism then evil and injustice never get resolved. Only theism allows the possibility for God to even all scores. Just because God hasn't punished all wrong doing yet doesn't mean that we won't one day at the appointed hour (John 5:22, Acts 17:31).

This is what Solomon's hopes rested on, "Though a sinner does evil a hundred times and prolongs his life, yet I know that it will be well with those who fear God, because they fear before him. But it will not be well with the wicked, neither will he prolong his days like a shadow, because he does not fear before God" (8:12-13). One day those who got away "scot-free" will have to stand before God and He will be judge, jury and executioner. There will be no appeals and no possibility for parole. So don't get worried that justice will not be carried out, because there will be a payday someday. Randy Alcorn writes:

> Do we criticize a great composer whose symphony doesn't end in ten minutes or half an hour? Do we complain when he moves from a major key to a minor key and back to a major? No, we celebrate his artistry. When we hear the dark and melancholic

---

9. Yiu, "Newborn Baby Rescued from Toilet Pipe in China," *ABC News*, 13 May 2013.

sections, we do not conclude he's made a mistake. One we reach the ending, we recognize the symphony as a far greater work than the one that consists of only bright melodies. A concert may last three hours. God's concert has lasted thousands of years. What if the melody and harmony, major and minor keys all prove in the end to have contributed to the whole . . . When we view life through the eyes of faith, we can say, "Things appear one way, but my God is sovereign, loving, merciful and kind. Through His grace and empowerment, I will cling to him. I will come out on the other side of this suffering a deeper and more Christ-like person, marked forever by Jesus' grave. And someday I will see that every minute was worth it."[10]

The story is told of two men who owned farms side-by-side. One was a bitter skeptic, the other a devout Christian. Constantly annoyed at the Christian for trusting God, the skeptic said to him one winter, "Let's plant our crops as usual this spring, each the same number of acres. You pray to your God and I'll curse Him. Then come August, let's see who has the bigger crop." When August came the skeptic was delighted because his crop was larger. "See you fool," he taunted, "what do you have to say for your God now?" "My God," the other farmer replied, "doesn't settle all his accounts in August."

If you think that God is doing a bad job running the affairs of the universe, just wait. He's not done. The Jefferson Memorial in Washington D.C. has these memorable words inscribed on them as a reminder that God will inevitably balance the scales, "I tremble for my country when I reflect that God is just and that his justice cannot sleep forever."

Wisdom to Be Content in this World (8:15)

"And I commend joy, for man has nothing better under the sun but to eat and drink and be joyful, for this will go with him in his toil through the days of his life that God has given him under the sun." Solomon is not just talking about the power of positive thinking nor is he speaking of making the best out of a bad situation. In spite of all the vanity in the world, the Preacher advises us to find pleasure in the simplicities of life's basics. This is the same advice he has given many times before in the so-called "enjoyment passages" (2:24–26, 3:12–13, 3:22, 5:18–20).

Some have wrongly misinterpreted these verses to take seriously the hedonistic mantra, "Eat, drink and be merry for tomorrow we die!"

---

10. Alcorn, *If God Is Good*, 340.

However, this view fails to take into account the God-centered view that the Preacher has in mind. This is Solomon's way of saying: "Life is a gift from God, make the most of it. Carpe Diem: Seize the Day!" The Preacher is trying to give balance to our perspective. Since there is little you and I can do to eradicate all evil and since there is always going be injustice that we cannot understand then we might as well trust that God has things under control and be content.

In other words, be like Jesus. Jesus was poor, homeless, and never formally educated. He was hated by the religious establishment, betrayed by someone in his inner circle and then executed under an evil political system at the hands of the Jews and Romans. On the outside his life looks like a complete failure. God is underachiever, or so it seems. Yet in the midst of all that injustice and suffering, Jesus was the most joyful person to have ever lived. He says in John 16:22 "So also you have sorrow now, but I will see you again and your hearts will rejoice, and no one will take your joy from you."

So here is your homework. What do you like to eat—cheeseburgers, banana splits, BBQ ribs, pepperoni pizza? Fix a delicious meal tonight and savor it. Thank God for the simple pleasure of being able to enjoy a meal together. Enjoy your spouse and your kids. Take a hike in the woods, skip stones across a pond, make a snow angel, go skydiving! Take time to stop and smell the roses. Enjoy your life, because sometimes you have to laugh to keep from crying.

The father of a wealthy family once took his son on a trip to the country to show his son how poor people live. They spent a couple of days and nights on the farm of what would be considered a very poor family. On their return from the trip, the father asked his son, "How was the trip?" "It was great, Dad." "Did you see how poor people can be?" the father asked. "Oh yeah," said the son. "So what did you learn from the trip?" asked the father. The son answered: "I saw that we have one dog, and they have four. We have a pool that reaches to the middle of our garden, and they have a creek that has no end. We have imported lanterns in our garden, and they have stars at night. Our patio reaches to the front yard, and they have the whole horizon. We have a small piece of land to live on, and they have fields that go beyond sight. We buy our food, but they grow theirs. We have walls around our property to protect us, but they have their friends to protect them." With this, the boy's father was speechless. Then his son added, "Thanks, Dad, for showing me how poor we are."

Contentment is an elusive treasure in our culture because we are constantly bombarded with advertisements which try to convince us that our lives are incomplete unless we own one more trinket, gadget or new-fangled creature comfort. However, I have found that contentment is not based on your possessions, but on who possesses your heart—Jesus, the one who never changes (Heb. 13:8), or the world, which is passing away (1 John 2:17). Cultivating contentment begins by counting our blessings and realizing that there is nothing in this world which can replace our relationship with Christ.

Wisdom to Know We Cannot Comprehend Everything God is Doing in the World (8:16–17)

Solomon's final instruction is to realize that as limited, finite, human creatures there is only so much we possibly know. "Then I saw all the work of God, that man cannot find out the work that is done under the sun. However much man may toil in seeking, he will not find it out." He discovered what he could not discover. The Preacher wants us to allow room in our theology for mystery. There are things that God in His wisdoms doesn't allow us to know as Deut. 29:29 says that "the secret things belong to the Lord."

An advanced student asked legendary martial arts master Bruce Lee if Lee would teach him everything he knew about martial arts. In response, Lee held up two cups, both filled with water: "This cup represents all I know, and the second cup represents all you know," Lee said. "If you want to fill your cup with my knowledge, you must first empty your cup of your knowledge."

Human wisdom can only take us so far and man's puffed-up knowledge gets in the way of true godly wisdom. The key to the beginning of wisdom is a fear of the Lord (Pro. 1:7). Rather than getting frustrated with all the things we do not know about the world or do not understand about the ways of God, we are invited to rest content with our own limitations and to worship God for his superior wisdom.[11]

In his book, *God's Undertaker*, scientist Dr. John Lennox explains the scope and limits of scientific inquiry with the following story:

> Let us imagine that Aunt Matilda has made a beautiful cake, and we take it along to be analyzed by a group of the world's top scientists . . . The nutrition scientists will tell us about the number of calories in the cake and its nutritional effect; the biochemists will inform us about the structure of proteins, fats, etc. in the cake . . . the physicists will be able to analyze the cake in terms of fundamental particles; and the mathematicians will no doubt offer us a set of elegant equations to describe the behavior of those particles. We have certainly been given a description of

---

11. Ryken, *Ecclesiastes*, 203.

how the cake was made and how its various ingredients relate to each other, but suppose I now ask the assembled group of experts a final question: Why was the cake made? The grin on Aunt Matilda's face shows she knows the answer, for she made it for a purpose. But all the scientists in the world will not be able to answer the question—and it is no insult to their disciplines to state their incapacity to answer it. Their disciplines . . . cannot answer the "why" questions connected with the purpose for which the cake was made. In fact, the only way we shall ever get an answer is if Aunt Matilda reveals it to us. But if she does not disclose the answer to us, the plain fact is that no amount of scientific analysis will enlighten us.[12]

In the same way, we look out at our world and have scores of data on file. Yet, with all our gigabytes of information many of the "why" questions remained unanswered. God has revealed Himself, this much is true. He has told us enough about Himself, the universe, the afterlife and His plan for history to trust Him as good. Although our knowledge is not exhaustive, we have been given enough to make an informed decision that trusting God is the logical and best option. We can say with the hymn writer:

> God moves in a mysterious way
> His wonders to perform;
> He plants his footsteps in the sea,
> and rides upon the storm.
>
> Deep in unfathomable mines
> of never failing skill,
> He treasures up his bright designs
> and works his sovereign will.[13]

---

12. Lennox, *God's Undertaker*, 41.
13. William Cowper, "God Moves in a Mysterious Way," 1774.

14

Straight Talk about Life and Death (9:1–10)

I SAW A BUMPER sticker not long ago which really put life into perspective; it read, "Don't take life too seriously—no one gets out alive." After reading that you feel like you should go ahead and begin planning your funeral. So what do you want on your tombstone? In an attempt to soften the blow we have devised many euphemisms to refer to the grim inevitability of death, "kicking the bucket," "biting the dust," "pushing up daisies," "six feet under." Perhaps the most appropriate designation for death considering our study of Ecclesiastes is "philosophy's greatest problem." Indeed, even the wisest of the wise have been stumped by this one.

In a morbid read, contemporary philosopher, Simon Critchley, describes how one-hundred-ninety of history's most famous philosophers died. Here are some of the honorable mentions:

- Zeno, the founder of Stoicism, died by holding his breath.
- Gottfried Leibniz, discredited as an atheist, died alone and was buried at night with only one friend in attendance.
- Thomas Hobbes, who wrote that, "Life is nasty, brutish, and short," died peacefully in bed at ninety-one.
- George Berkley died while his wife read him a sermon.
- The atheist, Julien Offray de La Mettrie, died of indigestion caused by eating a huge amount of truffle pate.
- Denis Diderot ate an apricot, choked, and died.

Straight Talk about Life and Death (9:1–10)

- Jean-Jacques Rousseau died of cerebral bleeding, probably caused by a collision with a Great Dane.
- Georg Hegel died in a cholera epidemic. His last words were: "Only one man understood me and he didn't understand me" (presumably referring to himself).
- Roland Barthes was hit by a dry cleaning van.
- Jean-Paul Sartre seemed to have a change of heart: prior to his death, this long-time atheist said, "I do not feel that I am the product of chance . . . but a being whom only a Creator could put here." He died in 1980 after years of alcohol and drug abuse.
- Albert Camus once said that he couldn't imagine a death more meaningless than dying in a car accident. In 1960, at the age of forty-seven, Camus died in a car accident.
- A. J. Ayer, a resolute atheist, choked on a piece of salmon, and technically died. Later he said that this near-death experience provided "strong evidence that death does not end consciousness." His wife reported, "Freddie has got so much nicer since he died." Ayer died for good a year later.

Despite the variety of ways to die, Critchley used a quote from Epicurus to highlight the certainty of death: "Against all other things it is possible to obtain security, but when it comes to death we human beings live in an unwalled city."[1]

It has been said that death is the last thing we talk about. It's that familiar stranger who is always lurking in the background. Max Lucado said that death is, "The bully on the block of life. He catches you in the alley. He taunts you in the playground. He badgers you on the way home, 'You, too, will die someday.'"[2] Death is always waiting around the next corner, he never sleeps and he never takes any holidays. It was Malcolm Muggeridge who quipped, "I have one foot in heaven and one foot on earth, and the foot on earth is on a banana peel."

The story is told of three men who were all riding in the same car when they crashed and were instantly killed. Before they were going into the gates of heaven one of the angels asked, "What would you like for people to say at your funeral?" The first guy said, "I want to be remembered as a man who loved his family and his kids." The second guy said, "I want to say that I was

---

1. Critchley, *The Book of Dead Philosophers*.
2. Lucado, *Six Hours One Friday*, 100.

a man who took care of the poor and used his life to help others." The third guy piped up and said, "I hope that people would say, 'Look he's moving!'"

The Reality of Death—We Are All Living to Die (9:1-6)

Death has been a recurring theme throughout Ecclesiastes. Solomon has already commented on the brevity of life and certainty of death on a number of occasions (2:14-15, 3:19-20, 5:15-16, 8:8). By the time Solomon sits down to pen the words in chapter nine of his journal, he must have spent some time walking through a graveyard because he has the end of life on his mind. He's going to level with us about the one subject none of us is really comfortable with—death.

First, Solomon touches on *the unknowable future with death (9:1)*. "But all this I laid to heart, examining it all, how the righteous and the wise and their deeds are in the hand of God. Whether it is love or hate, man does not know; both are before him." The Preacher again acknowledged the sovereignty of God. He states that nothing befalls the children of God that doesn't first pass through the hands of God. Life and death, good and evil, love and hatred are all under the control of God. The terms "love" and "hate" refer respectively to divine favor or disfavor. Solomon's point is this: there are no guarantees as to what life will bring, except of course death and taxes.

Just like your birth, you have no control over your death. You don't know how you're going to die; moreover, you don't know when you're going to die. Even the righteous man cannot gain an advantage over the wicked with respect to their death day. James 4:13-14 reminds us not to make presumptions that we will be alive from one day to the next, "Come now, you who say, "Today or tomorrow we will go into such and such a town and spend a year there and trade and make a profit"—yet you do not know what tomorrow will bring. What is your life? For you are a mist that appears for a little time and then vanishes."

The story is told of a boy who went to church one Sunday and listened to the pastor's sermon. At some point during the message the pastor said, "From dust we were created and to dust we will one day return." When the boy heard this he was very confused and he asked his pastor after the service to explain. The little boy said, "Pastor, if this is true then you've got to come to my house and look under my bed, because someone is either coming or going."

Second, Solomon ponders *the unavoidable fact of death (9:2-3)*. "It is the same for all, since the same event happens to the righteous and the wicked, to the good and the evil, to the clean and the unclean, to him who sacrifices and him who does not sacrifice." One could summarize these verses to say, "Whether rich or poor, sinner or saint, prince or pauper, one day we are all going to take a dirt nap." There is a plot of ground somewhere on one of these hillsides that has been reserved for you. Solomon is simply saying that the same destiny overtakes us all. You and I can work out, take our vitamins, drive under the speed limit, swear off fast food, but even with the best of care this flesh isn't going to stave off the grave.

In the Middle East a fable is told of a merchant in Baghdad who sent his servant to run an errand in the bazaar. When the servant completed his assignment he was about to leave the marketplace, but he turned a corner and unexpectedly met Death face-to-face all robed in black. The servant was so frightened that he left the market and ran home. The servant told his master what had happened and requested his fastest horse so that he could get as far away from Death as possible. So he got on the stallion and rode all the way to Damascus before nightfall. Later that same afternoon, the merchant himself went back to the marketplace and there he met Death bedecked in black. When he saw Death he asked, "Why did you startle my servant this morning?" Death looked back and I said, "I didn't intend to scare your servant; it was I who was startled. You see, I was surprised to see your servant in Baghdad in this morning, because I have an appointment with him in Damascus tonight!"

The great irony is that we live in a world where people may acknowledge that death is inevitable, but we go to extraordinary lengths to have as little contact with death as possible. The dying are cloistered away in nursing homes and hospital wards. We let the funeral homes take care of preparing the corpses because we don't want to deal with the ghastly reality. The magazines we read promote the impossible feat of outrunning death by way of plastic surgery, Botox and yoga. If you could see what I see during funeral services you would notice that there are many who are just not comfortable with the prospect of death. It makes people edgy, nervous and weird. David Jeremiah has written:

> You play the board game Monopoly. You buy railroads and place hotels on Park Place and Boardwalk. You pass "Go" and collect two hundred dollars. Everyone has fun. Then the game ends, and all the hotels and all the colorful tokens and all the funny money go back into the box. Solomon, held an empire much less plastic, he would tell us that whether you build in plastic or gold it's all the same. Build a temple, extend a dynasty, even

write three God-inspired books—in the end it all goes back into the box.[3]

Third, the Preacher points to *the unchangeable finality of death (9:4–6)*. Solomon's final remarks about death seem strange to us because he uses an ancient Middle Eastern expression that is foreign to the 21st century, "A living dog is better than a dead lion." In Solomon's day, dogs were despised, lowly creatures, but the lion was the king of the jungle. Still a lion cannot roar if there is no air in his lungs, thus a barking dog is better. Simply put, he is saying that living is better than dying. As long as you are alive there is always the prospect that you can prepare for death because with life comes the chance to leave a good legacy. The living still have time to make plans for where they will spend eternity.

According to these verses when the spirit leaves the body, then our eternal fate is sealed. "For the living know that they will die, but the dead know nothing, and they have no more reward, for the memory of them is forgotten. Their love and their hate and their envy have already perished, and forever they have no more share in all that is done under the sun." There is no second chance, no purgatory, no reincarnation, no soul sleep and you most certainly do not become an angel with wings, a halo and a harp. Your body is going to be painted up like a circus clown, filled full of preservatives, shut up in a box and thrown into a six-foot hole to become food for worms.[4] Meanwhile your spirit will either be in one of two places and there is no going back to change things if you end up in place you don't like. This was the lesson behind the story Jesus told about the rich man and Lazarus (Luke 16:19–31). If Solomon were here he might say this: "Life is like a parachute jump—you'd better get it right the first time around." Nineteenth century Anglican bishop J.C. Ryle wrote:

> Death is a mighty leveler. He spares no one. He will not tarry till you are ready. He will not be kept out by moats and doors and bars and bolts. The Englishman boasts that his home is his castle, but with all his boasting, he cannot exclude death. An Austrian nobleman forbade death and the smallpox to be named in his presence. But, named or unnamed, it matters little; in God's appointed hour death will come."[5]

3. Jeremiah, *Searching for Heaven on Earth*, 227.
4. Keith Krell, "Living While You Live (Ecclesiastes 9:1–12)."
5. Ryle, "A Common End."

A lawyer was on his deathbed. He asked his wife to go bring him the Bible. She thought this was a strange request because as long as she had known him he had never read the Bible seriously. So she went and found the family Bible of the house, blew the dust off its cover and brought it to the dying man. A few moments she came back and said, "What are you doing?" He said, "Looking for loopholes!"

The only loophole out of death is to know the One who holds the keys to life and death—Jesus Christ (Rev. 1:18).

The Response to Death: We Should All Be Dying to Live (9:7-10)

Some of you country music fans may be surprised that Tim McGraw wasn't the first to come up with the lyrics to his hit song, "Live Like You Were Dying." Solomon beat him by about 3,000 years. The Preacher's advice to the living is that they live each day to the fullest. Instead of waiting to die he says, "Roll your sleeves up, get up, and do some living!"

The first imperative is to *enjoy your life while you can (9:7-8)*. "Go then, eat your bread in happiness and drink your wine with a cheerful heart; for God has already approved your works." In so many words, Solomon says, "Have a blast while you last!" Again, the Preacher says that our enjoyment should be tied to our relationship with God. A merry heart has God's approval. So after dinner get an extra scoop of ice cream, throw a barbecue for your family, drink some strong black coffee in the morning and when you go the theme park scream at the top of your lungs when the roller-coaster goes speeding down the track.

Believe it or not, God is not a cosmic killjoy. He wants us to have sanctified, redeemed fun. It is not a sin to enjoy life. God made good food and drink and fellowship for our pleasure. Listen to what Paul says in 1 Cor. 10:31, "So whether you eat or drink or whatever you do, do it all for the glory of God."

In 9:8 Solomon gives a similar piece of advice, but in a different way, "Let your clothes be white all the time, and let not oil be lacking on your head." In the Old Testament, births, weddings, and harvest festivals were special occasions that required one to dress up. In the ancient world, black clothes and ashes on the head were a sign of mourning. Conversely, white clothes and oil on the head was a sign of rejoicing. Oil on your head was the ancient equivalent of perfume or cologne.

The Preacher is simply implying that we get dressed every day as if we were on the way to a celebration. One commentator said, "The Preacher is telling us to put on tuxedos and evening gowns so we can dance the night away."[6] This isn't a license to become a hedonist or a party animal because he says wear white garments. In other words, stay holy and pure before God, but have a good time while you serve Him.

The next imperative is to *enjoy your love while you can (9:9)*. "Enjoy life with the wife whom you love, all the days of your vain life that he has given you under the sun, because that is your portion in life and in your toil at which you toil under the sun." Solomon wasn't exactly the kind of guy to be giving marriage advice; after all he was the Hugh Hefner of his day. Apparently he learned the hard way that love, not lust, can only be experienced within the confines of marriage where sexual fulfillment is undefiled. Life is way too short to let the most intimate relationship God designed between two people be turned into drudgery. Proverbs 18:22 says, "He who finds a wife finds a good thing and obtains favor from the Lord."

When you're in love it doesn't matter where you are or what you are doing just as long as you are with the other person that's all that matters. So look for every excuse to go out on dates and weekend getaways. Men don't stop dating your wives. Pursue her heart every day. Find her love language and start filling up her love tank. As Max Lucado has said, "A woman's heart should be so hidden in God that a man has to seek Him just to find her."

This reminds me of the story I heard about an elderly couple who went into MacDonald's. They ordered one meal, sat down and started splitting everything up equally. They poured half of the coke into another cup, cut the Big Mac in half and divided up the fries. The husband started eating, but the wife just sat there calmly with her hands folded watching him eat. A young man sitting across from them noticed this and felt sorry for them. Thinking they were really poor the young man offered to pay for another meal. He walked over them and asked, "How long have you've been married?" "fifty years" they replied. He asked, "What is the secret of your marriage?" The husband said, "We have always tried to put the other person first and split everything down the line. We share everything fifty-fifty." The young man looked at the elderly lady and said, "Well, he's eating, why aren't you eating?" She said, "It's his turn to use the teeth."

Finally, we should make a point to *enjoy your labor while you can (9:10)*. Solomon wants us to know that we have only one life to make our contribution, ". . . for there is no activity or planning or knowledge or wisdom in Sheol where you are going." The Hebrew word *Sheol* refers to the abode of the dead. Solomon is saying, "When death overtakes us, our opportunities

---

6. Ryken, *Ecclesiastes*, 214.

to make ripples in eternity and leave a legacy will have come to a screeching halt."

Sadly, there are countless numbers of Americans out there who hate what they do for a living. The reason is because they are working at a job, not their passion. John Maxwell has some great career advice, "Find your passion and wrap your career around it." What has God gifted you to do—work with your hands, play beautiful music, care for the sick, build bridges? God put those desires and gifts in you for a reason, to glorify Him. As believers we should be the best at our jobs and put everything we've got into everything we do. That's much easier to do when you realize that God is your employer. The New Testament equivalent of this verse is Colossians 3:17, "Whatever you do in word or deed, do it all the in the name of the Lord Jesus, giving thanks through Him to God the Father."

An employer once asked a janitor why he took such pride in keeping his floors clean, he said, "Because the floors I clean are God's floors. I'm glad God put a mop and bucket in my hand instead of a pink slip."

One of the great heroes of the faith that was the personification of Ecclesiastes 9:10 was Matthew Henry, the famous preacher who left us with his voluminous commentary on the Bible. Spurgeon recommended that every minister of the Gospel read through the *Matthew Henry's Commentary* at least once during his lifetime. George Whitfield carried his set of Matthew Henry on all of his travels and read it from his knees. Born in 1662 Matthew Henry was physically weak but it was not long before his strength of intellect and character made him known. At the age of three, he was reading the Bible; by the time he was nine, he was competent in Latin and Greek. It is said that Matthew Henry was usually in his study before five o'clock each morning, devoting himself to preparation and exposition of the Word. He had breakfast with his family and always led them in worship, reading and expounding some passage from the Old Testament.

He returned to his study until afternoon, when he would set out to visit his people. Often in the late evening, he would put in a few hours of study before retiring. "Take heed of growing remiss in you work" he warned fellow pastors. "Take pains while you live . . . the Scripture still affords new things to those who search them." It was not unusual for him to preach seven times a week and he was always fresh and practical.

The key date in Matthew Henry's life is November 12, 1704; on this day he started writing his famous commentary. On April 17, 1714, he completed his comments on the book of Acts; but two months later on June 22, he suddenly took ill and died. Afterward, several of his pastor friends gathered up his notes and sermons and completed the *Commentary* from Romans to Revelation. When he was on his death bed, Matthew Henry said to a friend,

"You have been asked to take notice of the sayings of dying men—this is mine: that a life spent in the service of God and communion with Him is the most pleasant life that anyone can live in this world."[7]

---

7. Wiersbe, *50 People Every Christian Should Know*, 24–29.

15

Reckoning with Murphy's Law (9:11–18)

IMAGINE THAT YOU'RE SITTING in four lanes of bumper-to-bumper traffic. You're more than ready to get home, but you notice to your great dismay, that all of the other lanes seem to be moving. So you change lanes. But once you do, the cars in your new lane come to a dead halt. At a standstill, you notice every lane on the highway (including the one you just left) is moving except yours. What gives?

Welcome to the aggravation of living in a world under the influence of Murphy's Law. This common phrase says that whatever can go wrong will go wrong. When life goes well, little is made of it. After all, we expect that things should work out in our favor. But when things go badly, we look for reasons. Thus, Murphy's Law taps into our tendency to dwell on the negative and overlook the positive.[1]

You can see the effects of Murphy's Law all around us. In fact, you don't have to be a scientist to discern it; all you must do is look for the path of destruction left behind by its operation. For example, there is the curious case of Donald Peters, who bought two Connecticut lottery tickets on November 1, 2008—just as he had for the previous twenty years. As it turned out, one of his tickets was worth $10 million. But Peters was not as lucky as one might think, because he died of a heart attack later on the very day that he bought the winning lottery ticket.[2]

Murphy's Law has also thrown a monkey wrench in the space program on multiple occasions. It seems that no matter how well thought-out or cleverly engineered something may be, a system will fail because of a simple

---

1. Clark, "How Murphy's Law Works."
2. Ryken, *Ecclesiastes*, 222.

oversight. On April 24, 1990 NASA launched one of the most expensive camera's ever built to orbit around our planet. The Hubble Space telescope was the culmination of years of research, engineering and taxpayer dollars, coming in at a whopping $2.5 billion. Every ninety-seven minutes, Hubble was to complete a spin around Earth, moving at the speed of about five miles per second—fast enough to travel across the United States in about ten minutes. As it traveled, Hubble's instruments were supposed to capture unbelievable images from galaxies far, far away.

However, almost immediately after Hubble went into orbit, it became clear that something was wrong. While the pictures were clearer than those of ground-based telescopes, they weren't the pristine images promised. They were blurry. After months of investigation engineers finally located the problem. Hubble's primary mirror, polished so carefully and lovingly over the course of a full year, had a flaw called a "spherical aberration." The lens was just slightly the wrong shape. The tiny flaw—about 1/50th the thickness of a sheet of paper—was enough to distort the view. Finally by 1993 NASA astronauts fixed the problem after a painstaking five day spacewalk mission.

You might even say that Murphy's Law has changed the course of history. Look no further than the example of Thomas J. Jackson, a.k.a. "Stonewall Jackson." Many armchair historians have thought that Jackson's presence at Gettysburg would have undoubtedly tilted the outcome of battle in the direction of the South. But, Jackson never made it to Gettysburg thanks to what happened at the Battle of Chancellorsville in 1863.

During the battle, Jackson deftly moved around the battlefield to launch a surprise attack on the Union flank. Jackson and his 28,000 troops charged into Union soldiers who were leisurely playing cards. When Jackson and his staff tried to return to their own lines, they were met by a nervous Confederate sentry. Jackson could scarcely answer the sentry's call of, "Who goes there?" before he and his party were hit by a volley from Confederate rifles. One of the South's greatest leaders was shot by fellow rebels mistakenly convinced he was leading Union cavalry. General Robert E. Lee would go on to say that the death of Jackson was like "losing my right arm."

Life is notoriously unpredictable. Forrest Gump was no theologian, but he was right when he said, "Life is like a box of chocolates, you never know what you're going to get." Solomon knew this truth all too well. Life is messy, unfair, complicated and downright frustrating at times. Let's face it—we've all thought a time or two that the whole cosmic order was rigged so that we always get the short end of the stick.

One thing we can appreciate about Solomon is that he is brutally honest. He straddles a thin line of pessimism and realism so that many readers find his journal a bit unnerving. In the last verses of chapter nine Solomon launches into a meditation dealing with the uncertainty of life. "Time and chance," he would say, "happen to them all." The story book ending that we yearn for is often thwarted by unforeseen circumstances and unintended consequences. Plans can be altered by calamity. Good intentions often become the paving stones on the road to tragedy. Even though fail-safes are implemented, one wag has said, "Even if you make something idiot-proof, the world will create a better idiot."

What our culture popularly calls "Murphy's Law" Solomon called "time and chance." Actually, both of these terms are labels for a deeper theological truth—namely, that we live a fallen world (Rom. 8:20-22). In the following passage Solomon points out four facts we should come to expect in world which spins slightly left of center.

Fact 1: Failure Is Inevitable (9:11)

Just in case we are overly confident in our strengths, Solomon reminds us that human ability does not always equal success. "Again I saw that under the sun the race is not to the swift, nor the battle to the strong, nor bread to the wise, nor riches to the intelligent, nor favor to those with knowledge, but time and chance happen to them all." The fastest runners are not always the first ones to cross the finish line. The brave are often the ones who fall in battle. The intelligent are not always the ones with doctorate degrees. Sometimes the tortoise beats the hare. Sometimes giants fall to ruddy shepherds. Good things do not necessarily happen to good people. Turns out the best lessons God teaches are the ones gained through failure.

Solomon's simple point is this—if you put your stock in human ability then you will consistently be disappointed. The best man is still a man at best. Notice at the end of 9:11 he makes a reference to "time and chance." If one doesn't get us the other will. Don't misinterpret what the Preacher is saying, he's not being fatalistic when he uses these terms. First, time limits us. This is an echo of the teaching throughout Ecclesiastes that the seasons of our life are in the hand of God (3:1). Second, chance is the unexpected event which may throw the most accomplished off course despite carefully devised schemes.

However, it's important to keep failure in perspective. Often times, what you and I would call failures by unexplainable circumstances are God's appointed messengers of instruction. Failure is inevitable, but the question is whether we will fail forwards or fail backwards? Will we let failure crush our spirits or fuel us to keep going?

A famous Nike commercial from the 1990s featured shots of Michael Jordan and dub over of his voice, "I've missed more than 9000 shots in my career. I've lost almost 300 games. 26 times, I've been trusted to take the game winning shot and missed. I've failed over and over and over again in my life. And that is why I succeed."

In his book, *Failing Forward*, John Maxwell illustrated the paradigm of failure and success when he wrote about the renowned composer Handel:

> Despite George Fredrick Handel's talent and fame, he faced considerable adversity . . . several times he found himself penniless and on the verge of bankruptcy . . . Then his problems were compounded by failing health. He suffered a seizure or a stroke which left his right arm limp and caused him to lose the use of four fingers on his right hand . . . In 1741 Handel decided it was time to retire even though he was only fifty-six. He was discouraged, miserable and consumed with debt. But in August of 1741, some incredible happened. A wealthy friend named Charles Jennings gave him a libretto based on the life of Christ. The work intrigued Handel . . . He began writing and immediately the floodgates of inspiration opened up to him. His cycle of inactivity was broken. For twenty-one days he wrote almost nonstop. Then he spent another two days creating the orchestrations. In twenty-four days, he had completed the 260-page manuscript. He called the piece *Messiah* . . . Sir Newman Flower, one of Handel's biographers, said of the writing of *Messiah*, "Considering the immensity of the work and the short time involved, it will remain, perhaps, forever the greatest feat in the whole history of music composition."[3]

Failure should be our teacher, not our undertaker. If used properly, failure is merely a delay on the way to success not a final defeat. It is a temporary detour, not a dead-end street. Solomon warns that under the sun we should expect the elements of "time" and "chance" to come into play as tests of our character and faith.

Fact 2: Fiascos Are the Effects of a Fallen World (9:12)

A man thinks he is the captain of his own ship until the truth of Ecclesiastes 9:12 slaps him in the face, "Moreover, man does not know his time: like fish caught in a treacherous net and birds trapped in a snare, so the sons of men are ensnared at an evil time when it suddenly falls on them."

---

3. Maxwell, *Failing Forward*, 43–44.

Reckoning with Murphy's Law (9:11–18)

Instead of being the master of our destiny, we are more like creatures caught in a snare. Calamity and death are closer than we think. The sky is the limit until we are blindsided by a speeding delivery truck hurrying across town to make the next stop. We think, "That will never happen to me," then low-and-behold we discover that our house is built on an fault line. The earth shifts a quarter inch and everything we've worked for is lost. Cancer is the farthest thing from our mind, until a routine physical reveals a few malignant spots. Reluctantly, we must trade our two-week vacation to the Bahamas for six-weeks of radiation treatment. One commentator writes:

> In a sense, this verse [9:12] is a microcosm of the whole book of Ecclesiastes. So much of life is enigmatic and fails to conform to the rules we have learned. We've been taught that if you want to succeed you have to compete and be aggressive, get up earlier, go to bed later, put in more hours, do unto them before they do unto you. But, says Solomon, it doesn't always work that way. Nothing is guaranteed. This is how life is, but we shouldn't despair nor should we quit aiming to be swift, strong, wise, brilliant and learned. We should, however, quit thinking that life owes us anything, or for that matter, that God owes us anything under the sun.[4]

Job knew a lot about this. He was righteous and upright, but God allowed Satan to take everything he had and left him sitting on an ash heap scraping painful boils with a potshard. God gave Joseph dreams and visions. But before those dreams became reality he was sold into slavery by his brothers, wrongfully accused of a crime he didn't commit and thrown into jail for two years. Ruth saw her first husband die in a famine before she met her Prince Charming, Boaz. Paul was stoned and left for dead, snake bit and shipwrecked. Remember what Jesus said before he was executed? "In this life you shall face tribulation . . ." (John 16:33).

Reading this verse made me think of the lyrics to a Dave Matthew's Band song entitled, "Funny the Way It Is." The songwriter expresses with candor the absurdity of life and the ironies that contradict our expectations. A snippet of the lyrics read:

> Lying in the park on a beautiful day
> Sunshine in the grass and the children play
> Sirens pass in fire engine red
> Someone's house is burning down on a day like this
>
> The evening comes and we're hanging out

---

4. Krell, "Living While You Live (Ecclesiastes. 9:1–12)."

> On the front step and a car goes by with the windows rolled down
> And that War song is playing
> "Why can't we be friends?"
> Someone is screaming and crying in the apartment upstairs
>
> Funny the way it is
> If you think about it
> Somebody's going hungry and someone else is eating out
> Funny the way it is
> Not right or wrong
> Somebody's heart is broken and it becomes your favorite song
>
> The way your mouth feels in your lover's kiss
> Like a pretty bird on the breeze or water to a fish
> A bomb blast brings the building crashing to the floor
> Hear the laughter while the children play war
>
> Funny the way it is
> If you think about it
> One kid walks ten miles to school, another's dropping out
> Funny the way it is
> Not right or wrong
> On a soldier's last breath, his baby's being born[5]

Life is a constant lesson in getting used to what you never expected. Despite our attempts to control our environment, we must come to terms with the fact that we are in control of very little.

However, we must keep a balanced approach. There are those rare people who, by the grace of God, are not crippled by life's cruel circumstances. It was 1818 in France, and Louis, a boy of 9, was sitting in his father's workshop. The father was a harness-maker and the boy loved to watch his father work the leather. "Someday Father," said Louis, "I want to be a harness-maker, just like you." "Why not start now?" said the father. He took a piece of leather and drew a design on it. "Now, my son," he said, "take the hole-puncher and a hammer and follow this design, but be careful that you don't hit your hand." Excited, the boy began to work, but when he hit the hole-puncher it flew out of his hand and pierced his eye! He lost the sight of that eye immediately. Later, sight in the other eye failed. Louis was now totally blind. A few years later, Louis was sitting in the family garden when a friend handed him a pine cone. As he ran his sensitive fingers over the

---

5. Dave Matthews, "Funny the Way It Is," 2009.

cone, an idea came to him. He became enthusiastic and began to create an alphabet of raised dots on paper so that the blind could feel and interpret what was written. Thus, Louis Braille opened up a whole new world for the blind—all because of an accident.[6]

What makes the difference is if God is included in your worldview or not. For the man or woman "under the sun" with just a horizontal viewpoint then calamity is part of living on a cold, uncaring planet that is careening through space. However, with God the bad can be turned into good through His providence (Rom. 8:28).

E. Stanley Jones wrote, "Thank God for the unknown future. If we saw all the good things which are coming to us, we would sit down and degenerate. If we saw all the evil things, we would be paralyzed. How merciful God is to lift the curtain only on today; and as we get strength today to meet tomorrow, then to lift the curtain on the morrow. He is a considerate God." Have you ever praised God for what you didn't know? Thankfully, all we have to contend with is today.

Fact 3: Wisdom Fortifies against Folly (9:13-15)

Archimedes was born in the city of Syracuse on the island of Sicily in 287 BC. He was the son of an astronomer and mathematician named Phidias. Not only was the wise man known for his advances in math, but according to legend he also coined the phrase, "Eureka!" When Rome invaded Syracuse in 214 BC under General Marcellus, Archimedes was 72 years old. It would be his mechanical genius and wisdom that would preserve the city. Archimedes used his scientific mind to invent weapons that would defend his hometown against the Roman invasion.

The Roman historian Polybius relates that Archimedes made extensive preparations to repulse the enemy navy. He used his knowledge of levers to design catapults larger and more deadly than any built before. These tremendous catapults could hurl immense stones at the ships and sink them with a single blow. Ancient writers also claim that Archimedes carved huge mirrors and set up them on the walls of the city. As the Roman ships approached, the mirrors were positioned to reflect and focus the sun's rays directly onto the sails causing them to burst into flames.

However, Archimedes' most frightening weapons of all were probably the huge claw-shaped beams that jutted out from the city's walls. These "claws" were supported by counterweights on the interior side of the walls which allowed them to pick up the ships and drop them onto the cliffs and

---

6. "Louis Braille," *Bits and Pieces*, June 1990, p. 23-24.

rocks near shore. For three years Archimedes put up a fight and as a result many Romans began to think there was a supernatural force behind the walls of Syracuse. But, it wasn't the power of Mars aiding the people of Syracuse, just one wise man.

Apparently, the exploits of Archimedes were not just the stuff of legend, but Solomon had also witnessed something similar in his days. In his recollection, he tells of a wise man who outsmarts an invading force by wisdom. The city was sure to be overwhelmed by the superior forces of besieging army, but the wise man comes up with a brilliant strategy for victory. However, when the enemy is sent home with his tail tucked between his legs and the ticker tape parade is over the wise man who saved the city is forgotten. The statue they erected in the wise man's honor has crumbled and is covered in bird droppings. His name is lost with the passing of time and now it's like he never existed.

The meaning of the story is manifold. First, we see the advantage of wisdom. One wise man preserved his countrymen through the use of wisdom rather than brute force. Thus, wisdom should be sought after before strength. Proverbs 24:5 says, "A wise man is full of strength, and a man of knowledge enhances his might." Remember the example of Samson? Even though he was physically strong, he was morally and spiritually weak. Because of his lack of wisdom and discernment, the strong man was seduced by Delilah. The enemies of Israel plucked out Samson's eyes, bound him in fetters and made him grind meal like a beast of burden. There is strength in wisdom because it acts like high walls and a defensive mote against folly and ruin.

The second lesson we learn is that even the famous are forgotten. How many godly, wise people do you know whose names will never appear on the evening news for their charitable or courageous acts? I can think of scores of saints who will never see the recognition they deserve while under the sun. The real heroes usually aren't the ones in the public eye soaking up the limelight. They don't have million dollar shoe deals and they aren't promoting themselves on infomercials. The real heroes are the ones who live quiet lives of hard-work, holiness and dedication to the Lord.

In the annals of world history, you won't find many mentions of a lady named Pearl Goode. She never ran for political office, never commanded troops, and never served as the CEO of a Fortune 500 company. Pearl Goode was a widowed nurse in her mid-60s, living in Pasadena, California, in 1949 when a young evangelist came to hold tent meetings in Los Angeles at the corner of Washington and Hill streets. The very first night of the Crusade, she watched the fiery preacher Billy Graham and his team share the Gospel.

As Pearl later recounted in an interview, "That night God laid those boys on my heart as a burden."

Pearl then joined the volunteer prayer team for the greater Los Angeles Crusade and was a part of seeing the campaign extended from three weeks to eight weeks, with people cramming into the tent every night to hear the Good News. After that early Crusade, Pearl became a prayer warrior for the Crusades, without anybody on Graham's team even knowing. She would spend her own money to travel by Greyhound bus to wherever they were holding an event, quietly check herself into a motel near the venue, and immediately begin praying. Pearl estimated that she covered 48,000 miles by bus, simply to pray for the Crusades.

Even later in life when Pearl could no longer travel, or when Billy was preaching overseas, she would make it a point to know exactly when he would be preaching, and she would spend those exact hours in prayer. Ms. Goode lived to be ninety and at her funeral in 1994, Billy's wife, Ruth Graham, paid her this tribute: "Here lie the mortal remains of much of the secret of Bill's ministry."[7]

Pearle Goode wasn't a preacher, missionary, or author. She didn't have a hit song on Christian radio, but she did her part just as surely as Billy Graham did his. She was not famous on Earth, but something tells me that when the awards are given out in heaven she will be receiving a crown or two. Expect the nameless of Earth to be famous in heaven.

Fact 4: A Little Foolishness is Far-Reaching (9:16–18)

Solomon continues pulling applications from his story of the wise man, "But I say that wisdom is better than might, though the poor man's wisdom is despised and his words are not heard. The words of the wise heard in quiet are better than the shouting of a ruler among fools. Wisdom is better than weapons of war, but one sinner destroys much good."

Wisdom is the key to skillful living, yet it is not sought after and certainly not valued in our world. What was it that saved the little city under attack? It was not military might but wisdom. It may not bring accolades and popularity, but wisdom tends to win the day. Solomon is reinforcing a point he has already touched on earlier—wisdom is superior to strength (7:19). The world glorifies strength, but it is short-lived. Strength diminishes as we advance in years, but wisdom is like compounding interest; it only gets more valuable with time.

---

7. Graham, "The Power of Prayer," *Notes from the Cove*, 14 June 2011.

I think Solomon's final take-away point is that real insight for living is not found where you would normally expect. Wisdom is not behind the glossy covers of the *New York Times* best-selling self-help books. Wisdom is not found in the glitz and glamour of Hollywood. The people who really are skillful at living aren't the people constantly flapping their gums on the morning talk shows. In the event that you do find a person with godly wisdom, squeeze all you can out of them like a sponge. Mine them for every available nugget and praise God that he sent them to speak truth into your life.

Unfortunately, godly wisdom is seldom heeded. The wisdom of God is usually drowned out by the shouting of fools. Often, godly wisdom and counsel falls upon deaf ears, or at best, goes in one ear and out the other. Why is this so? Because the voice of God is not loud or flashy and most of the time God's perspective on life is counter-intuitive to everything we have heard before. Take up a cross, delay gratification for the next life, invest in eternity, trust in what you cannot see—this is not conventional wisdom. Remember what Paul said in 1 Cor. 1:27, "God chose what is foolish in the world to shame the wise and the; God chose what is weak in the world to shame the strong."

Fredrick Nietzsche, the famous atheistic philosopher from Germany who coined the phrase, "God is dead," wrote this about Christianity:

> Look at whom they worship. Look at this God whom they worship. How foolish and imbecilic to follow one who died, and then to claim that that death is victory! There is foolishness and there is foolishness. There is madness and there is madness, but to call death victory is the ultimate madness of all. This is a pathetic deity and he is followed by a pathetic people.[8]

Ironically, those words came from a man who was the son of a Lutheran minister. In 1900 Nietzsche died at the age of fifty-six. The last ten years of his life were spent in seclusion. Nietzsche had lost his mind and slipped into dementia. Yet, his writings influenced others, particularly one despondent youth who picked up his works and was profoundly impacted. His name? Adolf Hitler. In fact, Hitler often visited the Nietzsche museum in Weimar and published his veneration for the philosopher by posing for photographs of himself staring in rapture at the bust of the philosopher. Hitler appropriated Nietzsche's ideas and made them his own. It may not have been Nietzsche's intent to have his themes taken out of context, but few thinkers have the luxury of controlling what others do with their work. Hitler lived out what Nietzsche had envisioned, trying to prove himself to

---

8. Mohler, "The Foolishness of the Cross, Part III," 28 April 2006.

be the *Übermensch* and the precursor of "the master race." The result was a world war and the death of millions.

That's the truth of 9:18, "*Wisdom is better than weapons of warfare, but one sinner destroys much good.*" This last phrase is like our "one rotten apple ruins the whole barrel" or "one bad egg spoils the omelet." Throughout the Bible, there is an abiding principle: "A little leaven leavens the whole lump of dough" (1 Cor. 5:6). All it takes is a little foolishness to counteract the goodness of wisdom and if someone wants to be a fool the Devil will be there to help them.

What does Solomon mean in all of this? Life is full of failures, fiascos and fools. What you and I need to navigate through this twisted, cruel world is God's never-changing wisdom. Where do we find wisdom? Colossians 2:3 says it all, "In Christ are hidden all the treasures of wisdom and knowledge."

16

How to Spot a Fool (10:1–20)

A COLLEGE BUDDY OF mine proudly wore a t-shirt with the bold words printed across it, "You can't fix stupid." We laugh because we know it's true. Fools are a dime-a-dozen and after watching a few minutes of the evening news it's amazing that the human race has lasted as long as it has. I always get a good chuckle out of the short segments featuring the exploits of dumb criminals.

Radio personality, Paul Harvey, once told the story about a common thief who robbed a convenient store. But he didn't get very far because as the robber took off into the dark the police were able to track his every move. How? It wasn't because of a sophisticated GPS system. The criminal was wearing shoes with lights in the soles that blinked with every footfall. Every stride dropped an incandescent breadcrumb directly to his location.

Did you hear about the burglar in London who was arrested after using a manhole cover to break the plate-glass window of a store? To avoid the shattering glass, he stepped back away from the window, and fell into the open manhole.

Remember how your mom told you never to run with sharp objects? A man was running from a western Michigan store with stolen hunting knives hidden in his pants. As the shoplifter was in a frenzy to leave the store he tripped and fell. The $300 collection of knives in his waistband stabbed him in the stomach. After emergency surgery to save his impaled organs, the dim-witted derelict was taken down to the jailhouse.

In 2005 a duo of robbers held up an elderly couple on the streets of Bloemfontein, South Africa. The police heard the distress calls and began to give pursuit. One of the muggers jumped over a fence to hide from the perusing cops. What the man didn't realize was that he hopped the fence of the Bloemfontein Zoo and directly into the cage of Bengal tiger. The angry beast mauled the man to death.[1]

Perhaps one of my favorites was the recent story about a pair of thieves who tried to hold up a Stockton, California Burger King. As the two "hamburglars" stormed the restaurant brandishing guns and demanding cash, an employee sneaked out a back door. The quick-thinking cook found the thieves' idling getaway vehicle in the parking lot, hopped in and drove off, stashing the car around the block. When the thieves realized their car had been taken, they took off on foot and hid in a nearby field. The police soon found the two suspects and arrested them.[2]

In case you think that the world is getting dumber, take heart because fools have always been around. Solomon found himself constantly surrounded by foolish people. According to the Preacher the foolish came in all shapes and sizes. Not only were they committing petty crimes, but they were also the ones in the highest places of leadership. Fools are everywhere from the White House to the jail house.

Today if you turn on the TV and listen for a moment at where the world is going, it seems like the idiots are winning. Human knowledge may be doubling every year, but what ever happened to good ole' fashioned common sense? I think Solomon felt the same way, because in chapter ten the major theme is the antithesis of wisdom—folly. In fact he uses the word "fool" nine times in this passage alone.

Ecclesiastes chapter ten is like a lost chapter from Proverbs. This part of the journal is not a carefully constructed argument; rather it includes a variety of short stories, case studies, maxims, pithy sayings and exhortations. In this section Solomon warns us to say away from folly like the plague. Consider this Solomon's guide on how to spot a fool.

A Fool and His Character (10:1–3)

The Preacher has told us many things about the character of a fool already: he is lazy (4:5), ill-tempered (7:9), morally blind (2:14), refuses to heed sound counsel (9:17) and overall his life is not pleasing to God (5:4). When the Bible uses the term "fool," it is not necessarily referring to someone with

---

1. "Zoo Tiger Kills SA Crime Suspect," *BBC News*, 21 December 2005.
2. "Burger King Employee Foils Robbery by Stealing Thieves' Getaway Car," *ABC News*, 28 May 2013.

a low IQ; instead it points to a person who doesn't have a proper fear of God and is prone to go the wrong direction in life.[3]

Solomon begins by alerting us to the dangers a little foolishness can do. You may have heard the expression, "a fly in the ointment." This is where that saying originated. "Dead flies make a perfumer's oil stink, so a little foolishness is weightier than wisdom and honor." Notice, this proverb is connected to the previous statement in 9:18 that "one sinner destroys much good." The point being made is that it takes far less effort to ruin something than it does to create it. A pinch of folly sabotages a pound of wise living. The perfume metaphor is Solomon's vivid way of illustrating how a tiny bit of foolishness can destroy the integrity and reputation of a wise person. The KJV colorfully translates this verse, "Dead flies cause the ointment of the apothecary to send forth a stinking savour . . ."

What Solomon is trying to get across is that the pathway to foolish living begins with the little things of life. All it takes is a little compromise of character here, or a little sin there, or a careless move when no one is looking and you have begun to create to create a stink in your life. Solomon would also write in the Song of Solomon about, "little foxes that spoil the vines (Song 2:15)."

In September 2011 a giant came tumbling down. Along the Sierra Nevada's famed "Trail of 100 Giants," a mammoth sequoia had stood sentry since The Middle Ages. It witnessed the arrival of the first European settlers and the flurry of miners in search of gold. It stood, unperturbed, through the Civil War, the invention of the automobile and the onset of the digital age. Unexpectedly, the giant Sequoya shook the earth when its massive trunk slammed into the forest floor. The 1,500 year old tree, measuring over a football field in length, left a gaping crater in the soil from its overturned root ball. Amazingly a tourist caught the destruction on video as it happened. Turns out if a tree falls in the forest it makes a tremendous ruckus. What makes this hardwood's death even more eerie was that the Forest Service wasn't sure what caused the timber to topple. Was it extensive termite damage, or perhaps a weakened root structure that couldn't support the burgeoning trunk? Only God knows for sure.[4]

We must not tolerate the little evils that eat away at the roots of our lives. Many Christians appear to stand tall for God. They may resist temptations and weather storms. But little sins can begin to eat away at their lives and gradually erode their character. This is the danger of just a little folly. I

---

3. Ryken, *Ecclesiastes*, 232.

4. Boxall, "Giant Sequoia Falls, Raising Questions about What to Do Next," *Los Angeles Times*, 29 October 2011.

believe Solomon's simple point is that no one wakes up in the morning and decides, "Today I am going to be a fool." Rather, the lifestyle of a fool just like that of a wise person is cultivated in the small, everyday choices of life.

Fools also corrupt their character by consistently choosing poorly. The Preacher adds in 10:2, "A wise man's heart inclines him to the right, but a fool's heart to the left." No offense to you lefties out there, but in ancient times the right hand was considered the place of power and privilege. The left hand was considered the hand of weakness. The fool's heart and hand are turned away from godliness. Keep in mind that the heart in this context is not referring to the organ which pumps blood but to the center of a person's moral life. Since a foolish person lacks godly wisdom they naturally gravitate toward what is wrong.

Therefore a foolish person consistently goes against the counsel of God's Word. They choose their own way rather than God's way. The obvious outcome of this lifestyle is found in 10:3, "Even when the fool walks on the road, he lacks sense, and he says to everyone that he is a fool." The "road" is not a literal highway but the fool's metaphorical way of life. Solomon says in effect, "You can spot a fool a mile away because he's headed down the pathway of destruction."

The Preacher has said something similar in another proverb, "There is a way that seems right to man, but the end is the way of death" (Pro. 14:12). The fool seems to be the only person who doesn't know he's a fool as he whistles down the broad way (Matt. 7:13–14). Dan Allender says it well, "The fool will follow a path that seems to be right, even when the blacktop gives way to gravel and gravel to dirt and dirt to rocks and debris. Almost nothing will stop the fool from plunging ahead into peril."[5]

A Fool and His Conduct (10:4–10, 16–19)

In addition to telling us how to avoid folly, the Preacher also helps us know how to respond to the folly we see in the lives of others. Solomon moves on in his portrait of a fool to discuss the various kinds of behavior that is exhibited by those bereft of wisdom. He notes four specific qualities that the foolish person has missing in their life.

First, *a fool lacks composure* (10:4). "If the anger of the ruler rises against you, do not leave your place, for calmness will lay great offenses to rest." The basic point of this verse is that a wise person doesn't let another person's action determine their reaction. Cooler heads will always prevail.

---

5. Allender and Longman III, *Bold Love*, 263.

When someone loses their temper with you, whether warranted or not, the worst thing you can do is return anger with more anger.

In 2012 a New Zealand volcano that lay dormant for more than a century erupted without warning sending up ash clouds 20,000 feet into the atmosphere, disrupting flights and closing roads. Mount Tongariro, which hadn't been heard from since 1897, gave one volcanic belch and proved that it wasn't dead. Vehicles, homes and roads for miles around were caked in the thick grey soot, reminiscent of ancient Vesuvius. Ironically, it was this same mountain which filmmakers used as the backdrop for Mt. Doom in shooting *The Lord of the Rings* trilogy.[6]

That's a fitting picture of anger, wouldn't you say? Anger can be dormant but still destructive. Interior calderas of varying sizes can erupt when one least expects it—when someone cuts you off during rush hour traffic, when a heated conversation turns to rancor, when someone denies us something we believe we deserve. In such moments we find ourselves trembling with subterranean emotion. Solomon reminds us that a fool gives into his anger and blows a gasket while a wise person administers control over their emotions. A wise man steps away from a heated situation, accesses it methodically, and carefully chooses his words. Proverbs 25:28 adds, "Whoever has no rule over his spirit is like a city broken down, without walls." In other words, those not in control of their emotions are like a village ripe for pillaging by the enemy. Remember that anger, at some point, becomes a choice. It's hard to let go, but nursed anger leads to volcanic-like eruptions that destroy lives and leave us regretting that blow-up.

When Dwight D. Eisenhower was ten years old, his parents let his two older brothers go trick-or-treating one Halloween but told Ike he was too young to accompany them. Having eagerly anticipated a night of fun and freedom, young Dwight was crushed. He argued his case for why he should be allowed to go out, begging and pleading with his parents to change their minds until his brothers at last headed off into the night without him. Completely beside himself with rage, Ike went into the yard and starting pounding away at the trunk of an apple tree, pummeling the bark until his fists bled. His father finally pulled the boy away, gave him a few swats with a hickory stick, and sent him off to bed. Ike sobbed into his pillow, feeling like the whole world was against him.

After an hour, Eisenhower's mother came into his room and sat down in the rocking chair beside his bed. She rocked silently for a while, and then began to talk to young Dwight. She told him she was concerned about his anger and that of all her boys he had the most to learn about getting his

---

6. Andres Jauregui, "Mount Tongariro Erupts," *Huffington Post*, 21 November 2012.

temper under control. Mrs. Eisenhower quoted from Proverbs 16:32, "He that conquereth his own soul is greater than he who taketh a city." She explained to her son that there was little to be gained by harboring anger.

Eisenhower considered that conversation one of the most valuable moments in his life and it led to his developing a curious habit as an adult. Whenever someone angered him, he would write the person's name on a piece of scrap paper, drop it into the lowest drawer in his desk, and say to himself, "That finishes the incident."[7]

We also see that *a fool lacks competence (10:5–7, 16–17)*. "There is an evil I have seen under the sun, like an error which goes forth from the ruler—folly is set in many exalted places while rich men sit in humble places. I have seen slaves riding on horses and princes walking like slaves on the land." Solomon is talking about those infuriating role reversals in life where unqualified, incompetent people somehow get promoted to positions of leadership while those who have worked hard get passed over. It would appear from these verses that the world is being run by fools. An error that people in authority often make is that they appoint their incompetent cronies to office. This kind of bureaucratic backscratching spells doom for the people at the bottom. In our unfair hierarchies people are promoted based on favoritism, nepotism or "the good ole' boy system" not if they are actually capable of doing the job.

One of history's most scrutinized military generals of all time is George Armstrong Custer, who became infamous for leading a regimen of 231 troops to their death at the Battle of Little Big Horn. "Custer's Last Stand" is often remembered as one of the greatest military blunders of all time. Yet his recklessness can be traced back to the days of his youth. One historian writes about a particularly humiliating scene from Custer's early years that should have tipped officers off to the fact that Custer was unfit for leadership:

> In the spring of 1867, George Custer and his regiment were on a scouting expedition on the plains of Kansas. Suddenly Custer's English Greyhounds, his constant companions, began to chase some antelope over a distant hill. In spite of himself, Custer could not resist joining the chase. It was not long before the general, his horse, and his pack of dogs had left his regiment far behind. He quickly forgot his men and his mission when he crested the first hill and saw his first buffalo: an enormous, shaggy bull. He put the spurs to his horse's sides and began the chase. As the horse gained on the massive buffalo,

---

7. Eisenhower, *At Ease: Stories I Tell to Friends*.

Custer yelled with excitement. An avid hunter, he had to bring this trophy home. He drew his pearl-handled pistol. But as he came alongside the thundering beast and shoved the barrel into its thick shaggy side, Custer paused. Feeling the ground shake, hearing the ragged breathing of both animals side by side, he pulled the pistol back, to "prolong the enjoyment of the chase." After several minutes, Custer decided it was time for the kill. Again, He shoved the pistol into the side of the buffalo. But, as if sensing Custer's intentions, the buffalo abruptly turned toward the horse. The horse veered away from the buffalo's horns, and when Custer tried to grab the reins with both hands, his finger accidentally fired a bullet into his own horse's head, killing it instantly. Custer was thrown to the ground and then struggled quickly to his feet to face the animal that had been his prey only seconds before. Instead of charging, the buffalo stared at the strange, foolish man and walked off. Horseless and alone, Custer began the long, dangerous walk back to his regiment. In less than a decade, this same recklessness and arrogance would lead the General and his men to their death on a flat-topped hill next to a river called the Little Bighorn.[8]

Solomon's point is well taken—a position of leadership can often reveal the incompetence and immaturity of a foolish person promoted too soon. However, usually by that point it's too late and the fool has already done a lot of irreparable damage.

Jump down to 10:16–17 and we will see another parallel to incompetent leadership—immaturity. "Woe to you, O land, whose king is a lad and whose princes feast in the morning. Blessed are you, O land, whose king is of nobility and whose princes eat at the appropriate time—for strength and not for drunkenness."

These verses tell the story of a national disaster when a boy has been made king. To show how much trouble a country can get into when it lacks mature leadership, the Preacher describes the scene of a kingly court where a gluttonous prince feasts every morning. Instead of going out to build the country, this prince is hung-over from a night of hell-raising. Solomon's point is simply this: If your land is ruled by a fool then woe to you, because immature leadership is an act of judgment from God. Philip Ryken adds:

> A notable example from European history is Charles XII, who became the king of Sweden when he was only a teenager. The wild behavior of Charles and his friends included riding on horseback through his grandmother's apartment, knocking

---

8. Philbrick, *The Last Stand*, xv-xvi.

people to the ground on the city streets, and practicing firearms by shooting out the windows of the palace. In response the leading preachers of Stockholm all agreed to preach from Ecclesiastes 10:16 on the same Sunday, pronouncing woe on a land with a child for a king and princes that feasted in the morning . . . Woe to any nation characterized by sinful entertainment, lazy self-indulgence, and the widespread abuse of alcohol and other drugs, especially among its national leaders.[9]

Next we must notice that *a fool lacks caution (10:8–11)*. Eugene Peterson has paraphrased these verses like so, "Caution: The trap you set might catch you. Warning: Your accomplice in crime might double-cross you. Safety first: Quarrying stones is dangerous. Be alert: Felling trees is hazardous. Remember: The duller the ax the harder the work; Use your head: The more brains, the less muscle."[10] Sounds like a biblical injunction for workers compensation don't you think?

These verses describe those with a strong back but a weak mind. One man digging a ditch forgets to alert his partner of a sudden drop off, so he falls and breaks his neck. Another dope is clearing away rubble from a crumbling wall and discovers a copperhead nest. A guy quarrying stones wasn't paying attention when a boulder came crashing down on his head. Finally, a poor sap felling trees didn't calculate his cut correctly, so when gravity began to take the timber down it snapped backwards and crushed his pick-up truck.

Believe it or not these occupational mishaps occur every day with incredible regularity. In 2005 a fifty-four year old Colorado man, Brian Morse, was killed when his gloved hand got caught in a wood chipper and he was pulled into the machine.[11]

In 1993 a Toronto lawyer, Garry Hoy, was trying to impress a new workmate by running head-on into a window on the twenty-fourth floor of his office to prove that it was unbreakable. Mind you this was a stunt he had done multiple times without any injury. However this time the window gave way and he fell to his death.[12]

In 2010 the multi-millionaire owner of the company that makes Segway motorized scooters, Jimi Heselden, died at the age of sixty-two in a freak accident while riding one of his two-wheeled vehicles. In a twist of

9. Ryken, *Ecclesiastes*, 248–249.

10. Peterson, *The Message*, Ecc. 10:8–10.

11. "Man Killed in Wood Chipper Identified," *The Denver Channel*, 29 December 2005.

12. Bruce Demara, "Corporate Lawyer Plunges 24 Floors to Death," *The Toronto Star*, 10 July 1993.

fate, Heselden rode his ruggedized Segway off an eighty foot cliff and plummeted to his death.[13]

Ken Charles Barger accidentally shot himself to death in Newton, NC. He was in bed when the phone rang and when he reached for it he grabbed instead a Smith & Wesson .38 which discharged when he put it to his ear."[14]

Solomon strings together these short illustrations from the workplace to show how the fool seldom plans ahead and doesn't think before they act. The fool takes a short-range view of things and stumbles into situations haphazardly. The saying still holds true today, "fools rush in." God doesn't give us brownie points for being stupid. Solomon would tell us to work smarter, not harder; plan ahead; look before you leap; measure twice and cut once. Make good use of your grey matter and save yourself a trip to the emergency room.

The application of this passage arrives in 10:10, when the Preacher compares wisdom to a sharpened blade. "If the iron is blunt, and one does not sharpen the edge, he must use more strength, but wisdom helps one to succeed." It takes twice the energy and strength to wield a dull axe than a sharp one. Yet this is how foolish people operate. They never think to stop and sharpen their axe. They keep flailing away at their work, their addictions, their problems, and their relationships never really making any progress. If they were wise they would take time to prepare their mind and soul. How sharp is your blade? Are you hacking away at life like a fool, or are you staying on the sharp edge of wisdom?[15] Like sharpening an axe, learning to be wise may take more time in the beginning, but it is certainly a life-saver in the long run.

Solomon's follow-up statement in 10:11 seems obtuse and random, but it's also connected to the overall admonishment for wisdom. "If the serpent bites before it is charmed, there is no advantage to the charmer." The Preacher gives an illustration of a snake charmer which may seem foreign to our Western mindset. It takes years of patience and careful training to charm a snake. But if the charmer gets bitten before the snake is tamed, his talent didn't do him any good. The charmer had the skill but he didn't use it. Solomon's point is that you need to use the wisdom you have. It's not enough to know how to charm the serpent; you have to actually apply your knowledge before you're bitten.[16]

---

13. Chris Brooke, "Millionaire Segway Tycoon Dies in Cliff Plunge on One of His Own Scooters," 28 September 2010.

14. Jeremiah, *Searching for Heaven on Earth*, 270.

15. Ryken, *Ecclesiastes*, 239.

16. Krell, "Wise Beyond Words (Ecclesiastes 9:13–10:20)."

When the careful student considers 10:10 together with 10:11 the lesson the Preacher is trying to make becomes clear. Although wisdom is an invaluable resource it can be invalidated by improper timing. There are times in life when we need to plan methodically and carefully prepare before we set about an endeavor. This is the message of 10:10. However, there are other times when we must act quickly on what we know. We must not delay to put wisdom into practice. This is the counter balance of 10:11. Thus, a wise man knows the difference and acts accordingly.

It's also clear that *a fool lacks commitment (10:18)*. A farmer was sitting on the porch of his house when a stranger came by and asked, "How's things?" "Tolerable," The farmer continued, "Two weeks ago a tornado came along and knocked down all the trees I would have to chop down for this winter's firewood. Then last week lightning struck the brush I had planned to burn to clear the fields for planting." The stranger responded, "That's remarkable, what are you doing now?" The farmer answered, "Well, I'm just-a-waitin' for an earthquake to come along and shake the taters out of the ground."

Some people work hard at not working at all. Thus, Solomon's observation, "Through sloth the roof sinks in, and through indolence the house leaks." The Preacher thinks about a man who would do anything to keep from doing anything. Imagine a fellow who has given himself totally to the sin of sloth. His single-wide trailer will likely collapse before he can get his lazy carcass up the ladder to patch his crumbling roof. He is eaten up by apathy. Just give him nine thousands channels of cable television, some sweat pants, a case of beer and he will find a way to mooch his way through life. It's the Homer Simpson mentality. David Jeremiah comments on this passage like this:

> Picture a guy sitting at home with a bottle of beer in his hand, watching television. He's supposed to be doing work, taking care of things, providing for those for whom he is responsible. He's supposed to be a steward of the tasks entrusted to him. But the house is falling down. The roof is leaking. The bills are stacking up. The beer belly is growing larger.[17]

According to Solomon, the way a man takes care of his home says a lot about this character. If a guy won't even take care of the place where he lives, that is an indication that he's a waste of skin. Only a fool would neglect his home, his body, his family and ultimately his soul. Indeed, a man who will not provide for his family is worse than an infidel (1 Tim. 5:8). The problem with this man, or any other lazy good-for-nothing, is not that they

17. Jeremiah, *Searching for Heaven on Earth*, 265.

can't work; it's that they won't work. For every person who climbs the ladder of success, there a dozen waiting for the elevator. But there is no substitute for good old-fashioned elbow grease and manual labor. Poet F.O. Walsh explained the basis for laziness:

> While other men paint,
> Or water, or weed,
> I'm curled up in a chair,
> With a good book to read.
>
> While other men shop,
> Or shovel, or mow,
> I'm having a drink
> While watching some show.
>
> I offer to help,
> But my wife says, "Forget it,
> If you lend a hand,
> I know I'll regret it."
>
> And therein's my secret,
> I'm very adept
> At only one thing,
> And that's being inept.[18]

We should pair this verse with Proverbs 6:10 which says, "A little sleep, a little slumber, a little folding of the hands to rest and poverty will come upon you like a robber and want like an armed man." Laziness is an epidemic that can not only lead to the destruction of a home, and a life, but also a kingdom. The dangers of prosperity are just as bad as poverty. For those who are fat and sassy thinking they have it made, they will learn that their sense of entitlement will cause their good times to evaporate.

A Fool and His Conversation (10:12–15, 20)

According to Solomon you can tell a fool not only in the way he walks but also in the way he talks. Abraham Lincoln is credited with saying, "Better to remain silent and be thought a fool than to speak and remove all doubt." Keeping your mouth shut can keep a lot of ignorance from leaking out. Of course, a fool blathers on and on with no attempt to tame his tongue. Thus,

---

18. F.O. Walsh quoted by Michael P. Green, *1500 Illustrations for Biblical Preaching*, 213–214.

Solomon identifies three mistakes that a fool makes simply by opening his mouth. In fact, he spends more space discussing the lips of fool than the wise words of sage.

The Preacher points out that *a fool's words are ensnaring (10:12, 20)*. Someone has said that, "A slip of the foot you may soon recover from, but a slip of the tongue you may never get over." A wise man's words are seasoned with grace and gain him a good reputation with others. On the other hand, a fool's words are his own undoing. It's been said that if you give a man enough rope he'll hang himself; so it is with a tongue-wagging fool. Words that are poorly chosen are self-destructive to the speaker. The Preacher even gives us one specific example at the end of the chapter of how words can boomerang back to our ruin:

> Don't bad-mouth your leaders, not even under your breath,
> and don't abuse your betters, even in the privacy of your home.
> Loose talk has a way of getting picked up and spread around.
> Little birds drop the crumbs of your gossip far and wide.[19]

Do you know anyone like this? This is the kind of person who has no filter, whatever is on their mind is coming straight out of their mouth. How many times have you said something and the moment you said it you wished you could stuff those words back in? Solomon warns that those who hear juicy gossip and slander often use those details for self-interest (i.e. telling the king in order to gain favor). Just so happens that the word picture created in 10:20 is the origin of the expression, "A little bird told me." A wise person doesn't say something in private that he wouldn't want someone to hear in public. Moreover, you never know who might be listening—it could be the village blabbermouth.

I will never forget one of my first job interviews after college was for a teaching position at a high school I had been student teaching at. The principal was a gracious, but firm female who was all business. I don't know if it was nerves or what, but I uttered some of the most humiliating words in my life at this woman. After the interview process came to end I was shaking her hand to leave and she said, "Okay, Mr. McCarson we will contact you later." I replied, "Yes, Sir. Thank you for the interview." I don't know where that verbal slip came from, but I called that lady a man. Needless to say, I didn't get the job because one ill-fitting word consumed me.

In 10:13 we learn that *a fool's words are evil*. A fool's words may start out silly, but give the fool enough time and his words will turn coarse and vulgar. Soon the fool's words will be used for the evil purposes of the

---

19. Peterson, *The Message*, Ecc. 10:20.

Enemy—slander, gossip, criticism and profanity. Foolish words have a way of starting a chain reaction of hurt that is impossible to stop or contain.

In the summer of 2000 more than a thousand firefighters battled a wildfire for two weeks in the Black Hills of South Dakota. The fire started on August 24 and was not contained until September 8. Meanwhile, over eighty thousand acres of valuable timber were burned.

A 46-year-old woman, Janice Stevenson, was arrested on suspicion of starting the fire. She received five years in prison and a $250,000 fine. Federal investigators who filed charges against Ms. Stevenson say she admitted stopping by a road on August 24, lighting a cigarette, and tossing the still-burning match on the ground. "Rather than putting out the fire," an affidavit said, "she looked at it and decided to leave the area."

Like starting a forest fire, it requires little effort to produce a "wildfire" with our tongues. Rumors, half-truths, grumblings, sarcastic remarks, hurtful things said in the heat of anger—all of these smoldering matches have the potential for burning down acres of office morale, family peace, and church unity (James 3:5–7).[20]

A fool's words are also endless (10:14–15). Shakespeare's *Macbeth* has a good summation of this verse, "A tale told by an idiot is full of sound and fury and signifies nothing." Solomon's description in these verses brings to mind the image of a know-it-all. This is the kind of person who dominates the conversation and you can never get a single word in edge wise. Fools are notorious for being highly opinioned and they multiply words in their ignorant rants. Fools love to boast about their big plans for their future and weigh-in on matters in which they are ill-informed. Plato was right when he said, "Wise men speak because they have something to say, but fools speak because they have to say something."

Kevin Miller, Vice President of *Christianity Today International* once wrote about how his misfiring tongue got him in all kinds of hot water:

> I was flying from San Francisco to Chicago. Five minutes before takeoff from San Francisco, a gate agent from ATA came on the plane and said to me, "Get your bags and come with me." I got my bags out of the bin and followed her into the jetway and asked, "Why? Is this a random security check?" She said, "The captain refused to have you on this flight." In the terminal, she pointed me to the black vinyl seats and said, "Sit there. A supervisor will come talk to you." As I'm sitting there, it suddenly hits me: My friend had been ordered out of the security line and thus arrived on the plane much later than I. When he came on the

---

20. Larson and Elshof, *1001 Illustrations That Connect*, 224.

plane, I asked him, "Why were you stopped? Was it your beady terrorist eyes? Explosives?" My friend shook his head quickly, getting me to shut up. That was what was causing this. Soon four uniformed San Francisco cops, revolvers on their hips, walk up to me. "Do you know why you're here?" "Well," I said, "I did make a comment to my friend about looking like a terrorist. I know I shouldn't have said that. I was just making a private joke." The cop, steel hair and strong jaw, shoots back, "You can't joke about those things. They may not allow you to fly again in the future." Another cop grills me. One takes my driver's license and runs a criminal background check. Another calls the FAA, to see what they want to do with me. More huddled discussion, just out of earshot, between the leading cop and the airline rep. The airline rep walks over. "You realize that you can't talk about these things. We're in a new day." "I know that," I said. "It was stupid, and I shouldn't have said it." "We've decided to let you fly again on ATA." Inwardly I groan, but quickly say, "Thank you." The lead cop looks down at me: "You win the prize for Idiot of the Day."[21]

For good or evil, our words either make us or break us. Life and death are in the power of the tongue (Pro. 18:21). A prayer that I have learned to pray after sticking my foot in my mouth is "Lord, please fill my mouth with worthwhile stuff and nudge me when I've said enough."

---

21. Miller, "Busted over Careless Words," *Preaching Today,* 2002 January.

17

Living on the Edge (11:1–10)

A COACH ONCE SAID to me, "If you're going to steal second, then you have to take your foot off first base." He was right, no one who ever did anything exciting, bold or courageous tip-toed through life on eggshells. Columbus would have never discovered the Americas if he was too fond of the seashore. Edison couldn't have given the world the incandescent light bulb unless he was willing to fail a thousand times finding the right filament. Had he been content with a view through the telescope, Neil Armstrong would have never got moon dust on his boots. An old saying goes, "The best fruit is always out on a limb." Indeed, if we want the most out of life then we have to be willing to be bullish.

I was reminded of this while reading an excerpt from Palmer Chinchen's, *True Religion*. In that book he tells a funny story that explains how risk and adventure go hand in hand. He writes:

> My brothers and I had traveled to the western edge of Zimbabwe to raft the Zambezi River. We boarded our raft at the base of the Victoria Falls. Massive amounts of water spilled over the top of the giant falls and dropped almost a thousand feet; the roar was deafening. The falls are the largest in the world, more than a mile wide and three hundred feet high. Mist from the spray that fills the air like fog can be seen for fifty miles; the locals call it, "Smoke That Thunders." The water from the falls rushes down the gorge in torrents, creating the world's largest rapids. In the United States, the highest-class rapid you are allowed to raft is a Class 5. The Zambezi's whitewater rapids can top 7 and

8 . . . As I sat on the edge of the eight-person raft, all suited up in a tight, overstuffed jacket and a thick crash helmet, I felt like an over cautious tourist about to mount an overpowered moped in Honolulu or rent roller-blades on Huntington Beach. The Zambezi can't be that dangerous, can it? But then our guide said, "When the raft flips . . ." There was no "If the raft flips" or "on the off-chance we get flipped." But "When the raft flips." He went on, ". . . stay in the rough water. You will be tempted to swim toward the stagnate water at the edge of the banks. Don't do it. Because it is in the stagnate water that the crocs wait for you. They are large and hungry. Even when the raft flips, stay in the rough water."[1]

Staying in the rough waters is not something that comes natural for most people. For some of us the word "risk" disappeared from our vocabulary years ago. If you're like me—predictable and set in my ways—then about the most dangerous thing you've done lately is order something new off the menu. We like sure things. Anything that smacks of danger is an affront to what we know is tried and true. I think about the old poem that goes:

> There was a very cautious man
> Who never laughed or played;
> He never risked, he never tried,
> He never sang or prayed.
> And when he one day passed away
> His insurance was denied;
> For since he never really lived,
> They claimed he never died![2]

The Preacher was not one to just sit around and be a wallflower. Just look at his track record in this journal; you name it he tried it. Solomon was part philosopher, part architect, part politician, part playboy, part scientist and so much more. This was a guy who tried to get all the gusto out of life. In chapter eleven, the Preacher admonishes us to take some calculated risks. He wants us to get out of our comfort zone, try new things, venture out into the rough waters and not let the uncertainties of life keep us from stepping out on faith. Hudson Taylor, the man of faith who founded the China Inland Mission, integrated faith and risk. He said, "Unless there is an element of risk in our exploits for God, there is no need for faith." This is the point Solomon wants to sink into our hearts and minds. He is going to pass on some helpful tips on how to stop playing it safe and start living on the edge.

1. Chinchen, *True Religion*, 55–57.
2. Source Unknown.

The Uncertainty of Life (11:1–6)

One thing that Solomon discovered under the sun was that life was notoriously difficult to predict. One day your stock portfolio may be flying high, the next day the bottom could fall out and you could be penniless. Sickness, calamity and death never announce their arrival. On the other hand, you never know when some blessing might come your way. Underdogs do win. Life is as up and down as a knuckleball. Notice that three times in this section the Preacher makes the remark that we just don't know what a day may bring (10:2, 5, 6). In light of life's unpredictability how should we live? Solomon advises us to adopt two simple principles.

First, we should *invest generously (11:1–2)*. "Cast your bread upon the waters, for you will find it after many days. Give a portion to seven, or even to eight, for you know not what disaster may happen on earth." Admittedly, these verses are not exactly easy to interpret, because they contain an ancient expression that is foreign to our modern ears.

There are a couple of different lines of interpretation we can take. One school of thought claims that these verses talk primarily about taking wise financial risks. Solomon was a man of great enterprise; he was like the Warren Buffet of his day. In fact, 1 Kings informs us that he built a fleet of ships for trading all kind of goods far and wide (1 Kings 9:26, 28, 10:11, 14–15, 22). His ships would come back to Jerusalem loaded down with gold, silver, cedars from Lebanon and even exotic animals.

One commodity that Solomon would have traded was grain which was used for making bread. Thus, the phrase "cast your bread upon the waters." In other words, what Solomon could be saying is, "Diversify your investments and don't put all your grain on one ship." It's wise not to put all your grain on one ship because if the one ship sinks you will be financially ruined. That's why he says, "give a portion to seven or eight" because we can never be sure what financial calamity might occur—the stock market could crash, Social Security could run out, your business or home might burn down. Your broker might say, "Diversify your portfolio" and your grandma might say, "Don't put all your eggs in one basket," but Solomon says, "Cast your bread on the waters." Take calculated risks because no risk equals no reward. Nothing ventured, nothing gained.

Another school of thought says these verses are about generous philanthropy. In other words, the Preacher may be advising us not to be stingy with our resources but to give a helping portion to seven or eight people in need. Martin Luther commented on these verses, "Be generous to everyone while you can, use your riches wherever you can possibly do any good."[3] Chances are you know somebody who needs help paying their light bill, or someone who could use a sack of groceries. Perhaps you know of a friend raising money to go on a mission trip. Being open-handed rather than tight-fisted to the poor is certainly biblical (James 1:27; 1 John 3:17).

Proverbs 19:17 adds, "He who is gracious to a poor man lends to the Lord and He will repay him for his good deed." Thus, the general principle of these verses is that those who sow generously reap generously. The people you helped will help you when you find yourself in a pinch. When you invest in the Gospel, God takes notice and He will compensate you either on earth or in eternity for giving. Eugene Peterson translates, "Be generous: Invest in acts of charity. Charity yields high returns. Don't hoard your goods; spread them around. Be a blessing to others. This could be your last night."[4]

What many Christians don't realize is that God has a bigger shovel than us. What you shovel out as charity He can replenish abundantly. When you invest in heavenly things, the interest that accumulates will far exceed the initial investment. Make no mistake about it—God invites us to be venture capitalists for the Gospel.

The movie *Schindler's List* tells the story of the heroic efforts of the German industrialist Oskar Schindler to rescue as many Jews as he could from the Nazi concentration camps. When Schindler discovered what was happening inside the gates of Auschwitz he began bargaining for as many Jews as he could to work in his factory which made weapons for the German army. On one hand he was bringing in as many Jews as he could and on the other hand he was deliberately sabotaging the ammunition produced in his factory. He entered the war a wealthy industrialist, but by the end he was totally bankrupt. Finally when his factory was going to be shut down, he declared that the 1,000 or so Jewish men, women and children that worked in his factory could go free. The most emotional part of the film comes at the end when Schindler breaks down sobbing and says, "I could have done more." He looked at his automobile and said, "Why did I save this? This could have saved 10 people." He took off his gold watch and said, "This would have saved another one."

When you and I stand before God to give an account for our giving, there will be many selfish Christians who will realize they could have done a whole lot more for the cause of Christ. It's never a bad decision to invest in people and the Word of God because they are the only things that will last through eternity. What would happen if we had the guts to go "all-in" for

---

3. Martin Luther, "Notes on Ecclesiastes."
4. Peterson, *The Message*, Ecc. 11:1–2.

the Gospel and do all that we can to enlarge the Kingdom? You can't take your treasure with you, but you can send it on ahead. Invest in Kingdom enterprises and your goods will be in glory.

Second, we should *seize opportunity (11:3–6)*. Mark Twain once said "I was seldom able to see an opportunity until it had ceased to be one." The reason why so many cannot see an opportunity is because they are waiting for the stars to align and for God's booming voice to shout from heaven, "Here's your sign!" This is the kind of thinking that Solomon is warning against.

The Preacher is discussing things in life that are outside human control—the circulating winds of the jet stream, a falling tree, the cell division inside a mother's womb. Besides being out of our grasp, there are so many things we cannot understand because they belong to the secret, sovereign will of God. There is a danger in being overwhelmed by these things; I call it the paralysis of analysis. Solomon is describing the danger of watching life happen from the side lines because we are waiting for the most opportune time to do something. This proverb criticizes those who are overly cautious. In other words, stop procrastinating and start living!

Chuck Swindoll comments on this passage:

> There are certain things we cannot change. We cannot change the weather, taxes, bills, final scores of ball games, people's responses, the passing of time or the inevitably of death . . . Folks who focus only on the inevitable—the clouds, rain, falling trees and blowing wind—come dangerously close to that sign on the Alaskan High way which reads, "Choose your rut carefully. You'll be in it for the next 200 miles."[5]

If you are waiting for Prince Charming to come and sweep you off your feet; don't hold your breath sister because there is no such thing as a perfect man. If you are waiting for the ideal time to have children, stop over-planning. You'll never have enough money, energy or patience. Are you still looking for the right way to introduce Jesus into your daily conversations with your co-workers? Don't wait too much longer, the Rapture could happen any day or one of you may die unexpectedly. Stop trying to sound spiritual when you tell the pastoral staff, "I'll pray about it," when they ask you to volunteer in a church ministry. We all know that's a nice way to say "No" without actually saying "No."

There are people who are so paralyzed by the fear of failure that they never venture anything of significance. The simple point is this: don't waste the opportunities God has given you because this life is all you get. Fear

---

5. Swindoll, *Living on the Ragged Edge*, 304.

not that your life shall come to an end, but rather that it shall never have a beginning.

One of my favorite movies of all time is *Braveheart*. One of the most powerful moments in that film is when William Wallace, played by Mel Gibson, stands before his beleaguered countrymen at the Battle of Sterling. Outnumbered and facing sure defeat at the hands of superior enemy, Wallace mounts his horse and gives a stirring speech to arouse the courage of his men. As Wallace begins speaking of freedom and fighting one doubter from the crowd says, "We can run and live!" Wallace replies with the immortal words:

> Yes! Fight and you may die. Run and you will live at least awhile. And dying in your bed many years from now, would you be willing to trade all the days from this day to that for one chance, just one chance, to come back here as young men and tell our enemies that they may take our lives but they will never take our freedom!

With that the men of Scotland took the battlefield and began winning the war for their independence. Was there risk involved? No doubt. Was there great opportunity? Indeed, the prospect of being free men. In the end, the opportunity for real living outweighed the fear of never really living at all. This is the same attitude we must have if we are going to get the most out of our three score and ten.

The story of Jason McElwain captivated the sports nation in 2006. At the time McElwain was the enthusiastic seventeen-year-old manager for the varsity boys basketball team of Greece Athena High School in Rochester, New York. "J-Mac" as he was called by his teammates was not allowed to represent his team on the court because of his autism. On February 15, 2006, Greece Athena was playing Spencerport High School for a division title. Greece Athena got a large lead, so Coach Jim Johnson decided to let J-Mac play in the last four minutes. His teammates tried to pass him the ball and get him good looks at the basket, but J-Mac missed his first two shots. Finally, he delighted the home crowd by sinking a surprising three-pointer. But it didn't stop there, J-Mac caught fire. He did it again, and again and again. In a few minutes he scored twenty points hitting six three-pointers and one two-point basket. His teammates carried him off the court on their shoulders a hero.[6]

The ancient Romans had a phrase for such exploits: *Carpe Deim*, which means, "Seize the day." Make the most of the opportunities that God

---

6. Dakass, "Autistic Teen's Hoop Dreams Come True," *CBS News*, 1 March 2010.

has given you, even if it's just the final minutes of ball game. Sow your seed in the morning and evening and leave the results up to God.

The Brevity of Life (11:7–10)

It has been said that life is like a roll of toilet paper—the closer it gets to the end the faster it goes. Experts estimate that a lightning bolt flashes and then disappears in 45 to 55 microseconds, while the average running shoe lasts 350 to 500 miles. A hard pencil can write up to 30,000 words and a ball point pen can draw a line 7,500 feet long. Your run-of-the-mill 100 watt incandescent bulb lasts 750 hours. A $1 bill lasts 18 months in circulation. Yet, according the Bible the average lifespan is compared to vanishing vapor (James 4:14), a withering flower (Job 14:2) and a passing shadow (Ps. 102:11).

The Bible writers are constantly reminding us this brief stint on earth is merely a dress rehearsal for eternity. Amy Carmichael, the Irish missionary to India, once wrote, "We will have eternity to celebrate the victories, but only a few hours before sunset to win them." As the Preacher-King reflected back on his years he too was struck by their brevity. He closes this journal entry by reminding us that although we cannot control the length of our life, we can control its depth.

In light of life's shortness we should *live joyfully (11:7–8)*. "Light is sweet, and it is pleasant for the eyes to see the sun. So if a person lives many years, let him rejoice in them all; but let him remember that the days of darkness will be many. All that comes is vanity." Solomon reminds us that each day we rise to see the sun we receive a wonderful gift. We often take health and vitality for granted until we have a brush with death or find ourselves laying face up in a hospital bed.

When I was in my early twenties I was on my way to church one Wednesday evening. It was early spring and there was a light drizzle falling. The music was blaring on my stereo. I was singing. It was a happy, spring day. As I came around a bend in the road and headed into a straight-a-way I could see an oncoming truck gradually getting closer and closer to the yellow line. I kept thinking, "Surely this guy is going to get over." It seemed that time began to speed up. I was in a small Honda Accord and the missile heading toward me was a Dodge diesel truck. He drifted further over into my lane, by now he straddled the yellow line. I swerved on to the side of the road, but he didn't slow down. The two vehicles traded paint.

I can still remember the sound of breaking glass as my windshield cracked and the driver window shattered. My car careened into a ditch from the impact. The other guy kept driving, it was a classic hit-and-run. However, about an hour later, after the cops showed up he drove back to the scene of the accident. Turns out he was so drunk that he got home realized he had been in a wreck, so he got back in his truck and drove around looking to see if he killed anyone.

Miraculously, I didn't have a scratch on me. In retrospect, I should have died, but God protected me. He had another plan. Two things resulted from that: I drive defensively now and it taught me that life is so very precious and we should take every day as a gift from the Lord. At that point I had not really solidified my direction in the ministry, but it seemed like God used that event to compel me to get busy preaching the Gospel and to make the most of every minute.

In 2011 Steve Jobs, the co-founder of Apple Computer and Pixar, died after a prolonged battle with cancer. I was saddened to learn that he was not was a believer in Christ but a Buddhist. Before he passed, Jobs gave a commencement speech at Stanford University knowing already that cancer had invaded his body. Even though he was wrong about Christ, he said something that I think Solomon would have agreed with:

> Death is very likely the single best invention of life. It is life's change agent. It clears out the old to make way for the new . . . Remembering that I'll be dead soon is the most important tool I've ever encountered to help me make the big choices in life. Because almost everything—all external expectations, all pride, all fear of embarrassment or failure—these things just fall away in the face of death, leaving only what is truly important. Remembering that you are going to die is the best way I know to avoid the trap of thinking you have something to lose. You are already naked."[7]

Finally, because life is fleeting we should resolve to *be holy* (*11:9–10*). This command has a balance to it; we ought to enjoy life, but also fear God. Solomon says, "Get all you can out of life, learn all you can, accomplish your goals, dream big dreams, have lots of fun before the grey hairs set in, but remember that one day God will call into judgment everything we have done under the sun." The delight of God should add joy to our years and the fear of God should cause us to live righteously. Solomon's admonishment here can be summarized in a quote by Augustine who said, "Love God and do whatever you please." In other words, let your life be governed by your love of God and two things will happen: you'll be happy because God is the

---

7. Moria Forbes, "Steve Jobs: Death Is Very Likely the Single Best Invention of Life," *Forbes*, 5 October 2011.

source of all contentment and you'll be holy because your love of God will keep you from sin.

The Preacher ends with some advice to young people, "So, remove grief and anger from your heart and put away pain from your body, because childhood and the prime of life are fleeting." Solomon is speaking from the voice of experience. He had put his body through much aging and distress because of his wild living. Now in his later years he was paying for the wild oats he had sown. Imagine that he leans forward across the table, sips his coffee and says to you and me, "If you want to get the most out of life then don't destroy your best years with sex, drugs and rock n' roll."

The tragedy is that we get old too soon and wise too late. George Bernard Shaw said, "Youth is such a wonderful thing. It's a shame to waste it on young people." The irony is that when we finally get some wisdom and a handle on how to live skillfully we're in a rest home wearing diapers. Imagine if you could go back to being sixteen years old with all you know now. What advice would you give yourself? Would your older self say something like, "Stay away from the bottle. Save yourself for marriage. Give your heart to God and pray every day. Save more and spend less. Don't get caught up with getting things. Call your mother. Remember your family and tell them you love them."

Life is uncertain, but don't be afraid to take risks. Life is short, so live every day like it we're your last. In all that you do fear God. Perhaps the best way to summarize Solomon's meditation is to adopt the words of "The Paradoxical Commandments" by Kent Keith:

> People are illogical, unreasonable, and self-centered. Love them anyway. If you do good people will accuse you of selfish ulterior motives. Do good anyway. If you are successful you will win false friends and true enemies. Succeed anyway. The good you do today will be forgotten tomorrow. Do good anyway. Honesty and frankness make you vulnerable. Be honest and frank anyway. The biggest men and women with the biggest ideas can be shot down by the smallest men and women with the smallest minds. Think big anyway. People favor underdogs but follow only top dogs. Fight for a few underdogs anyway. What you spend years building may be destroyed overnight. Build anyway. People really need help but may attack you if you do help them. Help people anyway. Give the world the best you have and you'll get kicked in the teeth. Give the world the best you have anyway."[8]

---

8. Keith, *Do It Anyway*, 170–171.

18

Passing the Final Exam (12:1-14)

THERE IS A HUMOROUS story about a group of friends who attended their high school reunion and decided that in order to keep their relationships intact that every few years they would meet, have dinner, catch up on life and reminisce about the good ole' days. They made this pact as many of them were just breaking into their thirties. As they were discussing where they should go for dinner somebody suggested that they meet at the Glowing Embers Restaurant because it was a chic, happening place to be. They all agreed.

Fifteen years later, at age forty-five, they called one another and discussed again where they should have dinner. Somebody suggested the Glowing Embers because the food selection there was very good. They all agreed.

Another fifteen years later many of them were getting into their sixties, they once again discussed where to meet. Somebody suggested the Glowing Embers because you can eat there in peace and quiet and the restaurant is smoke free. They all agreed.

Another fifteen years later, as many of them were now retiring, the group discussed again where they should meet. Somebody suggested that they should meet at the Glowing Embers because the restaurant was easily accessible and they even have an elevator. They all agreed.

Finally, another fifteen years rolled off the calendar and those that were left were well into their nineties. The same group of friends discussed one more time where they should meet for dinner. Somebody suggested that they should meet at the Glowing Embers because they had never been there before. And they all agreed.

For those of you who are moving into the twilight of your years here is a little bit of encouragement. Moses was eighty when God called him to deliver the children of Israel from bondage (Acts 7:23, 30). J.C. Penny still kept office hours at the age of eighty-five. Michelangelo was seventy-one when he began the architectural designs on St. Peter's Basilica in Rome. John Wesley preached until he was eighty-eight and Billy Graham gave his last public sermon at eighty-six. Golda Meir was seventy-one when she became Israeli Prime Minister and Ronald Reagan was seventy-seven when he left the Oval Office. Benjamin Franklin helped to frame the US Constitution at age eighty-one. Noah Webster completed his monumental dictionary at seventy, Thomas Edison was eighty-three when his last invention was patented and Galileo made his greatest discoveries in astronomy at age seventy-three.

For some folks age is just a number. In 2011 a New Jersey man, Fred Mack, celebrated his centennial birthday with a fall from the clouds.[1] Could you imagine going skydiving at one-hundred? Better yet, what about competing athletically? In 2013 Fauja Singh became the oldest runner ever to complete a full marathon. He hung up his competitive running shoes for good at age one-hundred-one! The elderly marathoner credited his longevity to a strictly vegetarian diet.[2] Yet, these amazing stories are the exception rather than the rule.

The final entry in Solomon's journal is about how to finish the race of life well. Remember, this book is like the Preacher's last will and testament, so it is fitting that he closes these meditations with some pearls of wisdom about the end of life. Once again, Solomon is true to his ragged-edge look at life. You won't find any mention of the "golden years" from this greybeard. The final words of admonition that Solomon shares with us parallel what Billy Graham wrote in his book *Nearing Home*:

> I never thought I'd live to be this old. All my life I was taught how to die as a Christian, but no one every taught me how I ought to live in the years before I die. I wish they had because I am an old man now, and believe me, it's not easy. Whoever said it was right: old age is not for sissies. Get any group of older people together, and I can almost guarantee what their favorite topic of conversations will be: their latest aches and pains. I will soon

---

1. "100-Year-Old Man Goes Skydiving," *ABC News*, 22 March 2011.
2. Rick Chandler, "101-Year-Old Vegetarian Runner Completes His Final Marathon," *NBC Sports*, 25 February 2013.

celebrate my ninety-third birthday, and I know it won't be long before God calls me home to Heaven. More than ever I look forward to that day—not just because of the wonders I know Heaven holds in store for me and for every believer but because I know that finally all the burdens and sorrows that press down upon me at this stage in my life will be over.[3]

Now as a tired, old man Solomon has his life flash before his eyes like a highlight reel. He leaves us with his final words of wisdom so that we do not make the same mistakes he did. Clearly his lasting legacy was not is his many achievements but the truths contained in the pages of this book. Every lesson came by way of the school of hard-knocks. We would be wise to learn that the best way to meet the challenges of old age is to prepare for them now, before they arrive.

Remember God Before You Reach the End of Life (12:1-7)

Solomon's words are directed towards those who still have some youth left in their bones (11:9, 12:1-2). His advice is for you and me to live life to the fullest before old age sets in and death starts drawing the blinds. Imagine Grandpa Solomon stroking his beard while turning his patient gaze to the young whippersnappers and saying, "Listen to what I've got to say and get a hold of this while you're young."

When he says to "Remember thy Creator" he's not talking about jogging your memory. Instead, what he means is to have an ever-present commitment to love and fear God before grey hairs, senility and adult diapers enter the picture. We must live in light of judgment and as stewards who will one day give an account to our Creator. Remember your Creator now before you forget the God who made you lest you make bad decisions that you will regret later. Remember God while you're young and you will have a whole lifetime to live for His glory.

The Preacher launches into an extended poem on the grueling process of aging. This is one of the most imaginative and creative descriptions of growing old in the Bible. The metaphor that he uses is that of a house that is steadily falling apart. As you meditate on the double entendre of the imagery you get the sense that very soon the crumbling castle is fit to be condemned.

The "keepers of the house" refers to the arms and the hands that tremble as we get older. Solomon's words here remind me of Muhammad Ali. Because of time and Parkinson's disease "The Louisville Lip" neither floats like a butterfly nor stings like a bee. Those mighty biceps and fists which

---

3. Billy Graham, *Nearing Home*, vii-viii.

crumpled his opponents in the ring now shake uncontrollably. What a sad commentary on the fleeting glory of man.

The "strong men" bowing down refers to the knees and shoulders which weaken and bend with age. As you grow older expect to lose some of your height as your bones bend and become weaker with osteoporosis. "The grinders" are the teeth that start falling out. Someone has said, "One thing about getting old is that you can sing in the bathroom while brushing your teeth." You laugh now, but beware. One day you may have to gum your food.

The "windows" which grow dim refers to the eyes. Solomon is saying that vision deteriorates, cataracts set in and things become blurry. I joke with my father about this because he has had perfect vision all his life until recently. Now he owns stock in Lens Crafters. He relies on reading glasses and I have even found some of his spectacles left behind at my house.

The Preacher continues, "and the doors are shut in the streets and the sound of the grinding is low." Excuse me? What did you say? Solomon is telling us to turn-up our hearing aid because the ears don't detect sound as well. To make matters worse, old fogies are gone to bed with the chickens and up before the sun rises. That's the meaning of the expression, "one will arise at the sound of the bird." The meaning of "all the daughters of music are brought low" pertains to the quivering voice that sets in as the elderly don't talk as loud or as clearly as they once did. I have had to lean in close so that I could hear an old-timer tell me a story.

"Also they are afraid of height and of terrors in the way." Heights and long walks become major obstacles for the elderly. Leave the climbing of ladders and stairways for the young. The blossoming of the almond tree is a reference to greying hair. This makes me think of my papaw's head of snow white hair. No Rogaine for him, he earned every strand of silver. "The grasshopper becomes a burden," is a picture of the elderly shuffling their feet. Think canes, walkers, and motorized carts and you've got the idea. "And desire fails." One word: Viagra. Finally, "*man goes to his eternal home and the mourners go about in the streets.*" This refers to the endless funerals that we attend at the end of life as we watch our contemporaries go on before us.

A friend of mine sent me a modernized version of Solomon's poem in an email, "Eight Ways You Know You're Getting Old." I offer it for your humor:

1. When all the names in your contact book end in MD.
2. When you get winded playing chess.
3. When you look forward to a dull evening.
4. When your knees buckle and your belt won't.

5. When you sink your teeth into a steak and they stay there.
6. When you try to fix the wrinkles in your socks and you find you're not wearing any.
7. When your pacemaker accidently opens your garage door.
8. When you bend over to tie your shoes and you wonder what else you can do while you're down there.

Late in his life, a colleague wrote John Quincy Adams, the 6th president of the United States, and asked him how he was doing. The former president replied, "John Quincy Adams is quite well sir. The house in which he has been living is feeble. The shingles are coming off the roof. The foundation is a bit shaky and he has received word from his Maker that he must vacate the premises soon. But, Mr. Adam's is fine, just fine sir." That's a great attitude to have about the end of life. In fact, after reading through Solomon's poem I am convinced that if you don't have a sense of humor then growing older will be doubly difficult.

Why does Solomon go to these elaborate lengths to talk about growing old and frail? He's painting a vivid picture so that those who have a few years ahead will wake up and realize that "man's days are few and full of trouble" (Job 14:1). His simple point is this: we had better live for God now because when you're shut up in a nursing home, playing bingo and eating through a straw it's too late.

How many senior citizens come to Christ? Very few. The older people become the more set in their ways they become and they are less likely to give their life to Christ. What makes things more difficult when health begins to fail is that the reality of old age sets in as well and with it comes all kinds of fears. There is the fear of growing old alone, regret over missed opportunities in life, anger and bitterness over being hurt by others, the realization that you are past your prime and your dreams will not be fulfilled.

Woody Allen is a good example of what happens when a cynic faces the end of the life. He admitted:

> I find aging a lousy deal. There's no advantage in getting older. I'm seventy-four now. You don't get smarter, you don't get wiser, you don't get more mellow, you don't get more kindly. Nothing good happens. Your back hurts more. You get more indigestion. Your eyesight isn't as good. You need a hearing aid. It's a bad business getting older, and I would advise you not to do it."

In regards to death he said, "My relationship with death remains the same. I am very strongly against it."[4]

Without Christ death is the worst enemy of all. In fact, Solomon ends with a few poetic descriptions of how we might face death in 12:6–8. The first is a picture of lamp hanging from the ceiling by a silver chord, when the chord snaps the lamp hits the ground and light is extinguished. The second is a well with a broken wheel and when it stops working the pitcher shatters and life is over. Chuck Swindoll comments on these verses:

> Life simply isn't a great big bowl of cherries and don't let anyone try to convince you it is. Life is a challenge. Life is tough and only the power of Jesus Christ can give you the resiliency to handle it. Life is sickness and terminal illness. Life is brokenness—broken hearts, broken marriages, broken relationships. Life is not enough food and not enough hope. Life is discouragement and depression, times and bewilderment and uncertainty. Life is deterioration, disappointment, and ragged-edge reality. I honestly cannot imagine how anyone copes with that ragged edge apart from a relationship with Jesus Christ.[5]

According to an old fable, a man made an unusual agreement with Death. He told the Grim Reaper that he would willingly accompany him when it came time to die, but only on one condition—that Death would send a messenger well in advance to warn him. Weeks winged away into months, and months into years. Then one bitter winter evening, as the man sat thinking about all his possessions, Death suddenly entered the room and tapped him on the shoulder. Startled, the man cried out, "You're here so soon and without warning! I thought we had an agreement." Death replied, "I've more than kept my part. I've sent you many messengers. Look in the mirror and you'll see some of them." As the man complied, Death whispered, "Notice your hair! Once it was full and black, now it is thin and white. Look at the way you cock your head to listen to me because you can't hear very well. Observe how close to the mirror you must stand to see yourself clearly. Yes, I've sent many messengers through the years. I'm sorry you're not ready, but the time has come to leave." May we learn to pay attention to the messengers!

Have you ever thought of why God allows believers to grow old and weak? The former president of Columbia Bible College, J. Robertson

---

4. Woody Allen, "Woody Allen: Getting Older 'A Lousy Deal,'" *CBS News*, 15 May 2010.

5. Swindoll, *Living on the Ragged Edge*, 347.

McQuilkin, pointed out that God has a wise purpose in letting us grow old and weak:

> I think God has planned the strength and beauty of youth to be physical. But the strength and beauty of age is spiritual. We gradually lose the strength and beauty that is temporary so we'll be sure to concentrate on the strength and beauty which is forever. And so we'll be eager to leave the temporary, deteriorating part of us and be truly homesick for our eternal home. If we stayed young and strong and beautiful, we might never want to leave.[6]

That explains why older saints are more homesick for heaven than younger ones, because heaven is where their bodily redemption lies.

Know God As You Search for the Meaning of Life (12:8-12)

Someone has said that, "Life is like a school, except that sometimes you don't know what the lessons are until after you have failed the exam." In a sense, that is what the book of Ecclesiastes has been. It's been the Preacher's trial and error attempts to find ultimate meaning and contentment. Yet it was only through failure, disillusionment, and discovering the empty promises of pleasure under the sun that he learned the enduring lesson—life without God is like groping for the wind.

Solomon doesn't want us to end up missing the point of this exercise. That is why he repeats the theme of his writing over again, "Vanity of Vanities . . . all is vanity." Notice that the journal ends the same way it started (1:2, 12:8). We have now come full circle. The Preacher's elaborations have expanded our understanding of what is possible and what is merely a pipe dream. If we live merely on a horizontal plane, with no transcendent reference point, then vanity is the sum total of life's pursuits.

Newspaper publishing giant William Randolph Hearst built a media empire and was the inspiration for Orson Welles' Oscar-winning film *Citizen Kane*. During his life Hearst invested a fortune collecting priceless art and other treasures from around the world. It is said that one day Mr. Hearst read the description of a valuable art item which he sent his agent abroad to find. After months of searching, the agent reported that he had finally found the treasure. To the surprise of Hearst, the priceless masterpiece was stored in none other than the warehouse of William Randolph Hearst. The

---

6. J. Robertson McQuilkin, "Land of Eternal Spring," *Our Daily Bread*, 10 July 2009.

multi-millionaire had been searching all over the world for a treasure he already possessed. Had he read the catalog of his treasures, he would have saved himself a lot of time and money.[7]

That illustration is a microcosm of Solomon's whole search for meaning. He looked under every nook and cranny of Earth to find the contentment that already belonged to him in God. In the same way, we would do well to read the record of his quest and heed the conclusions of the Preacher for in doing so we will save ourselves a lot of trouble.

Some scholars believe that 12:9–12 are the words of an editor that came along after Solomon and added this epilogue. However, it could also be just as likely that in these verses the Preacher speaks in the third person. Phillip Yancey accurately states:

> Some view the final chapter as a form of invitational hymn, as if the author disingenuously led us along toward a final appeal. Some see it as a later addition, tacked on by scribes worried about the oval message of Ecclesiastes. I get a different image, of a tired old man, not unlike Solomon, who has earnestly sought the answer to the riddles of life. In the first part of chapter 12, he gives a brilliant Shakespearian depiction of aging. Now overwhelmed by his mistakes and his morality, he sighs and says, "One thing is worthwhile. Somehow, in the midst of this meaningless world, remember your Creator."[8]

These closing verses in this epilogue give an overall appraisal and summation of the Preacher's work.

Notice that the words of Ecclesiastes are *intelligent*, "Besides being wise, the Preacher also taught the people knowledge, weighing and studying and arranging many proverbs with great care." A proverb is merely heaven's wisdom distilled for earthly application. 1 Kings 4:32 informs us that Solomon wrote thousands of proverbs. The Preacher-King heard many wise sayings over his lifetime and, no doubt, coined a few himself. This journal is a compilation of all his diligence and hard work to sift through what he learned and to select the choicest nuggets of wisdom. Thus, this journal flows with a logical clarity expounding on his main theme, "Vanity of vanities."

The Preacher's words were also written with great *integrity*, "The Preacher sought to find words of delight, and uprightly he wrote words of truth." The phrase "words of delight" speaks of the great beauty and poetry in his writing style. The Bible is not only true, but it is also well-written. The words of the Preacher are graceful, eloquent and articulate. The famous

---

7. "William Randolph Hearst," *Today in the Word*, 13 December 1995, 20.
8. Yancey, *The Bible Jesus Read*, 165.

American writer Thomas Wolfe described Ecclesiastes as "the highest flower of poetry, eloquence and truth—the greatest single piece of writing I have known."[9]

The expression, "words of truth" is also connected to the integrity of this book. Solomon never pulled any punches with his audience. It was never his intention to present a picture of life filled with rainbows and rose gardens. He's telling his readers, "I lived a long full life and here are all my conclusions. I didn't edit anything out. I didn't candy-coat the difficult things, or shy away from though stuff. This is my ragged-edged look at life in the fast lane. Take notes and be sure to apply these timeless truths."

The words of Ecclesiastes are also *instructional*. Solomon gives us another word picture to ponder in 12:11, "The words of wise men are like goads, and masters of these collections are like well-driven nails." Goads were tools of the trade for shepherds—long wooden rods with an iron point used for driving oxen and other animals forward. The sharp point of the goad would prod the stubborn animal to cooperate with the herdsman. Ecclesiastes does this for its serious readers. The words may be well written, but they are also blunt and often inflict a certain amount of pain. The words of the Preacher are like goads to the conscience, nudging us to steer clear of sin and folly. Think of Ecclesiastes as God's cattle prod.[10] It's truth keep us pointed in the right direction and act as a guardrails to keep us on the straight and narrow path.

Solomon's wisdom also acts as "well driven nails," meaning that the truth of the Bible finds a deep lodging place in the mind. The wisdom that comes from the Preacher's experience gives us an anchoring point for life. As the principles and morals of the world move in and out like the tide, the words of wisdom give us a stable mooring. Solomon wrote his proverbs in such a way that they would be memorable and stick-out in our soul. Moreover, the Scriptures stay with us over the years even when the externals are stripped from us.

The biography of Geoffery Bull, a British missionary to Tibet who was captured and imprisoned by Chinese Communists, tells how his captors took his possessions from him, threw him into a series of prisons, robbed him of his Bible, and made him suffer terribly at their hands for three years. In addition to extreme temperatures and miserable physical conditions, bodily abuse and near starvation, Bull was subjected to such mental and psychological torture that he feared he would go insane.

---

9. Wolfe, quoted in Short, *A Time to Be Born—A Time to Die*, ix.
10. Ryken, *Ecclesiastes*, 277.

How did he keep his mind at peace? He had no Bible now, but he had studied the Bible all his life. So he began to systematically go over the Scriptures in his mind. He found it took him about six months to go all the way through the Bible mentally. He started at Genesis and recalled each incident and story as best he could, first concentrating on the content, then musing on certain points and seeking light in prayer. He continued through the Old Testament, reconstructing the books and chapters, then into the New Testament—Matthew to Revelation. When he was done he started all over again. He later wrote, "The strength received though the meditation was, I believe, a vital factor in bringing me through, kept by the faith to the very end."[11]

Lastly we see that the words of Ecclesiastes are *inspired*. Take notice of the last phrase in 12:11, "... they are given by one Shepherd." In the Old Testament, the title "shepherd" is often used of God (Ps. 23:1). In the New Testament, Jesus referred to himself as the Good Shepherd (John 10:11). Solomon is saying that his words are given straight from God. This is a strong argument for the inspiration of Ecclesiastes. The doctrine of inspiration refers to ministry of the Holy Spirit whereby He supernaturally guided the biblical authors to write the exact things that He wanted expressed. Therefore, the Preacher's words are not merely the musings of some skeptical philosopher; they are part of the inspired, infallible and inerrant revelation of Almighty God.[12] It's almost as if the Holy Spirit looked down the corridors of time and could foresee the controversy that this book would cause when it came to its canonization. Therefore, this phrase is tagged on as a preemptive strike against any who might want to call its inspiration into question.

In light of the inspiration of Ecclesiastes, we are given a warning about our study habits in 12:12, "My son, beware of anything beyond these. Of making many books there is no end, and much study is a weariness of the flesh." At first glance this sounds anti-educational, but Solomon is simply saying, "There are many books out there filled with wonderful facts, but studying them can be an endless chore. So don't let secular sources rob you from God's wisdom." If you tried to keep up with all the bestsellers and periodicals you would be reading yourself to death since millions of publications are released every year. Solomon is warning us that we shouldn't study other books to the exclusion of Scripture. Other books were given for our information, but the Bible was given for our transformation.[13] Ruth Graham

---

11. Bull, *When Iron Gates Yield*.
12. Ryken, *Ecclesiastes*, 278.
13. Nelson, *The Problem of Life with God*, 199.

gave a practical piece of advice when she said, "Read, read, read, but use the Bible as home base."[14]

When I was in seminary once in a blue moon a professor would give us a take home exam. A take home exam is a life-saver for a stressed out student because in a take home exam, we got to use all our notes and refer to all our text books while taking the test. This was great because we weren't forced to memorize every fact and we didn't have to be worried about being unprepared for certain topics. In reality, there was no reason why anyone should make below an "A" on a take home exam because we had access to all the answers.

In a way, Solomon has given us a "cheat sheet" with his journal. Contained within are the revelations of his studies in the classroom of life. The deepest questions have been explored and the answers recorded. It is all here for our instruction and study. He's already done the hard work for us. All we have to do is read and apply the truth. We should not be so foolish to neglect the study of this book because if we do our homework we can pass the final exam with flying colors.

Fear God While You Prepare for the Afterlife (12:13-14)

If you're not of a fan already, then you've probably heard of Bono, the lead singer for the world famous rock band U2. Besides being an international star and humanitarian activist, Bono is also a committed follower of Christ and is vocal about his faith. In fact, U2 and Johnny Cash collaborated on a song in 1993 entitled "The Wanderer" which Bono likened to the Preacher's quest for meaning and purpose in life.[15] Bono said this about Ecclesiastes:

> Ecclesiastes is one of my favorite books. It's about a character who wants to find out why he's alive, why he was created. He tries knowledge. He tries wealth. He tries experience. He tries everything. You hurry to the end of the book to find out why, and it says, "Remember your Creator." In a way, it's such a letdown. Yet it isn't."[16]

You may feel like Bono reading the last verses of Ecclesiastes. Here you've invested all this time and diligence to understand the words of the Preacher and to get to the bottom of the meaning of life. Yet, here at the end

---

14. Graham, *Legacy of a Pack Rat*, 187.

15. Christianson, *Ecclesiastes through the Centuries*, 82–83.

16. Bono, quoted by Dennis Haack, "Johnny Cash: Colored by Sin, Colored by Grace," *By Faith* (July/August 2005), 39.

we find the simple commands, "Remember thy Creator," and "Fear God." There's got to be more, right? I mean—this is just too simple.

However, we must realize that the final verses of Ecclesiastes summarize man's ultimate purpose and response to God's Word. "The end of the matter; all has been heard. Fear God and keep his commandments, for this is the whole duty of man." The secret to finding the meaning of life is summed up in just two words: "Fear God." Just for the record, Solomon has been saying this all along so we shouldn't be surprised that this is how he ends the book (3:14, 5:7, 7:18, 8:12-13).

To fear God means to be struck by a reverential awe in His holy presence and to live in such a way that our lives reflect the fact that one day we will have to stand before Him and give an account for our words and works. Fearing God is not cowering before Him because we expect His condemnation. On the other hand, loving God is not an emotional heart palpitation, but both are evidenced in our obedience to His word, and both are rooted in our understanding of Him as our Creator, Savior and Judge.

For years, the opening of ABC's *The Wide World of Sports* illustrated "the agony of defeat" through the painful ending of an attempted ski jump. The skier appeared in good form as he headed down the slope, but then, for no apparent reason, he tumbled head-over-heels off the side of the jump and bounced off the supporting structure. What viewers didn't know was that he chose to fall. Why? As he explained later, the jump surface had become too fast, and midway down the ramp he realized that if he completed the jump, he would land on the level ground, beyond the safe landing zone, which could have been fatal. As it was, the skier suffered no more than a headache from the tumble. The fear of the slope, the fear of flying too high, and the fear of the fall led him to change course. In the same manner, a proper fear of God ought to lead us to a course correction. For this passage and the entire book of Ecclesiastes teaches that the fear of God leads to life.[17]

Moreover, the fear of God leads us to the conclusion that our lives are ultimately a stewardship to God, "For God will bring every deed into judgment, with every secret thing, whether good or evil." The Bible is clear that one day the Judge of the universe will give an instant replay of our lives. He will examine every facet of our time on Earth and scrutinize our thoughts, words, deeds and motivations (Matt. 13:26, Acts, 17:31, 1 Cor. 4:5). Nothing will be exempted and we will be unable to appeal if we receive a ruling we don't like. His judgment will be totally just and fair. So if you fear God in life, then you need not fear God in death. A life lived in the fear of the Lord removes any shame or trepidation from our final job review (1 John 2:28).

---

17. Krell, "Life's Final Exam (Ecclesiastes 12:9-14)."

Philip Ryken brilliantly adds his insight to the final lesson of Ecclesiastes when he writes:

> Why does Ecclesiastes tell us about the final judgment here? Because it means that everything matters. The Preacher began and ended his spiritual quest by saying that everything is vanity and that without God there is no meaning or purpose in life. "Is this all there is?" he kept asking. "Isn't there more to life than what I see under the sun?" If there is no God, and therefore no final judgment, then it is hard to see how anything we do really matters. But if there is a God who will Judge the world then *everything* matters . . . The final message of Ecclesiastes is not that nothing matters but that *everything* does. What we did, how we did it and why we did it will all have eternal significance. The reason everything matters is because everything in the universe is subject to the final verdict of a righteous God who knows every secret.[18]

In 1866, D.L. Moody was conducting a series of evangelistic meetings in Brockton, Massachusetts. Daniel B. Towner, director of the music department at Moody Bible Institute in Chicago, was leading the music for those meetings. A young man rose to give his testimony of following Christ and he included in his remarks these words: "I am not quite sure—but I am going to trust, and I am going to obey." Mr. Towner was so touched by these words that he jotted them down and sent them to the Reverend J.H. Sammis, a Presbyterian minister and later a teacher at Moody Institute.[19] Sammis turned that simple confession into one of the Church's most beloved hymns. Perhaps the final admonition of the Preacher can be summed up by the simple chorus of that immortal song:

> Trust and obey for there's no other way
> To be happy in Jesus, but to trust and obey.[20]

---

18. Ryken, *Ecclesiastes*, 281.
19. Jeremiah, *Searching for Heaven on Earth*, 311.
20. Sammis, "Trust and Obey," 1887.

Bibliography

Alabaster, Jay. "Japanese Man Dies of Overworking," *The Huffington Post*, 9 July 2008, <http://www.huffingtonpost.com/2008/07/09/japanese-man-dies-of-over_n_111707.html> accessed 24 May 2013.

Alcorn, Randy. *Heaven*. Wheaton, IL: Tyndale House, 2004.

Alcorn, Randy. *If God Is Good: Faith in the Midst of Suffering and Evil*. Colorado Springs, CO: Multnomah, 2009.

Allen, Woody. "Woody Allen: Getting Older 'A Lousy Deal,'" *CBS News*, 15 May 2010 <http://www.cbsnews.com/news/woody-allen-getting-older-a-lousy-deal/> accessed 21 December 2013.

Allender, Dan B. and Longman III, Tremper. *Bold Love*. Colorado Springs, CO: NavPress.

Ames, Paul. "Hungary Interdicts 98-Year-Old for Nazi War Crimes." *Global Post*, 18 June 2013 <http://www.cbsnews.com/8301-202_162-57589879/hungary-indicts-98-year-old-for-nazi-war-crimes/> accessed 19 June 2013.

Barrett, Katherine. "An Epidemic Called Loneliness." *Ladies Home Journal*, May 1983, p.90.

"Beaver's Make Big-Bucks Dam," *Associated Press*, 15 November 2004 <http://www.msnbc.msn.com/id/6494941/ns/us_news-weird_news/t/beavers-make-big-bucks-dam/> accessed 7 June 2013.

Bender, Doug and Sterrett, Dave. *I Am Second: Real Stories. Changed Lives*. Nashville, TN: Thomas Nelson, 2011.

Bono. Quoted by Haack, Dennis. "Johnny Cash: Colored by Sin, Colored by Grace." *By Faith*, July/August 2005.

Boxall, Bettina. "Giant Sequoia Falls, Raising Questions about What to Do Next." *Los Angeles Times*, 29 October 2011 <http://articles.latimes.com/2011/oct/29/local/la-me-fallen-sequoia-20111029> accessed 26 June 2013.

Brooke, Chris. "Millionaire Segway Tycoon Dies in Cliff Plunge on One of His Own Scooters," 28 September 2010 <http://www.dailymail.co.uk/news/article-1315518/Segway-tycoon-Jimi-Heselden-dies-cliff-plunge-scooters.html#ixzz2XQHy1GAT> accessed 27 June 2013.

Bull, Geoffrey T. *When Iron Gates Yield*. Chicago, IL: Moody, n.d.

"Burger King Employee Foils Robbery by Stealing Thieves' Getaway Car." *ABC News*, 28 May 2013 <http://gma.yahoo.com/blogs/abc-blogs/burger-king-employee-foils-robbery-stealing-thieves-getaway-191035044.html> accessed 26 June 2013.

Bibliography

Cain, Frasier. "The Life of the Sun." *Universe Today*, 10 March 2012 <http://www.universetoday.com/18847/life-of-the-sun/> accessed 22 March 2013.

Chandler, Rick. "101-Year-Old Vegetarian Runner Completes His Final Marathon." *NBC Sports*, 25 February 2013 <http://offthebench.nbcsports.com/2013/02/25/101-year-old-vegetarian-runner-completes-his-final-marathon/> accessed 2 July 2013.

Chinchen, Palmer. *True Religion*. Colorado Springs, CO: David C. Cook, 2010.

Christianson, Eric S. *Ecclesiastes through the Centuries*. Malden, MA: Blackwell Publishing, 2007.

Clark, Josh. "How Murphy's Law Works."<http://people.howstuffworks.com/murphys-law.htm> accessed 21 June 2013

Colson, Charles. *Loving God*. Grand Rapids, MI: Zondervan, 1983.

Cowper, William. "God Moves in a Mysterious Way," 1774.

Critchley, Simon. *The Book of Dead Philosophers*. New York, NY: Vintage Books, 2008.

Dakass, Brian. "Autistic Teen's Hoop Dreams Come True." *CBS News*, 1 March 2010 <http://www.cbsnews.com/2100-500202_162-1339324.html> accessed 30 October 2013.

Dawkins, Richard. *Out of Eden*. New York, NY: Basic Books, 1992.

DeHann, Dennis J. "Relevant Routine." *Our Daily Bread*, 24 April 2006 <http://odb.org/2006/04/24/relevant-routine/> accessed 26 April 2013.

Demara, Bruce. "Corporate Lawyer Plunges 24 Floors to Death." *The Toronto Star*, 10 July 1993.

Dillon, Sam. "Survey Finds Teenagers Ignorant on Basic History and Literature Questions," *The New York Times*, 27 February 2008 <http://www.nytimes.com/2008/02/27/us/27history.html?_r=0> accessed 29 March 2013.

Disney, Walt. Quoted by Arterburn Stephen and Farrel, Bill. *The One Year Devotions for Men on the Go*. Wheaton, IL: Tyndale, 2004.

Dobson, James C. *Straight Talk to Men and their Wives*. Waco, TX: Word Books, 1980.

Dubay, Thomas. *The Evidential Power of Beauty: Science and Theology Meet*. San Francisco, CA: Ignatius, 1999.

Eaton, Michael A. *Ecclesiastes: An Introduction and Commentary*. Leicester, England and Downers Grove, IL: InterVarsity, 1983.

Ehrman, Bart D. *God's Problem: How the Bible Fails to Answer Our Most Important Question—Why We Suffer*. New York, NY: Harper Collins, 2008.

Eisenhower, Dwight. *At Ease: Stories I Tell to Friends*. New York, NY: Doubleday, 1998.

Evans, Tony. *Tony Evans Book of Illustrations*. Chicago, IL: Moody Press, 2009.

Forbes, Moria. "Steve Jobs: Death Is Very Likely The Single Best Invention Of Life." *Forbes*, 5 October 2011 <http://www.forbes.com/sites/moiraforbes/2011/10/05/steve-jobs-death-is-very-likely-the-single-best-invention-of-life/> accessed 29 June 2013.

Ford, Henry. "The Twenty Most Influential Americans of All Time." *Time*, 25 July 2012 <http://newsfeed.time.com/2012/07/25/the-20-most-influential-americans-of-all-time/slide/henry-ford/> accessed 12 April 2013.

Foreman, George. *God in My Corner*. Nashville, TN: Thomas Nelson, 2007.

Frank, Robert. "How A Secretary Made and Gave Away $7 Million." *The Wall Street Journal*, 8 March 2010, <http://finance.yahoo.com/news/pf_article_109018.html> accessed 28 May 2013.

Freud, Sigmund. "Sigmund Freud." *Discoveries*. Summer 1991, vol. 2, no. 3, p. 1.

Geisler, Norman. *If God, Why Evil?* Minneapolis, MN: Bethany House, 2011.
Glenn, Donald R. "Ecclesiastes" in *The Bible Knowledge Commentary: Old Testament*, eds. Walvoord, Jon F. and Zuck, Roy B. Wheaton, IL: Victor, 1985.
Graham, Billy. *Just As I Am*. San Francisco, CA: Harper Collins, 1997.
Graham, Billy. *Nearing Home: Life, Faith and Finishing Well*. Nashville, TN: Thomas Nelson, 2011.
Graham, Ruth Bell. *Legacy of a Pack Rat*. Nashville, TN: Thomas Nelson, 1989.
Graham, Will. "The Power of Prayer." *Notes from the Cove*, 14 June 2011 <http://notesfromthecove.com/2011/06/14/the-power-of-prayer/> accessed 21 June 2013.
Haley, Jen. "Seduced into Spending Thousands on Lottery Tickets," *CNN News*, 4 January 2010 <http://articles.cnn.com/2010-01-04/living/lottery.tix.add.up_1_lotto-lucky-numbers-bills?_s=PM:LIVING> accessed 7 June 2013.
Hawking, Stephen and Mlodinow, Leonard. *The Grand Design*. New York, NY: Bantam, 2010.
Harvey Jr., Paul. *Paul Harvey's For What It's Worth*. New York: NY Bantam Books, 1991.
Hilary, Sir Edmund. Quoted by Abba Eban. *An Autobiography*. New York, NY: Random House, 1977).
Hilton, George W. "A History of Track Gauge." *Trains*, 1 May 2006 <http://trn.trains.com/sitecore/content/Home/Railroad%20Reference/Railroad%20History/2006/05/A%20history%20of%20track%20gauge.aspx?sc_lang=en> accessed 19 December 2013.
Hume, David. *Dialogues Concerning Natural Religion*, Part 10. Aiken, Henry D., ed. New York: NY, Hafner Publishing, 1963.
Jauregui, Andres. "Mount Tongariro Erupts." *Huffington Post*, 21 November 2012 <http://www.huffingtonpost.com/2012/11/21/mount-tongariro-erupts-new-zealand-eruption-video_n_2172511.html> accessed 25 October 2013.
Jeremiah, David. *Searching for Heaven on Earth*. Nashville, TN: Thomas Nelson, 2004.
Keith, Kent M. *Do It Anyway*. Novato, CA: New World Library, 2003.
Kinder, Derek. *The Bible Speaks Today: The Message of Ecclesiastes*. Downers Grove, IL: InterVarsity, 1976.
Kreeft, Peter. Quoted by Strobel, Lee. *The Case for Faith: A Journalist Investigates the Toughest Objections to Christianity*. Grand Rapids, MI: Zondervan, 2000.
Krell, Keith. "Alone at the Top (Ecclesiastes 4:4-16)." 1 July 2008 <http://bible.org/seriespage/alone-top-ecclesiastes-44-16> accessed 1 November 2013.
Krell, Keith. "The Naked Truth (Ecclesiastes 5:10-20)." 3 July 2008 <http://bible.org/seriespage/naked-truth-ecclesiastes-510-20> accessed 7 June 2013.
Krell, Keith. "Living Under the Thumb (Ecclesiastes 8:1-17)." 15 July 2008 <https://bible.org/seriespage/living-under-thumb-ecclesiastes-81-17> accessed 19 June 2013.
Krell, Keith. "Living While You Live (Ecclesiastes 9:1-12)." 17 July 2008 <https://bible.org/seriespage/living-while-you-live-ecclesiastes-91-12#P887_314544> accessed 20 June 2013.
Krell, Keith. "Wise Beyond Words (Ecclesiastes 9:13-10:20)." 21 July 2008 <https://bible.org/seriespage/wise-beyond-words-ecclesiastes-913-1020> accessed 26 June 2013.

Bibliography

Krell, Keith. "Life's Final Exam (Ecclesiastes 12:9–14)." 24 July 2008 <https://bible.org/seriespage/life%E2%80%99s-final-exam-ecclesiastes-129-14#P1255_452553> accessed 5 July 2013.

Kroll, Luisa. "Inside The 2013 Billionaires List: Facts and Figures." *Forbes*, 25 March 2013 <http://www.forbes.com/sites/luisakroll/2013/03/04/inside-the-2013-billionaires-list-facts-and-figures/> accessed 12 April 2013.

Kushner, Harold. *When All You've Wanted Isn't Enough*. New York, NY: Random House, 1988.

Larson, Craig Brian and Elshof, Phyllis Ten. *1001 Illustrations That Connect*. Grand Rapids, MI: Zondervan, 2008.

Lennox, John C. *God's Undertaker: Has Science Buried God?* Oxford, UK: Lion Books, 2009.

Leupold, H.C. *Exposition of Ecclesiastes*. Grand Rapids, MI: Baker, 1952.

Lewis, C.S. *Mere Christianity*. San Francisco, CA: Harper Collins, 2001.

Lewis, C.S. *Prince Caspian*. New York, NY: HarperCollins, 1979.

Lewis, C.S. *The Complete Chronicles of Narania*. San Francisco, CA: Harper Collins, 1998.

Livgren, Kerry. "Dust in the Wind." Kirshner, 1977.

Longley, Robert. "*Mint Survey Shows Most Americans Can't Name Founding Fathers*." 21 August 2007, <http://usgovinfo.about.com/od/thepresidentandcabinet/a/mintsurvey.htm> accessed 19 April 2013.

"Louis Braille." *Bits and Pieces*. June 1990, p. 23–24.

Lucado, Max. *And the Angels Were Silent*. Nashville, TN: Thomas Nelson, 1987.

Lucado, Max. *Six Hours One Friday*. Nashville, TN: W Publishing Group, 2004.

Luther, Martin. Quoted by Powell, Mark Allan. *Giving to God: The Bible's Good News about Living a Generous Life*. Grand Rapids, MI: Eerdmans, 2006).

Luther, Martin. "Notes on Ecclesiastes," in *Luther's Works*, trans. and ed. Pelikan, Jarolsav, 56 vols. St. Louis, MO: Concordia, 1972.

MacDonald, Gordon. *The Life God Blesses*. Nashville, TN: Thomas Nelson, 1994.

MacDonald, William. *Chasing the Wind*. Chicago, IL: Moody Press, 1975.

"Madeoff Investor Commits Suicide." *The New York Times*, 23 November 2008 <http://www.nytimes.com/2008/12/23/business/worldbusiness/23iht-23suicide.18901765.html?_r=0> accessed 11 June 2013.

Martinez, Luis. "Medal of Honor Awarded to Ranger Leroy Petry." *ABC News*, 12 July 2011 <http://abcnews.go.com/Politics/medal-honor-awarded-ranger-leroy-petry/story?id=14048891> accessed 11 October 2013.

"Man Killed in Wood Chipper Identified." *The Denver Channel*, 29 December 2005 <http://www.thedenverchannel.com/news/man-killed-in-wood-chipper-identified> accessed 26 June 2013.

Matthews, Dave. "Funny the Way It Is." RCA, 2009.

Maxwell, John. *Failing Forward*. Nashville, TN: Thomas Nelson, 2000.

McDowell, Josh. *Evidence for Christianity*. Nashville, TN: Thomas Nelson, 2006.

McQuilkin, J. Robertson. "Land of Eternal Spring." *Our Daily Bread*, 10 July 2009 <http://odb.org/2009/06/10/land-of-eternal-spring/> accessed 5 July 2012.

Miller, Kevin. "Busted over Careless Words." *Preaching Today*, 2002 January <http://www.preachingtoday.com/illustrations/2002/january/13483.html?start=1> accessed 27 June 2013.

Mohler, Albert. "The Foolishness of the Cross, Part III," 28 April 2006 <http://www.albertmohler.com/2006/04/28/the-foolishness-of-the-cross-part-three/> accessed 21 June 2013.

Morgan, Robert J. *More Real Stories for the Soul*. Nashville, TN: Thomas Nelson, 2000.

Morgan, Robert J. *Nelson's Completes Book of Stories, Illustrations, and Quotes*. Nashville, TN: Thomas Nelson, 2000.

Nelson, Tommy. *The Problem of Life with God: Living with a Perfect God in an Imperfect World*. Nashville, TN: Broadman & Holman, 2002.

Nichols, Michelle. "Paris Loses Out: Hilton Fortune Pledged to Charity." *Reuters*, 26 December 2007, <http://www.reuters.com/article/2007/12/26/uk-hilton-charity-idUKN2636653220071226> accessed 26 April 2013.

NPR Staff. "What Makes Paul McCartney Nervous?" *NPR: All Things Considered*, 15 October 2013, <http://www.npr.org/2013/10/15/231639159/what-makes-paul-mccartney-nervous> accessed 21 December 2013.

Pascal, Blaise. "Blaise Pascal: Scientific and Spiritual Prodigy," *Christianity Today*, 8 August 2008 <http://www.christianitytoday.com/ch/131christians/evangelistsandapologists/pascal.html> accessed 29 March 2013.

Park, Madison. "Small Choices, Saved Lives: Near Misses of 9/11." *CNN News*, 5 September 2011 <http://www.cnn.com/2011/US/09/03/near.death.decisions/index.html> accessed 7 May 2013.

Peterson, Eugene. *The Message: The Bible in Contemporary Language*. Colorado Springs, CO: NavPress, 1998.

Perot, Ross. Quoted by Larson, Craig Brian. *750 Engaging Illustrations for Preachers, Teachers and Writers*. Grand Rapids, MI: Baker Books, 2008.

Pfeiffer, Eric. "Man Allegedly Steals $100K Coin Collection, Then Spends at Face Value on Pizza and a Movie," *Yahoo! News*, 21 September 2012 <http://news.yahoo.com/blogs/sideshow/ man-allegedly-steals-100k-coin-collection-then-spends-214047054.html> accessed 29 May 2013.

Philbrick, Nathaniel. *The Last Stand*. New York, NY: Viking Press, 2010.

Piper, John. *The Pleasures of God*. Colorado Springs, CO: Multnomah, 1991.

Platt, David. *Radical: Taking Back Your Faith from the American Dream*. Colorado Springs, CO: Multnomah, 2010.

Richardson, Don. *Eternity in Their Hearts*. Ventura, CA: Regal, 1981.

Robinson, Haddon. "Funeral or Birthday?" *Our Daily Bread*, 15 July 1994 <http://odb.org/1994/01/15/funeral-or-birthday/> accessed 14 June 2013.

Rowell, Edward K. *1001 Quotes, Illustrations, and Humorous Stories for Preachers, Teachers and Writers*. Grand Rapids, MI: Baker Books, 2008).

Ryken, Philip Graham. *Ecclesiastes: Why Everything Matters*. Wheaton, IL: Crossway, 2010.

Ryle, J.C. "A Common End." <http://www.christianbeliefs.org/articles/death.html> accessed 20 June 2013.

Sammis, John H. "Trust and Obey," 1887.

Sample, Ian. "Stephen Hawking: 'There Is No Heaven; It's A Fairy Story.'" *The Guardian*, 15 May 2011 <http://www.guardian.co.uk/science/2011/may/15/stephen-hawking-interview-there-is-no-heaven> accessed 5 April 2013.

Schaeffer, Francis. *A Christian Manifesto*. Wheaton, IL: Crossway, 1981.

Schorn, Daniel. "Transcript: Tom Brady, part 3." *60 Minutes*, 11 February 2009 <http://www.cbsnews.com/8301-18560_162-1015331.html> accessed 15 March 2013.

Siegel, Joel. "Dewey Bozella: Wrongfully Convicted Man Wins Pro Boxing Debut Match." *ABC News*, 16 October 2011, <http://abcnews.go.com/US/dewey-bozella-wrongfully-convicted-man-wins-pro-boxing/story?id=14747101#.UZY9K7W1E28> accessed 17 May 2013.

Spurgeon, Charles. *Lectures to My Students*. Grand Rapids, MI: Zondervan, 1953.

Stedman, Ray. "The Search for Meaning." <http://www.raystedman.org/old-testament/ecclesiastes/the-search-for-meaning> accessed 15 March 2013.

Strobel, Lee. *The Case for Faith: A Journalist Investigates the Toughest Objections to Christianity*. Grand Rapids, MI: Zondervan, 2000.

"Storms over Everest: Life After Everest." *PBS: Frontline*, 13 May 2008 <http://www.pbs.org/wgbh/pages/frontline/everest/stories/lifeafter.html> accessed 14 June 2013.

"Surviving Everest Heightens Texan's Priorities about Life." *Atlanta Journal Constitution*, November 14, 1988, E22.

Swindoll, Charles R. *Living on the Ragged Edge*. Nashville, TN: W Publishing Group, 2004.

Swindoll, Charles R. *The Quest for Character*. Grand Rapids, MI: Zondervan, 1982.

Swindoll, Charles R. *Swindoll's Ultimate Book of Illustrations & Quotes*. Nashville, TN: Thomas Nelson, 1998.

Thomas, Gary. "Wise Christians Clip Obituaries." *Christianity Today*, 3 October 1994<http://www.christianitytoday.com/ct/1994/october3/4tb024.html> accessed 1 November 2013.

Tolkien, J.R.R. *The Hobbit*. New York, NY: Del Ray, 1982.

Vander Lught, Herbert. Quoted by Zuck, Roy B. *The Speaker's Quote Book*. Grand Rapids, MI: Kregel, 2009.

Walsh, F.O. Quoted by Green, Michael P. *1500 Illustrations for Biblical Preaching*. Grand Rapids, MI: Baker, 1989.

Warren, Rick. *The Purpose Driven Life*. Grand Rapids, MI: Zondervan, 2002.

Wesley, John. Quoted by Whybray, R.N. *The New Century Bible Commentary: Ecclesiastes*. Grand Rapids, MI: Eerdmans, 1999.

Webster, George. "The Little Cube that Changed the World." *CNN News*, 11 October 2012 <http://www.cnn.com/2012/10/10/tech/rubiks-cube-inventor> accessed 19 June 2013.

Wiersbe, Warren. *The Wiersbe Bible Commentary: Old Testament*. Colorado Springs, CO: David C. Cook, 2007.

Wiersbe, Warren. *50 People Every Christian Should Know*. Grand Rapids, MI: Baker, 2009.

"William Randolph Hearst." *Today in the Word*, 13 December 1995.

Wolfe, Thomas. Quoted in Short, Robert. *A Time to Be Born—A Time to Die*. New York, NY: Harper and Row, 1973.

Yancey, Philip. *Disappointment with God*. Grand Rapids, MI: Zondervan, 1988.

Yancey, Philip. *The Bible Jesus Read*. Grand Rapids, MI: Zondervan, 1999.

Yiu, Karson. "Newborn Baby Rescued from Toilet Pipe in China," *ABC News*, 13 May 2013 <http://abcnews.go.com/blogs/headlines/2013/05/newborn-baby-rescued-from-toilet-pipe-in-china/> accessed 19 June 2013.

Zacharias, Ravi. *The Real Face of Atheism*. Grand Rapids, MI: Baker, 2004.

"Zoo Tiger Kills SA Crime Suspect." *BBC News*, 21 December 2005 <http://news.bbc.co.uk/2/hi/africa/4548494.stm> accessed 27 June 2013.

"100-Year-Old Man Goes Skydiving." *ABC News*, 22 March 2011 <http://abcnews.go.com/WNT/video/100-year-old-man-goes-skydiving-13195329> accessed 2 July 2012.

www.ingramcontent.com/pod-product-compliance
Lightning Source LLC
Chambersburg PA
CBHW062027220426
43662CB00010B/1507